COLORADO *Colore*

A PALATE OF TASTES

COLORADO *Colore*

A PALATE OF TASTES

An inspired collection of recipes,
menus, and entertaining tips from
The Junior League of Denver,
creators of the best-selling
Colorado Cache, Crème de Colorado,
and Colorado Collage cookbooks.

COLORADO Colore

A PALATE OF TASTES

Copyright © 2002
The Junior League of Denver, Inc.
6300 East Yale Avenue
Denver, Colorado 80222
800-552-9244
Fax: 303-753-6846
www.jld.org

This cookbook is a collection of favorite recipes, which are not necessarily original recipes.

Library of Congress Number:
2002110954
ISBN: 0-9603946-7-2

Edited, Designed, and
Manufactured by
Favorite Recipes® Press
An imprint of

FRP

PO Box 305142
Nashville Tennessee 37230
1-800-358-0560

Art Director: Steve Newman
Project Manager: Susan Larson
Project Editor: Debbie Van Mol

Manufactured in the United States of America
First Printing 2002   70,000 copies
Second Printing 2002   40,000 copies

The Junior League of Denver, Incorporated, is an organization of women committed to promoting volunteerism and to improving the community through the effective action and leadership of trained volunteers. Its purpose is exclusively educational and charitable.

The proceeds from the sale of *Colorado Colore: A Palate of Tastes* support the purpose and programs of The Junior League of Denver, Inc.

Additional copies of *Colorado Colore: A Palate of Tastes* and other cookbooks published by The Junior League of Denver may be obtained on-line at www.jld.org, by using a reorder form at the end of this book, or by contacting The Junior League of Denver, Inc.

roduction

Just as the artist's inspiration is often found in his surroundings, *Colorado Colore* is inspired by the dazzling magnificence of our colorful state. Imagine creating a menu for family or friends as memorable as a fiery Colorado sunset or as inviting as a cool Rocky Mountain lake. The philosophy behind this collection is that every recipe, no matter how simple, should present a rich culinary experience for all of the senses.

The palette of 300 recipes in this book was thoughtfully selected from more than 2,500 entries, then exhaustively tested. Each was chosen for its representation of a vivid spectrum of colors and flavors that is uniquely Colorado. By design, many of the ingredients used throughout *Colorado Colore,* from chile peppers and sugar beets to wheat and beef, are found in our state's colorful agricultural abundance.

The fourth in a series of nationally renowned cookbooks, which together have sold more than 1.8 million copies to date, *Colorado Colore* follows in the tradition of offering recipes that will be favored, talked about, and shared for years. In keeping with recent food trends, *Colorado Colore* presents our first-ever section dedicated entirely to vegetarian fare with an incredible array of healthful recipes and complete meal possibilities. Other new additions include easy-to-read sidebars, featuring helpful entertaining and food presentation tips, and suggested wine pairings to enhance a recipe or round out a menu.

Everything in *Colorado Colore,* from its spectacular theme-style menus to its vivid photographic images shot on backdrops of natural textures, is designed to inspire and awaken creativity in food preparation, tastes, and presentation.

contents
TABLE OF CONTENTS

8   Committees

10   Acknowledgments

12   Appetizers

38   Salads

60   Soups and Sandwiches

84   Breads and Brunch

110   Vegetables and Sides

130   Poultry

150   Meats

174   Seafood

198   Noodles

220   Vegetarian

250   Desserts

272   Menus

274   Sponsors

276   Submitters

278   Testers

280   Index

287   Order Form

  *City and County of Denver*

Wellington E. Webb
MAYOR

OFFICE OF THE MAYOR
CITY AND COUNTY BUILDING
DENVER, COLORADO • 80202-5390
TELEPHONE: 720-865-9000 • FAX: 720-865-9040
TTY/TTD: 720-865-9010

October 14, 2002

Greetings!

As Mayor of Denver, I am honored to endorse *Colorado Colore* as the official cookbook of our city. In the tradition of the Junior League of Denver, they have once again created a regional cookbook worthy of nationwide recognition.

There is no doubt that *Colorado Colore* reflects the colorful lifestyle, tastes and cultures of Denver, and of our state. More importantly, it's creation is a reflection of our community - a community that values and embraces the spirit of volunteerism that has long been the foundation for the activities and works of the Junior League.

Your purchase of this cookbook will support the many Junior League of Denver's programs that, for more than eight decades, have contributed to the enrichment and strength of Denver and continue to help make our community what it is today.

Yours truly,

Wellington E. Webb
Mayor

Steering Committee

Editors
Alissa Gutin Crowley
Wendy Zerr

Recipe Coordinators
Stephani C. Davis
Julia Romeo Haen

Marketing Chair
Kelley O'Connor Digby

Non-Recipe Text Coordinators
Terri Fennell
Lesa Gerlach
Melissa Redmond

C & C Liaisons
Nicole Bigler
Lauren Eigner
Kathleen Gallagher

Distribution Chair
Margaret Ansted

Sustaining Advisor
Fran Yeddis

Marketing

Marketing Chair
Kelley O'Connor Digby

Marketing Committee
Kameron Abbott
Katie Benson
Nicole Bigler
Kellye Boehme
Carey Brandt
Kristen Carucci
Alexis Ciesla
Jen Cortese
Tracy DeHoop
Angela Drennan
Mary DuBois
Lauren Eigner
Stephanie Farnsworth
Sarah Feist
Janie Fletcher
Nanette Gamily
Kathleen Gallagher
Michelle Garnsey
Michele Goldman
Dana Gordon
Sevi Hanley
Amy Harming
Kristin Hartman

Katrina Heim
Julie Hodges
Sandie Hopkins
Molly Jansen
Faith Johnston
Keli Kinsella
Tammy Krause
Meghan Mortimer
Melanie Orth
Mary Peterson
Jackie Rafferty
Katie Schlenker
Elizabeth Schneider
Susan Schneider
Donna Shelton
Andrea Showalter
Cristina Sigdestad
Ashley Slupe
Cheryl Stephens
Amy Stern
Karen Taylor
Sharon Thomas
Kimberly Walsh
Shannon Wanebo
Tracy Weise
Mary White

8

Recipe Committee and Section Heads

Distribution Committee
Kimberly Abele
Ann Bohn
Karlene Butler
Anne Hammer
Tricia MacHendrie
Ellie McKenzie
Kristine McMullan
Susan Parker
Tracy Thomas

Recipe Coordinators
Stephani C. Davis
Julia Romeo Haen

Recipe Committee
Holly Curtis
Lee Dabberdt
Katie Harrell

Appetizers—Section Heads
Nikki Feltz
Kathleen Morton

Salads—Section Heads
Haley Hayes
Stacy Stokes

Soups and Sandwiches—Section Heads
Barb Anderson
Jennifer Turner

Breads and Brunch—Section Heads
Tana Rosenberg
Michelle Weinraub

Vegetables and Sides—Section Heads
Gail Berliner
Janice Cortez

Poultry—Section Head
Cami Cooper

Meats—Section Head
Susie McLain

Seafood—Section Head
Catherine Hollis

Noodles—Section Heads
Nancy Gargan
Jane Siekmeier

Vegetarian—Section Heads
Susan James
Cara Kimsey

Desserts—Section Head
Christine McLaughlin-Trigg

acknowled

ACKNOWLEDGMENTS

Food Photography
  Rick Souders, Souders Studios

Photography Assistant
  Trevor Moore,
  Souders Studios

2nd Photography Assistant
  Rob Jones

Scenic Photography
  T. J. Rhine &
  Rick Souders

Photography Representative
  Christelle Newkirk, aRep

Food and Prop Styling
  Stephen Shern Creative
  Food Styling

Props
  Peppercorn Gourmet Goods

Book Title
  Hayley Hartman

Cover Designs
  Timothy Stortz, Stortz Design

Copywriter
  Jo Fukaye, The Copy Shop

Wine Consultant
  Mark W. Price

Rick Souders

Rick Souders is a commercial photographer based in Denver, Colorado, who specializes in food and beverage photography. After being in the business for 18 years, his passion for photography only grows stronger while his imagery gets more conceptual, colorful, and graphic. Rick's work can be seen worldwide in advertising print campaigns, magazines, and books, as well as on the Internet.

Rick graduated from the Art Center College of Design in Pasadena, California, with honors. He has won numerous local and national awards. Rick's work has been featured by Kodak and the International Photography Hall of Fame, and he has been named one of "America's Top Pros" by Mamiya America Corporation. Rick has also been featured in *Studio Photography & Design* magazine. *The Art and Attitude of Commercial Photography* is a new book from Rick, published in July 2002.

Some of Rick's clients include Coca-Cola, Pepsi, Coors, Smirnoff, Boston Market, ConAgra, Frito-Lay, Nabisco, and Kraft. For more information on Rick Souders and Souders Studios, visit the website at www.soudersstudios.com

gments

Stephen Shern

"I love food. I love everything about food. I love buying it, creating it, tasting it, touching it, and talking about it. I have been involved with food for over 25 years and I never tire of it."

Stephen Shern began his food styling career in New York City 18 years ago. There, he worked closely with nationally recognized chefs Leslie Revsin and Michel Fitoussi, contributing recipes for new menus at 24 Fifth Avenue in Greenwich Village. Over the next seven years, as a Consulting Chef, he specialized in recipe development, menu and kitchen design, restaurant and cookbook reviews, and private cooking lessons with celebrities. Fresh from being a chef, he had the artist's eye and creative touch to cultivate his food styling focus. He worked in both New York and Los Angeles before relocating to Boulder, Colorado.

His work has graced the covers of *Bon Appétit* and the *New York Times* and *Los Angeles Times* magazines. Some of his clients include Contadina, Jack-in-the-Box, Einstein Bagel, Taco Johns, Con Agra, Leprino Cheese, the Beef and Lamb Councils, and Celestial Seasonings.

His website is available for viewing at www.stephenshern.com

T. J. Rhine

T. J. Rhine comes to the photography arena from a creative background. T. J. has been in the advertising industry for many years. He has been a Creative Director for such companies as the Coors Brewing Company and Planet Hollywood.

Having that creative eye has always kept him keenly interested in his environment, and it was an easy transition for T. J. to incorporate landscape and scenic photography into his career. His unique camera angle and use of color in his landscape photographs blends well with the contents of the food photography in *Colorado Colore.* T. J. currently resides in Colorado and is now a partner in a brand creation and development agency known as Greenhouse.

T. J. Rhine's scenic photography has appeared in calendars and ads by such companies as Coors Brewing Company, CoorsTek, and Celestial Seasonings, as well as other national companies.

CONTENTS

14 Zucchini Tomato Bites
15 Bleu Cheese Quesadillas with Pear Salsa
16 Chèvre, Marmalade and Ripe Pear Crostini
16 Pesto Hots
17 Endive with Brandied Gorgonzola
18 Bacon-Wrapped Grissini
19 Spicy Black Bean Cakes
20 Beef and Pepper Bundles
22 Asian Chicken Lettuce Wraps
23 Spicy Sashimi Triangles
24 King Crab Cups with Avocado
25 Ceviche
26 Lemon Shrimp
26 Mango, Shrimp and Prosciutto Kabobs
27 Pistachio Shrimp with Dipping Sauces
28 Avocado Lime Cream Dip
28 Roasted Red Pepper, Feta and Mint Dip
29 Hot Soufflé Dip
30 Figs with Prosciutto
31 Layered Ginger Chicken Dip
32 Asian Salsa with Won Ton Chips
32 Papaya Salsa
34 Mediterranean Salsa
34 Watermelon Salsa
35 Stacked Caviar Dip
35 Montrachet Spread
36 White Wine Sangria
36 Coconut Margarita
36 Pear and Ginger Martini
37 Pisco Sour
37 The Ruby
37 Ramos Gin Fizz

APPETIZERS

Zucchini Tomato Bites

5 small zucchini, cut into 1/2-inch slices
4 ounces Gorgonzola cheese, crumbled
   and chilled
1 pint cherry tomatoes, thinly sliced
Fresh small basil leaves
Freshly ground white pepper to taste
5 1/3 ounces Parmesan cheese, finely grated

Line a baking sheet with baking parchment. Scoop out the center of each zucchini slice carefully with a melon baller, creating a shell that resembles a bowl. Fill each shell with about 1/2 teaspoon of the Gorgonzola cheese. Top each bite with 1 tomato slice and 1 basil leaf. Sprinkle with white pepper and Parmesan cheese.

Arrange the bites on the prepared baking sheet. Bake at 400 degrees for 5 to 7 minutes or until the cheese melts. Do not allow to brown. You may prepare several hours in advance and store, covered, in the refrigerator. Bake just before serving.

Makes 50 to 60 appetizers

Bleu Cheese Quesadillas with Pear Salsa

Pear Salsa

2 fresh ripe pears, peeled and cut into
    1/4-inch pieces
2 dried pear halves, cut into 1/4-inch pieces
1/2 cup chopped red onion
2 tablespoons chopped fresh cilantro
2 tablespoons chopped fresh mint
Juice and grated zest of 1 lime
1 tablespoon minced fresh gingerroot
1 large jalapeño chile, seeded and minced
1/4 teaspoon crushed red pepper

Quesadillas

8 ounces creamy bleu cheese such as
    Gorgonzola or Danish Bleu
8 (8-inch) flour tortillas
2 tablespoons vegetable oil
2 tablespoons honey

For the salsa, combine the pears, onion, cilantro, mint, lime juice, lime zest, gingerroot, jalapeño chile and red pepper in a bowl and toss gently to mix. Chill, covered, in the refrigerator.

For the quesadillas, freeze the cheese for 1 hour or until firm. Brush 1 side of 4 of the tortillas with 1 tablespoon of the oil. Arrange the tortillas oil side down on a baking sheet.

Chop the frozen cheese into 1/2-inch pieces. Sprinkle about 1/2 cup of the cheese over each of the 4 tortillas on the baking sheet. Spread 2 to 3 tablespoons of the salsa over the cheese using a slotted spoon. Top with the remaining tortillas. Brush with the remaining 1 tablespoon oil.

Bake at 500 degrees for 5 to 7 minutes or until the cheese melts and the quesadillas are light brown. Cut each quesadilla into 8 wedges using a pizza wheel or sharp knife. Drizzle with the honey. Serve with the remaining salsa. Great with grilled chicken or pork.

Serves 8

Beverages

Keeping the beverages cold is always an important element to any gathering. Simply fill any big container with ice, and place sodas, beer, or wine in it to keep cold. To keep the drinks cold longer, fill the container with ice, water, and salt and submerge the drinks. Add about 1 tablespoon of salt per quart of water. Try one of these ideas for containers or think of some of your own:

- Fill a wheelbarrow with ice.
- For a poolside party, fill a children's wading pool with ice.
- Large terra-cotta pots in different shapes.
- For a tropical theme, dress up an ordinary tin bucket with palm fonds, holding the leaves in place with raffia.

Chèvre, Marmalade and Ripe Pear Crostini

Crostini ("little toasts" in Italian) begin with slices of country bread or baguettes that are either grilled, toasted, or fried in oil.

2 ounces chèvre, such as Montrachet
8 to 12 crostini
1 ripe pear
2 to 3 tablespoons marmalade
    (ginger, orange or lemon)
Grated lemon zest or orange zest
    (optional)

Spread some of the chèvre on each crostini. Cut the pear lengthwise into halves. Remove the core and thinly slice the pear along the width of the fruit, producing half-moon shape slices. Arrange 2 or 3 pear slices in a fan shape on each crostini. Spread 1/4 to 1/2 teaspoon of the marmalade over the top of each with the back of a spoon. Garnish with lemon zest or orange zest.

Makes 8 to 12 appetizers

Pesto Hots

1/2 cup fresh basil, finely chopped
1/2 cup (2 ounces) shredded Parmesan cheese
6 tablespoons mayonnaise
1 garlic clove, chopped
1 French baguette, cut into 1/4-inch slices

Combine the basil, cheese, mayonnaise and garlic in a bowl and mix well. Arrange the baguette slices in a single layer on a baking sheet.

Broil until light brown. Turn the slices and spread with the mayonnaise mixture. Broil until light brown and heated through. Serve immediately.

Makes (about) 20 appetizers

Cojita Cheese Rounds

Preheat a nonstick skillet over medium-high heat. Once the pan is hot, sprinkle cojita cheese into 1/4-inch-thick rounds. When firm and toasted on one side, turn and toast the other side. If desired, you can form the rounds into shapes by immediately removing from the pan and forming over a small bowl or rolling pin. Serve as a tasty addition to chips and salsa or use as a plate garnish for your Mexican dishes.

Endive with Brandied Gorgonzola

1/4 cup sliced almonds

1 cup (4 ounces) crumbled Gorgonzola
    cheese

4 ounces cream cheese, softened

2 teaspoons brandy

4 medium heads Belgian endive, separated
    into spears

Spread the sliced almonds in a single layer on a baking sheet. Toast at 325 degrees for 5 to 7 minutes or until light brown, stirring occasionally. Let stand until cool and coarsely chop.

Process the Gorgonzola cheese, cream cheese and brandy in a food processor or beat with an electric mixer in a bowl until smooth.

To assemble, spoon a heaping teaspoon of the cheese mixture inside each endive spear toward the stem end. Sprinkle the cheese mixture with toasted almonds. Arrange the endive spears with the tips of the spears facing out in concentric circles on a serving platter.

For a festive dish, mound cranberries in the middle of the circle and serve.

Makes 2 dozen appetizers

The Favored Guest

Surprise your guests with a little memento of your special event. Here are some fun ideas:

- Picture frames with each guest's picture inserted, which can also double as place card settings.
- Bars of scented soap wrapped in tissue with a gold seal sticker.
- Gourmet chocolates wrapped in clear cellophane bags and tied with raffia, ribbon, or twine.
- Put together a tape or CD to play during the evening. Make a copy for each guest and wrap it in old sheet music or music-theme paper.
- Bottles of their favorite wine adorned with flowers and homemade name tags.
- Seed packet with a small cellophane bag of potting soil in hand-painted flowerpots.

Bacon-Wrapped Grissini

1 pound smokehouse bacon
1 package grissini (long thin Italian
   breadsticks)
$1/3$ cup packed brown sugar
$1^1/_2$ to 2 tablespoons dark chili powder

Let the bacon stand at room temperature until slightly softened. Wrap 1 slice of the bacon around each breadstick to resemble a candy cane or old-fashioned barbershop pole. You may prepare this portion of the recipe up to 2 hours in advance and store, covered, in the refrigerator.

Mix the brown sugar and chili powder in a shallow dish. Roll each breadstick in the brown sugar mixture until coated. Arrange the breadsticks $1/2$ inch apart on the rack of a broiler pan. Bake at 350 degrees for 20 minutes or until the coating caramelizes and the bacon is deep golden in color and cooked through.

Loosen each breadstick from the broiler rack. Cut the breadsticks into halves while warm if desired. Cool for 10 to 15 minutes or until firm. Serve at room temperature.

Makes 2 dozen breadsticks

Marinated Mushrooms

Combine 3 tablespoons minced shallots, 1/4 cup fresh orange juice, 2 tablespoons white wine vinegar, 1 tablespoon grated orange zest, 2 teaspoons minced fresh thyme, 1/2 teaspoon salt and 2 teaspoons olive oil in a bowl and mix well. Add 3 cups small mushrooms and toss to coat well. Season with freshly ground pepper. Chill, covered, for 1 hour or longer, stirring occasionally.

Spicy Black Bean Cakes

2 (15-ounce) cans black beans, drained and
    rinsed
3/4 cup (3 ounces) shredded Monterey Jack
    cheese
8 green onions, finely chopped
1/2 cup finely chopped red bell pepper
1/3 cup chopped fresh cilantro
2 tablespoons minced seeded jalapeño chile
3 large garlic cloves, minced
2 teaspoons cumin
1 teaspoon salt
1/2 teaspoon freshly ground pepper
2 tablespoons yellow cornmeal
1 egg, lightly beaten
1 cup yellow cornmeal
1/4 cup vegetable oil
Sour cream
Salsa
Guacamole

Mash the beans slightly in a bowl. Stir in the cheese, green onions, bell pepper, cilantro, jalapeño chile, garlic, cumin, salt and pepper. Add 2 tablespoons cornmeal and the egg and mix well. Chill, covered, for 1 hour.

Place 1 cup cornmeal in a small bowl. Drop 1 heaping tablespoon of the bean mixture into the cornmeal and roll to coat. Flatten into a 1/2-inch cake. Repeat the process with the remaining cornmeal and remaining black bean mixture, forming approximately 20 to 25 cakes.

Heat the oil in a large heavy skillet over medium heat. Fry the cakes in batches in the hot oil for 5 to 6 minutes per side or until firm and crisp; drain on paper towels. Serve warm with sour cream, salsa and guacamole.

Makes 20 to 25 appetizers

*A classic cocktail party takes less
preparation than a meal, entertains more
people, and allows guests to mingle, all within a
two-hour time frame before dinner.*

Beef and Pepper Bundles

1 cup reduced-sodium soy sauce
1/2 cup packed light brown sugar
2 pounds beef tenderloin, trimmed
Kosher salt and freshly ground pepper
    to taste
4 scallions
1 green bell pepper, julienned
1 yellow bell pepper, julienned
1 red bell pepper, julienned
2 teaspoons olive oil

Whisk the soy sauce and brown sugar in a bowl until the brown sugar dissolves. Cut the beef crosswise into 1/4-inch slices. Trim any excess fat or connective tissue. Place 1 slice of the beef between 2 sheets of plastic wrap. Pound into a 1/8-inch-thick rectangle with a meat mallet, being careful to avoid tearing the slices. Repeat the process with the remaining beef.

Dip the beef slices 1 at a time into the soy sauce mixture. Arrange the slices on a baking sheet with sides. Sprinkle with kosher salt and pepper. Marinate, covered, in the refrigerator for 8 to 10 hours. Reserve the remaining marinade.

Cut the green tops of the scallions into 3-inch lengths. Cut each length lengthwise into 2 strips. Cut the scallion bulbs into 1/8-inch slices and separate into rings.

To assemble, arrange 2 strips of the scallion tops and 1 strip of each color of the bell peppers parallel to the shorter side of the beef slice. Equal amounts of the bell pepper strips and scallion strips should extend on either side of the beef slice. Roll the beef tightly to enclose the vegetables and secure with 2 wooden picks. Repeat the process with the remaining tenderloin, remaining scallion tops and remaining bell pepper strips.

Brush a broiler rack, grill rack or grill pan with the olive oil. Arrange the beef bundles on the broiler rack of a broiler pan. Brush each with some of the reserved marinade. Broil for 2 to 4 minutes or until the beef is medium-rare, turning and basting frequently with the reserved marinade.

Pour the remaining marinade into a small saucepan. Bring to a boil. Boil for 3 to 5 minutes. Pour the marinade into a small bowl and stir in the scallion rings. Serve as a dipping sauce with the bundles.

This impressive appetizer pairs nicely with a California Syrah or Australian Shiraz. Try Justin Syrah or Leasingham Bin 61 Shiraz.

Makes (about) 30 appetizers

*To prevent dilution of drinks,
fill ice cube trays with the same beverage
or a complementary one (lemonade for iced tea
or limeade for vodka tonics) and freeze.*

Asian Chicken Lettuce Wraps

To make lettuce leaves more pliable, trim off the raised portion of the vein on each leaf.

Soy Marinade
2 tablespoons light soy sauce
2 tablespoons white wine
2 tablespoons brown sugar
2 tablespoons water
2 garlic cloves, minced

Chicken Filling
2 boneless skinless chicken breasts
4 ounces water chestnuts, chopped
4 ounces fresh shiitake mushrooms, chopped
2 scallions, chopped (green and white parts)
2 tablespoons sesame oil or peanut oil

Hot Sauce and Assembly
1/4 cup white vinegar
1/4 cup chili paste
1 tablespoon soy sauce
1 teaspoon hot Chinese chili oil
1 teaspoon hot Chinese mustard

Wraps
8 to 10 iceberg lettuce leaves

For the marinade, combine the soy sauce, wine, brown sugar, water and garlic in a bowl and mix well.

For the filling, process the chicken in a food processor until finely chopped. Combine the chicken, water chestnuts, mushrooms and scallions in a bowl and mix well. Spoon the chicken mixture into a sealable plastic bag. Add the marinade and seal tightly. Turn to mix. Marinate in the refrigerator for 3 to 10 hours, turning occasionally.

Heat a wok or sauté pan over high heat. Add the sesame oil and heat until the sesame oil is hot but not smoking. Add the filling to the wok. Reduce the heat to medium-high. Cook for 10 minutes or until the chicken is cooked through, stirring frequently.

For the sauce, whisk the vinegar, chili paste, soy sauce, chili oil and Chinese mustard in a bowl until blended.

For the wraps, spoon 2 to 3 spoonfuls of the chicken filling onto each lettuce leaf and drizzle with the desired amount of sauce. Roll like a burrito to enclose the chicken filling.

Serves 8 to 10

Spicy Sashimi Triangles

It is essential to use sashimi-grade tuna whenever tuna is left even partially uncooked. You can find sashimi-grade tuna in a reputable fish market.

8 won ton wrappers, diagonally
    sliced into quarters
1 (8-ounce) sashimi-grade tuna fillet,
    finely chopped
2 tablespoons flaked unsweetened coconut
2 tablespoons sliced almonds
2 tablespoons dried currants
1 tablespoon minced fresh chives
2 teaspoons soy sauce
1 1/2 teaspoons minced garlic
1 1/2 teaspoons minced fresh gingerroot
1 teaspoon lemon juice
1 teaspoon hot pepper sauce
1/2 teaspoon salt
1/4 teaspoon minced habanero chile
Chopped fresh chives to taste

Arrange the won ton triangles in a single layer on a baking sheet. Bake at 350 degrees for 3 minutes or until light brown. Remove to a wire rack to cool.

Combine the tuna, coconut, almonds, currants and 1 tablespoon chives in a bowl and mix well. Stir in the soy sauce, garlic, gingerroot, lemon juice, hot pepper sauce, salt and habanero chile.

Spoon about 1 tablespoon of the tuna mixture onto each won ton triangle. Sprinkle with chopped chives to taste.

Make preparation an easier task by freezing the tuna for 10 to 15 minutes prior to chopping.

Makes 32 appetizers

Asian Table

For setting an Asian table, tie green bamboo shoots together into a rectangular "plate frame." An arrangement of ornamental grasses or a bowl of goldfish would make a whimsically elegant centerpiece.

King Crab Cups with Avocado

Won Ton Cups

    2 dozen won ton wrappers
    2 tablespoons vegetable oil
    Salt to taste

Filling

    1 ripe avocado
    1 scallion, finely chopped
    1^1/$_2$ tablespoons lime juice
    ^{1}/$_2$ teaspoon minced garlic
    ^{1}/$_2$ to ^{3}/$_4$ teaspoon wasabi paste
    ^{1}/$_2$ teaspoon salt
    12 ounces fresh or thawed frozen steamed
        king crab in shell
    1 tablespoon lime juice

For the cups, stack 1 dozen won ton wrappers and trim the stack to a 3-inch square. Repeat the process with the remaining won ton wrappers.

Brush lightly a 3-inch square on your work surface with some of the oil. Arrange 1 won ton square over the oil. Brush the top of that square with oil. Top with another square and brush with oil. Repeat the process with the remaining won ton squares and remaining oil. Both sides of the squares should be coated with oil.

Place 1 won ton wrapper in each cup of miniature muffin tins. Press the wrapper gently into the bottom and the side of each cup. Sprinkle with salt. Bake at 350 degrees for 7 to 10 minutes or until crisp and golden brown. Remove to a wire rack to cool. The cups will continue to crisp. You may prepare the won ton cups up to 2 days in advance and store in an airtight container in a cool environment.

For the filling, mash the avocado in a bowl with a fork. Stir in the scallion, 1^1/$_2$ tablespoons lime juice, garlic, wasabi paste and salt. You may prepare the filling up to 4 hours in advance. Cover the surface with plastic wrap and store in the refrigerator.

Split the crab lengthwise. Remove the crab meat from the shell and chop into small pieces. Toss the crab meat with 1 tablespoon lime juice in a bowl. Do not use canned crab meat in this recipe.

To assemble, spoon an equal amount of the avocado filling into each of the won ton cups. Top each with some of the crab meat. Serve immediately.

Makes 2 dozen appetizers

Brie Butter

Combine 8 ounces Brie cheese with ^{1}/$_2$ cup (1 stick) softened butter and ^{1}/$_4$ cup white wine in a food processor or blender and process until smooth. Serve immediately or store, tightly covered, in the refrigerator until needed. Serve at room temperature with French baguettes, apples, pears, peaches or crackers.

Ceviche

8 ounces large shrimp, peeled and deveined
8 ounces tilapia or other white meaty fish
Salt and pepper to taste
1/2 cup fresh lime juice
1/4 cup fresh lemon juice
1/4 cup fresh orange juice
1 or 2 garlic cloves, finely chopped
1 medium tomato, seeded and cut into
    1/4-inch pieces
1/2 large cucumber, seeded and cut into
    1/4-inch pieces
1/4 cup (1/4-inch pieces) red onion
1/2 to 1 jalapeño chile, seeded and finely
    minced
2 tablespoons olive oil
1 avocado
1/4 cup fresh cilantro sprigs

Add the shrimp to a stockpot of boiling water. Cook for 1 minute or just until the shrimp turn pink; drain. Plunge the shrimp into a bowl of ice water to stop the cooking process. Drain and pat dry with paper towels. Cut each shrimp into halves. Rinse the tilapia and pat dry with paper towels. Cut the fish into 1/2-inch pieces. Combine the shrimp and fish in a large shallow dish. Season with salt and pepper.

Combine the lime juice, lemon juice, orange juice and garlic in a bowl and mix well. Pour the lime juice mixture over the shrimp mixture and toss to coat. Marinate, covered, for 2 hours, stirring every 30 minutes. The citrus juices will "cook" the shrimp and fish, turning the fish opaque. Add the tomato, cucumber, onion, jalapeño chile and olive oil to the shrimp mixture and mix gently. Marinate, covered, for up to 1 hour or until the shrimp and fish are fully opaque.

Chop the avocado into 1/4- to 1/2-inch pieces. Using a slotted spoon, mound the ceviche in martini glasses or individual serving dishes. Drizzle each with 1 or 2 spoonfuls of the citrus marinade. Top with the chopped avocado and sprigs of fresh cilantro. Serve immediately.

A California Sauvignon Blanc such as Beckmen from Santa Barbara or Dry Creek Vineyards pairs nicely with this dish.

Serves 4 to 6

Lemon Shrimp

2¹/₂ pounds large shrimp, steamed, peeled, deveined

2 medium red onions, thinly sliced

4 large lemons, thinly sliced

1¹/₂ teaspoons crushed rosemary

Garlic salt to taste

4 garlic cloves, minced

1 (34-ounce) bottle olive oil

Juice of 2 lemons

Layer the shrimp, onions and lemon slices in a large serving bowl until all of the ingredients are used, sprinkling each layer with rosemary and garlic salt. Sprinkle the minced garlic over the top.

Pour the olive oil over the layers just until the top layer is covered. Drizzle with the lemon juice. Marinate, covered, in the refrigerator for 2 days. Drain before serving.

Serves 10

Mango, Shrimp and Prosciutto Kabobs

12 bamboo skewers

12 jumbo shrimp, peeled and deveined

1 firm ripe mango, cut into 12 strips

12 arugula leaves

12 paper-thin slices prosciutto

1 tablespoon chili oil

1 lemon, cut into wedges

1 lime, cut into wedges

Soak 12 bamboo skewers in hot water in a bowl for 1 hour or longer. Layer 1 shrimp, 1 mango strip and 1 arugula leaf to create a stack. Wrap 1 slice of the prosciutto around the stack. The prosciutto should wrap around the stack only once, so trim accordingly.

Thread the skewer through the middle of the stack. Brush with the chili oil to coat. Grill the kabobs over high heat for 5 minutes or until the shrimp turn pink. Cut each kabob into bite-size pieces. Serve immediately with lemon and lime wedges.

Serves 4

When making a crudité platter, consider generous amounts of just one or two vegetables, which can be an impressive display. Use vegetables at their seasonal best rather than aiming for a broad selection.

Pistachio Shrimp with Dipping Sauces

Mint Dipping Sauce

1/2 cup shelled pistachios, coarsely chopped
1/2 cup fresh cilantro leaves
1/2 cup fresh mint leaves
3 scallions, chopped
1 garlic clove
1/2 cup unsweetened coconut milk
1/3 cup lime juice
1/2 teaspoon red chili paste

Ginger Dipping Sauce

1/4 cup minced fresh gingerroot
1/4 cup rice vinegar
2 tablespoons honey
4 teaspoons soy sauce

Shrimp

2 cups whole shelled pistachios
1 1/2 pounds medium shrimp, peeled and
   deveined
2 egg whites
1 tablespoon ice water

For the mint sauce, process the pistachios, cilantro, mint, scallions and garlic in a food processor until the pistachios are finely chopped and the mixture is of a pasty consistency. Add the coconut milk, lime juice and chili paste. Process until blended. Serve at room temperature.

For the ginger sauce, combine the gingerroot, vinegar, honey and soy sauce in a bowl and mix well. Serve at room temperature.

For the shrimp, process the pistachios in a food processor or blender just until finely chopped. Be careful not to process to a pasty consistency. Spread the pistachios in a shallow dish.

Using a sharp knife, butterfly the shrimp by slicing to but not through the inside curl of the shrimp, starting about 1/4 inch below the tip of the tail. Continue slicing down the inside length of the shrimp. Separate the two sides of the shrimp enough that the shrimp can "stand" upright using the thicker body portion of the shrimp as a base.

Beat the egg whites and ice water in a mixing bowl. Dip the shrimp in the egg white mixture and coat with the chopped pistachios. Arrange the shrimp upright in a single layer on a baking sheet. Bake at 375 degrees for 8 to 10 minutes or until the shrimp are cooked through. Serve immediately with one or both of the dipping sauces.

Serves (about) 8

Avocado Lime Cream Dip

2 medium avocados, coarsely chopped
4 scallions, chopped
1 teaspoon finely minced jalapeño chile
2 green chiles, seeded and finely chopped
1/2 cup fresh cilantro leaves
Juice of 2 limes
1 tablespoon olive oil
1/3 cup sour cream
Salt to taste

Combine the avocados, scallions, jalapeño chile, green chiles, cilantro, lime juice, olive oil and sour cream in a food processor. Pulse until smooth. Season with salt. Chill, covered, for 15 minutes to allow the flavors to blend. Serve cold with chips and/or crudités. You may prepare up to 8 hours in advance and store, covered, in the refrigerator.

To prevent the dip from discoloring, press a sheet of plastic wrap directly on the surface. The oxygen in the air turns the avocados brown, so the less air that comes in contact with the dip the greater the chances of no discoloration.

Makes (about) 2 cups

Roasted Red Pepper, Feta and Mint Dip

3 roasted red bell peppers, seeded and
    coarsely chopped
1 1/2 cups (6 ounces) crumbled feta cheese
8 ounces lite cream cheese, softened
3 tablespoons finely chopped fresh mint
2 tablespoons olive oil
1 tablespoon lemon juice
1 garlic clove, minced
Salt and pepper to taste

Combine the roasted bell peppers, feta cheese, cream cheese, mint, olive oil, lemon juice and garlic in a food processor. Pulse until blended but with some texture. You may alter the consistency of the dip by adding water 1 teaspoon at a time. Taste and season with salt and pepper.

Chill, covered, for 30 minutes to allow the flavors to blend. Serve cold with chips and/or crudités.

Makes (about) 2 cups

Serve dips in cappuccino mugs for a fun look.

Hot Soufflé Dip

Start with the simple Hot Dip Base and add one of the following variations to create an unforgettable appetizer.

Hot Dip Base
> 16 ounces cream cheese, softened
> 1 1/3 cups grated Parmesan cheese
> 6 tablespoons mayonnaise

Sweet Onion Dip
> 1 cup finely chopped sweet onion, such as
>   Maui, Vidalia or Walla Walla

Roma Dip
> 1/2 cup pine nuts, toasted
> 1/4 cup basil pesto
> 1/3 cup drained oil-pack sun-dried tomatoes,
>   minced

Santa Fe Dip
> Reduce Hot Dip Base Parmesan cheese
>   quantity to 2/3 cup
> 1 (10-ounce) package frozen chopped
>   spinach, thawed, drained, squeezed dry
> 2/3 cup shredded Monterey Jack cheese
> 1/2 cup drained canned green chiles, chopped
> 2 teaspoons (or more) hot sauce
> 1/2 teaspoon cumin

Danube Dip
> Reduce Hot Dip Base Parmesan cheese
>   quantity to 2/3 cup
> 2/3 cup bleu cheese crumbles
> 1 cup praline chopped walnuts

For the dip base, beat the cream cheese, Parmesan cheese and mayonnaise in a mixing bowl until blended. Stir in the ingredients of one of the dip variations. Spoon the cream cheese mixture into a 1-quart soufflé dish or baking dish.

Bake at 350 degrees for 25 to 30 minutes or until brown and bubbly. Serve hot with assorted party crackers, French bread, toasted pita triangles and/or chips.

To make praline walnuts, heat 1/2 cup sugar in a heavy skillet over medium heat until caramelized. Remove from the heat. Stir in 1 cup chopped walnut pieces until coated. Spread the walnut mixture in a thin layer on a sheet of foil brushed with butter. Let stand until cool.

Serves 12 to 14

Sun-Dried Tomato Dip

Heat 2 tablespoons olive oil in a small skillet and add 2 minced garlic cloves. Sauté over medium heat until golden brown. Add 1/4 cup minced sun-dried tomatoes and cook until heated through. Remove from the heat and add 4 ounces goat cheese and 4 ounces softened cream cheese. Season with pepper and mix well. Serve with fresh vegetables and crackers.

Figs with Prosciutto

Figs are a classic Mediterranean fruit and can be eaten whole. Choose firm, unblemished figs that yield slightly to gentle pressure. Figs are very perishable and can be stored in the refrigerator for up to 3 days.

1/3 cup crème fraîche
2 teaspoons chopped fresh mint
2 teaspoons fresh lemon juice
2 to 3 teaspoons milk
1/8 teaspoon salt
12 fresh ripe figs
3 ounces prosciutto, thinly sliced
Sprigs of fresh mint

Whisk the crème fraîche, chopped mint and lemon juice in a bowl until mixed. Whisk in enough milk to produce a thick and creamy mixture. Season with the salt.

Cut the figs into halves and arrange on individual plates or a serving platter. Drape the prosciutto around the figs and drizzle with the crème fraîche mixture. Garnish with sprigs of mint.

Try this dish with a classic Italian white wine like Orvieto Classico or Vernaccia from Rocca della Macie.

Honeydew melon may be substituted for the fresh figs.

Serves 6

Crème Fraîche

Crème Fraîche is a cultured mixture of buttermilk and whipping cream. It has the consistency of thin sour cream and a tangy, nutty flavor. It may be purchased in the gourmet cheese section of some supermarkets, or in specialty food stores.

Layered Ginger Chicken Dip

Sweet-and-Sour Sauce

1 cup water
1/4 cup packed brown sugar
2 teaspoons cornstarch
1/4 cup ketchup
2 tablespoons rice vinegar
1 tablespoon Worcestershire sauce
Tabasco sauce to taste

Chicken Layer

3/4 cup shredded or chopped cooked
   chicken
1/2 cup shredded carrot
1/4 cup chopped unsalted peanuts
3 tablespoons sliced scallions
2 tablespoons soy sauce
1 tablespoon chopped fresh cilantro
1 tablespoon grated fresh gingerroot
1 teaspoon sesame oil
1 garlic clove, minced

Cream Cheese Layer

8 ounces cream cheese, softened
1 tablespoon milk

For the sauce, combine the water, brown sugar and cornstarch in a saucepan and mix well. Cook over medium heat until the brown sugar and cornstarch dissolve, stirring frequently. Stir in the ketchup, vinegar, Worcestershire sauce and Tabasco sauce. Simmer until thickened, stirring frequently. Let stand until cool.

For the chicken layer, combine the chicken, carrot, peanuts and scallions in a bowl and mix well. Stir in the soy sauce, cilantro, gingerroot, sesame oil and garlic. Chill, covered, in the refrigerator.

For the cream cheese layer, beat the cream cheese and milk in a mixing bowl until light and fluffy, scraping the bowl occasionally.

To assemble, spread the cream cheese mixture over the bottom of a flat 12-inch serving plate. Spread with the chicken mixture. Pour the sauce into a squeeze bottle. Drizzle the sauce in a decorative pattern over the top of the prepared layers or drizzle the sauce from a spoon. Chill, covered, until serving time. Serve with rice crackers.

Serves (about) 8

Place Cards

It is always nice to take the time before guests arrive to decide where people are sitting at the table. This eliminates any confusion and you can place people where you want them. Use your imagination and let your creative side show! Some simple ideas are:

- Paint names on rocks with paint or magic marker.
- Using metallic paint pens, write names on dried leaves.
- Buy or make sugar cookies in desired shapes, then write names in icing.
- Cut slits in apples or squash and insert place cards.

Asian Salsa with Won Ton Chips

Won Ton Chips

12 won ton wrappers, cut diagonally
    into halves
1/2 teaspoon garlic salt

Asian Salsa

1 cup chopped cucumber
1/2 cup chopped red bell pepper
1/2 cup thinly sliced scallions
1/3 cup coarsely chopped fresh cilantro
3 tablespoons soy sauce
1 garlic clove, minced
1 tablespoon rice vinegar
1 teaspoon sesame oil
1/2 teaspoon crushed red pepper

For the chips, coat each won ton half lightly with nonstick cooking spray and sprinkle with the garlic salt. Arrange the won ton halves in a single layer on a baking sheet. Bake at 375 degrees for 4 to 6 minutes or until light brown and crisp, turning halfway through the baking process. Remove to a wire rack to cool.

For the salsa, combine the cucumber, bell pepper, scallions, cilantro, soy sauce, garlic, vinegar, sesame oil and red pepper in a bowl and mix well. Chill, covered, until serving time. Serve with the chips.

Serves 4 to 6

Papaya Salsa

1 ripe papaya, peeled and chopped
1 small red bell pepper, chopped
1 small red onion, chopped
6 tablespoons lime juice (2 or 3 limes)
1/4 cup fresh cilantro, minced
1/4 cup pineapple juice
1/4 cup pine nuts, toasted
1 jalapeño chile, finely chopped
1 tablespoon gold tequila (optional)
Salt and pepper to taste

Combine the papaya, bell pepper, onion, lime juice, cilantro, pineapple juice, pine nuts, jalapeño chile and tequila in a bowl and mix gently. Season with salt and pepper. Chill, covered, until serving time. The salsa may be stored, covered, in the refrigerator for up to 4 days.

Serves 6 to 8

To add flair to your next Asian-theme dinner, set your table with woven mats, bamboo plants, and orchids. Just for fun, set a shiny black stone, available at garden shops, for each of the guests to rest their chopsticks on.

Mediterranean Salsa

Pita Chips

6 white or whole wheat pita rounds, split

Salsa

1 (6-ounce) jar marinated artichoke hearts
4 medium plum tomatoes, chopped
1/2 cup drained pitted black olives, chopped
2 to 3 tablespoons snipped or chopped
    fresh basil
2 tablespoons chopped red onion
2 garlic cloves, chopped
Juice of 1/2 lemon
1 tablespoon olive oil
1 teaspoon Cavender's seasoning or oregano
1/8 teaspoon balsamic vinegar
Salt and pepper to taste

For the chips, cut each pita round into 8 wedges. Arrange the wedges in a single layer on a baking sheet. Bake at 400 degrees for 8 to 10 minutes or until light brown. Cool slightly to crisp. Store in a sealable plastic bag.

For the salsa, drain the artichokes and chop, reserving the marinade. Combine the artichokes, tomatoes, olives, basil, onion and garlic in a bowl and mix well. Stir in the lemon juice, olive oil, Cavender's seasoning, balsamic vinegar, salt and pepper. Stir in the reserved marinade 1 tablespoon at a time if needed for the desired consistency. Let stand at room temperature for 1 hour to allow the flavors to blend, stirring occasionally. Serve with the baked pita chips.

Serves 4 to 6

Watermelon Salsa

1/4 cup fresh lime juice
1 tablespoon light brown sugar
3 cups finely chopped seeded watermelon
1 cup finely chopped honeydew melon or
    cantaloupe
1 medium cucumber, peeled, seeded, chopped
1/2 cup chopped red onion
1/4 cup fresh mint, chopped
2 to 3 tablespoons minced seeded jalapeño
    chile
2 tablespoons finely chopped candied ginger
1 tablespoon rice vinegar
1 teaspoon salt
1/2 teaspoon white pepper

Whisk the lime juice and brown sugar in a large bowl until the brown sugar dissolves. Add the watermelon, honeydew melon, cucumber, onion, mint, jalapeño chile, candied ginger, vinegar, salt and white pepper and mix gently. Drain the excess liquid before serving. Serve with tortilla chips, pita chips or won ton chips.

May be served as an accompaniment to chicken or fish.

Serves 4 to 6

Stacked Caviar Dip

6 hard-cooked eggs, finely chopped
3 tablespoons mayonnaise
3/4 cup chopped red onion
8 ounces cream cheese, softened
2/3 cup sour cream
2 tablespoons drained rinsed capers
1 (4-ounce) jar lumpfish red or black caviar
Lemon wedges
Snipped fresh parsley
Capers, drained and rinsed

Combine the eggs and mayonnaise in a bowl and mix well. Spread the egg mixture over the bottom of a greased 8-inch springform pan. Sprinkle with the onion. Beat the cream cheese and sour cream in a mixing bowl until smooth. Spread the cream cheese mixture over the prepared layers. Chill, covered, for 3 to 10 hours.

Remove the sides of the pan just before serving. Mound the capers in a circle in the center of the chilled layers. Spread the caviar evenly around the capers. Garnish with lemon wedges, parsley and/or capers. Serve with assorted party crackers, thin baguette slices, toast points and/or slices of cold baked potatoes.

Serves 8 to 12

Montrachet Spread

12 large garlic cloves, peeled
1 tablespoon olive oil
1 medium red onion, thinly sliced
2 tablespoons butter
1 tablespoon brown sugar
10 ounces Montrachet or other goat cheese, crumbled
1 tablespoon balsamic vinegar
1/4 cup fresh basil, thinly sliced

Place the garlic in a baking dish and drizzle with the olive oil. Roast, covered with foil, at 350 degrees for 35 minutes. Let stand until cool.

Cook the onion in the butter in a large skillet over medium heat for 10 minutes, stirring frequently. Sprinkle the brown sugar over the onion. Cook until the brown sugar dissolves, stirring constantly. Spoon the onion mixture into an 8×8-inch baking dish. Sprinkle with the cheese and roasted garlic cloves. Chill, covered, for 8 to 10 hours.

Bake, uncovered, at 350 degrees for 25 minutes or until the cheese melts. Drizzle with the balsamic vinegar and sprinkle with the basil just before serving. Serve with assorted party crackers or baguette slices.

Serves 10

White Wine Sangria

1/2 cup fresh orange juice
1/2 cup pineapple juice
1/4 cup water
1/4 cup sugar
11 ounces white wine
2 ounces Orange Curaçao
1/4 cup lemon-lime soda
1 ounce brandy
1 ounce crème de banana
1 lemon, thinly sliced and seeded
1 lime, thinly sliced and seeded
2 oranges, thinly sliced and seeded
Pineapple chunks
Maraschino cherries

Bring the orange juice, pineapple juice, water and sugar to a boil in a saucepan, stirring occasionally. Remove from the heat. Let stand until cool. Combine the wine, Orange Curaçao, soda, brandy and crème de banana in a pitcher and mix well. Stir in the cooled syrup. Add the lemon slices, lime slices and orange slices and mix well.

Pour the sangria into 4- to 6-ounce glasses. Garnish with pineapple chunks and/or cherries. You may prepare up to 12 hours in advance, adding the fruit just before serving. Double the recipe with little or no additional fruit.

Makes 6 servings

Coconut Margarita

Honey
Toasted shredded coconut
1/3 tequila
1/3 Coco Lopez
1/3 margarita mix

Rim margarita glasses with honey and toasted coconut. Process the tequila, Coco Lopez, margarita mix and ice in a blender until of a slushy consistency. Pour into the prepared margarita glasses.

Serves variable

Pear and Ginger Martini

3 cups pear nectar
12 ounces vodka
1 1/2 tablespoons fresh lemon juice
1 1/2 teaspoons fresh ginger juice
Ice cubes
Sliced pears

Mix the nectar, vodka, lemon juice and ginger juice in a large pitcher. Add enough ice to fill the pitcher and stir to chill. Pour into martini glasses. Garnish with sliced pears.

Serves 6 to 8

Pisco Sour

4 ounces Pisco (Chilean or Peruvian brandy)
4 teaspoons lemon juice or lime juice
2 teaspoons egg white (optional)
2 teaspoons sugar
Crushed ice
Angostura bitters (optional)

Combine the Pisco, lemon juice, egg white, sugar and crushed ice in a cocktail shaker. Cover and shake. Strain into 2 small glasses and serve straight up or add more crushed ice. Top with a few drops of angostura bitters.

Serves 2

The Ruby

12 ounces red grapefruit juice, chilled
Sugar to taste
6 ounces citrus vodka
2 slices fresh grapefruit, chilled
Sprigs of fresh mint

Dampen the rim of 2 martini glasses with some of the grapefruit juice and dip in sugar. Mix the remaining grapefruit juice and vodka in a cocktail shaker. Cover and shake. Pour into the prepared martini glasses. Garnish with grapefruit slices and fresh mint.

Serves 2

Ramos Gin Fizz

3 ounces gin
1 ounce Orange Curaçao
6 dashes of orange-flower water
4 teaspoons superfine sugar
2 egg whites
6 ounces half-and-half
Juice of 1 lemon

Flash-blend all the ingredients with a small amount of crushed ice. Pour into a stemmed glass and dust with nutmeg and serve.

Serves 2

CONTENTS

40   Asian Pear and Watercress Salad with Sesame Dressing
40   Cantaloupe and Avocado Salad with Chili Dressing
41   Baby Bleu Salad with Sweet and Spicy Pecans
42   Curried Couscous Salad
43   Edamame Salad
44   Stuffed Fresh Figs on Greens
44   Greek Potato Salad
45   Green and White Bean Salad
45   Indian Waldorf Salad
46   Multicolor Southwest Tomato Salad
46   Island Paradise Salad
47   Mixed Greens with Baked Goat Cheese and
     Roasted Red Pepper Vinaigrette
48   Mustard Greens with Grapefruit
49   Pacific Flavors Salad
50   Roasted Beet, Caraway and Red Cabbage Slaw
50   Tofu Coleslaw
51   Spinach and Berries Salad with Dill
52   Spinach Salad with Grilled Chicken and Mango Chutney
53   Spinach Salad with Crisp Red Chiles
54   Summer Orange Salad with Rhubarb Salsa
54   Front Range Steak Salad
55   Ham, Gruyère and Cabbage Salad
55   Pecan Chicken and Wild Rice
56   Grilled Salmon and Pear Salad
57   Cranberry Lemon Tuna Salad
57   Tuna, White Bean and Roasted Pepper Salad with
     Creamy Dijon Dressing
58   Japanese Shrimp Salad
59   Irish Mist Salad Dressing
59   Easy Balsamic Salad Dressing
59   Asian Sesame Dressing

SALADS

Asian Pear and Watercress Salad with Sesame Dressing

Try using watercress as a garnish—it looks great and gives a peppery taste to your dishes.

Sesame Dressing
1 (1/2-inch) slice fresh gingerroot
1/4 cup smooth peanut butter
1/4 cup rice vinegar
3 tablespoons Asian sesame oil
2 tablespoons water
1 1/2 teaspoons sugar
1 teaspoon Asian chili paste with garlic
1/4 teaspoon salt

Salad
2 medium Asian pears, peeled and
　　cut into 1/4-inch slices
2 bunches (5 cups) trimmed fresh
　　watercress sprigs
2 carrots, finely shredded

For the dressing, combine the gingerroot, peanut butter, vinegar, sesame oil, water, sugar, chili paste and salt in a blender. Process until smooth.

For the salad, toss the pears and watercress in a bowl. Divide the salad evenly among 6 salad plates. Drizzle with the desired amount of dressing and sprinkle with the carrots.

Serves 6

Cantaloupe and Avocado Salad with Chili Dressing

Chili Dressing
1/4 cup prepared chili sauce
1/4 cup honey
3 tablespoons white vinegar
2 teaspoons Worcestershire sauce
2 teaspoons minced onion
1/2 cup canola oil

Salad
1 small head butterhead lettuce, torn
1 small head red leaf lettuce, torn
1/2 cup chopped celery
1 small cantaloupe, sliced
1 large avocado, sliced

For the dressing, combine the chili sauce, honey, vinegar, Worcestershire sauce and onion in a bowl and mix well. Add the canola oil and whisk until blended. Chill, covered, in the refrigerator. Whisk before serving.

For the salad, toss the lettuce and celery in a large salad bowl. Add the desired amount of dressing and toss to coat lightly. Add the cantaloupe and avocado and toss gently.

Serves 6

Baby Bleu Salad with Sweet and Spicy Pecans

Sweet and Spicy Pecans

1/4 cup sugar

1 cup warm water

1 cup pecan halves

2 tablespoons sugar

1 tablespoon chili powder

1/8 teaspoon ground red pepper

Dijon Vinaigrette

1/2 cup fig vinegar or balsamic vinegar

3 tablespoons Dijon mustard

3 tablespoons honey

2 small shallots, minced

2 garlic cloves, minced

1/4 teaspoon salt

1/4 teaspoon pepper

1 cup olive oil

Salad

12 ounces salad greens

2 to 4 ounces bleu cheese, crumbled

1 pint fresh strawberries or any fresh
  seasonal fruit

For the pecans, dissolve 1/4 cup sugar in the warm water in a bowl and mix well. Stir in the pecans. Let stand for 10 minutes; drain. Combine 2 tablespoons sugar, chili powder and red pepper in a bowl and mix well. Add the pecans and toss to coat.

Spread the pecans in a single layer on a lightly greased baking sheet. Bake at 350 degrees for 10 minutes, stirring once. Let stand until cool. The pecans should be prepared 1 day in advance and stored in an airtight container. You may chill or freeze the pecans for up to 1 week.

For the vinaigrette, whisk the vinegar, Dijon mustard, honey, shallots, garlic, salt and pepper in a bowl. Whisk in the olive oil. You may prepare the vinaigrette up to 1 day in advance and store, covered, in the refrigerator.

For the salad, toss the salad greens with the vinaigrette and bleu cheese in a salad bowl. Divide the salad evenly among 8 salad plates. Top with the strawberries and sprinkle with the pecans.

Serves 8

Serving Suggestions

- Try serving dips in natural containers. They add a lot of color and are interesting to look at. Be creative and use hollowed-out pineapples; squash; red, green, and yellow peppers; purple cabbage; or radicchio.
- Pedestal cake stands make interesting serving trays.
- Baskets can be used to hold napkins or silverware for a buffet. Put a dish towel in them and they can hold bread, chips, raw veggies, crackers, or sandwiches. Best of all, you do not have to wash them. Just give them a little shake.
- Scatter rose petals on silver trays to serve your dessert.

Curried Couscous Salad

Orange Curry Vinaigrette
- 1/3 cup red wine vinegar
- 1/3 cup orange juice
- 1 tablespoon curry powder
- 1 teaspoon turmeric
- 1 teaspoon Dijon mustard
- 1/2 cup olive oil
- Salt and pepper to taste

Salad
- 2 1/4 cups chicken broth
- 10 ounces couscous
- 3/4 cup raisins
- 1/3 cup orange juice
- 2 cups fresh or frozen peas
- 1 1/2 cups chopped scallions
- 1 cup chopped carrot
- 1 cup chopped red bell pepper
- 3/4 cup pine nuts

For the vinaigrette, combine the vinegar, orange juice, curry powder, turmeric and Dijon mustard in a food processor fitted with a knife blade. Process until mixed. Add the olive oil, salt and pepper gradually, processing constantly until blended.

For the salad, bring the broth to a boil in a saucepan. Stir in the couscous. Remove from the heat. Let stand, covered, for 15 minutes; fluff with a fork. Let stand until cool. Plump the raisins in the orange juice in a small bowl.

Combine the cooled couscous, undrained raisins, peas, scallions, carrot, bell pepper and pine nuts in a salad bowl. Add the vinaigrette and toss to coat. Let stand for 30 to 60 minutes to allow the flavors to blend. Serve as an accompaniment to grilled meats or as a side dish on a buffet or take to your next potluck.

Serves 8

Couscous is semolina, a high-protein wheat that's been cooked and dried. The texture of cooked couscous is softer than that of rice and firmer than Cream of Wheat. Couscous, by itself, is bland until you add sauce or seasonings.

Edamame Salad

1¹/2 cups cooked shelled edamame beans
    (about 20 ounces of pods)
3 large carrots, coarsely grated
¹/3 cup thinly sliced green onions
2 tablespoons chopped fresh cilantro
2 tablespoons rice vinegar
2 tablespoons fresh lemon juice
1 tablespoon vegetable oil
1 teaspoon minced garlic
Salt and pepper to taste

Toss the edamame beans, carrots, green onions and cilantro in a bowl. Whisk the vinegar, lemon juice, oil and garlic in a small bowl. Add the vinaigrette to the bean mixture and toss to coat. Season with salt and pepper.

Chill, covered, until serving time. You may prepare up to 3 hours in advance and store, covered, in the refrigerator.

Serves 6

Edamame

Edamame, the Japanese name for fresh whole soybeans, is a trendy snack with major nutritional credentials. Look for the pods in the produce section or frozen in Asian markets, health food stores, or in any large grocery store.

Stuffed Fresh Figs on Greens

Mustard Vinaigrette

2 tablespoons red wine vinegar or white
    wine vinegar
1 teaspoon Dijon mustard
1 garlic clove, minced
1/2 cup olive oil
Salt and freshly ground pepper to taste

Salad

1 bunch watercress, stems removed and
    coarsely chopped
1/2 cup walnuts, toasted and coarsely chopped
31/2 tablespoons snipped fresh chives
3 tablespoons mayonnaise
2 tablespoons plain yogurt
1 teaspoon fresh lemon juice
1/4 teaspoon salt
1/8 teaspoon cayenne pepper
16 fresh figs
8 to 10 cups seasonal salad greens

For the vinaigrette, whisk the vinegar, Dijon mustard and garlic in a bowl until mixed. Add the olive oil gradually, whisking constantly until combined. Season with salt and pepper.

For the salad, toss the watercress, walnuts and chives in a bowl. Stir in a mixture of the mayonnaise, yogurt, lemon juice, salt and cayenne pepper.

Stand the figs upright on a hard surface. Cut an X through the stem end of each fig with sharp scissors. Pull apart gently, creating a cavity in each fig. Fill each fig with 1 tablespoon of the watercress mixture. Toss the salad greens with the desired amount of the vinaigrette in a bowl. Mound the salad greens evenly on 8 serving plates. Top each serving with 2 stuffed figs. Serve immediately.

Serves 8

Greek Potato Salad

1/2 cup olive oil
4 garlic cloves, minced
2 pounds red potatoes, peeled and cut into
    11/2-inch pieces
1 (16-ounce) package frozen pearl onions,
    thawed and drained
6 carrots, cut into halves lengthwise and cut
    into 11/2-inch pieces
4 (8-ounce) cans artichoke bottoms, drained
    and cut into halves
1 cup kalamata olives, cut into halves,
    rinsed, dried
1/4 cup fresh lemon juice
2 teaspoons dill weed
Salt and freshly ground pepper to taste

Heat the olive oil and garlic in a large heavy saucepan over low heat. Add the potatoes, onions and carrots and mix well. Cook for 30 minutes or until the vegetables are tender, stirring occasionally. Stir in the artichokes. Cook for 2 to 3 minutes longer or until the artichokes are tender. Remove from the heat.

Add the olives, lemon juice and dill weed to the potato mixture and mix gently. Season with salt and pepper. Serve at room temperature.

Serves 8 to 10

Green and White Bean Salad

Toasted Walnuts
1/2 cup walnuts, coarsely chopped
1/2 cup milk

Herb Vinaigrette
2 large shallots, minced
2 garlic cloves, minced
3 to 4 tablespoons red wine vinegar
1 to 2 tablespoons fresh lemon juice
1 tablespoon Dijon mustard
1 to 2 tablespoons minced fresh winter savory
    or tarragon
1 tablespoon minced fresh flat-leaf parsley
2 tablespoons olive oil
Salt and white pepper to taste

Salad
1/4 cup drained canned baby lima beans,
    rinsed and drained
1/4 cup drained canned white cannellini beans,
    rinsed and drained
1 pound fresh thin green beans, trimmed
Salt to taste
4 ounces Stilton cheese, crumbled

For the walnuts, soak the walnuts in the milk in a bowl for 1 hour; drain. Spread the walnuts in a single layer on a baking sheet. Toast at 400 degrees until light brown. Let stand until cool.

For the vinaigrette, whisk the shallots, garlic, vinegar, lemon juice, Dijon mustard, savory and parsley in a bowl. Add the olive oil a few drops at a time, whisking constantly. Season with salt and white pepper.

For the salad, toss the canned beans with enough vinaigrette to coat in a bowl. Cook the fresh green beans in boiling salted water in a saucepan until tender-crisp but very green; drain. Rinse the green beans with cold water until the beans are cool; drain. Toss the lima beans, cannellini beans and green beans in a bowl. Add the desired amount of remaining vinaigrette and mix well. Sprinkle with the walnuts and cheese.

Serves 4

Indian Waldorf Salad

3 cups chopped unpeeled Granny Smith apples
1/2 cup chopped celery
1/2 cup golden raisins
1/4 cup minced red onion
1/4 cup lite mayonnaise
2 teaspoons lime juice
1/2 teaspoon curry powder
1/2 teaspoon ground ginger
1/4 cup chopped raw or toasted almonds

Toss the apples, celery, raisins and onion in a bowl. Combine the mayonnaise, lime juice, curry powder and ginger in a small bowl and mix well. Fold the mayonnaise mixture into the apple mixture. Chill, tightly covered, for 30 minutes to several hours. Stir in the almonds just before serving.

Serves 4

Multicolor Southwest Tomato Salad

3 pounds ripe cherry tomatoes or teardrop
    tomatoes
10 medium tomatillos, husks removed,
    cored, thinly sliced
1 fresh jalapeño chile, seeded and minced
1/4 cup lightly packed fresh cilantro leaves
1/4 cup lime juice
Salt and pepper to taste
Lime wedges

Shop for tomatoes of varied colors. Include some tomatoes that are 1/2 inch or smaller in diameter. Cut any tomatoes larger than 3/4 inch in diameter into halves. Combine the tomatoes, tomatillos, jalapeño chile, cilantro and lime juice in a bowl and mix gently. Season with salt and pepper. Serve with lime wedges.

Serves 8

Island Paradise Salad

Honey Lime Dressing
    3 tablespoons honey
    2 tablespoons fresh lime juice
    1 tablespoon canola oil or vegetable oil
    1 teaspoon grated lime zest

Salad
    1 1/2 to 2 cups frozen sugar snap peas
    3 cups torn romaine
    1 avocado, cut into 1/2-inch pieces
    1 large ripe mango, peeled and cut into
        1/2-inch pieces
    1 small red onion, thinly sliced and
        separated into rings
    1/2 cup shredded unsweetened coconut,
        lightly toasted

For the dressing, combine the honey, lime juice, canola oil and lime zest in a jar with a tight-fitting lid. Shake to mix.

For the salad, cook the sugar snap peas using package directions; drain. Rinse with cold water to cool and stop the cooking process; drain. Combine the sugar snap peas, romaine, avocado, mango and onion in a bowl and mix gently. Add the dressing and toss to coat. Sprinkle with the coconut.

Serves 4 to 6

Tomatillos

Tomatillo, a fruit, is called the Mexican green tomato and belongs to the tomato family. After removing the thin parchment-like covering, wash the fruit and use uncooked in salads. If preferred, cook the tomatillo to soften its thick skin and enhance its flavor.

Mixed Greens with Baked Goat Cheese and Roasted Red Pepper Vinaigrette

Roasted Red Pepper Vinaigrette
1 (8-ounce) jar roasted red peppers, drained
1 cup olive oil
1/3 cup red wine vinegar
1/4 cup fresh cilantro leaves
1/2 teaspoon salt
1/4 teaspoon black pepper
1/4 teaspoon sugar
1/8 teaspoon crushed red pepper

Baked Goat Cheese
1 (5-ounce) log soft fresh goat cheese,
   such as Montrachet, chilled
1/2 cup flour
2 eggs, beaten
1/2 cup bread crumbs
Olive oil

Salad
12 ounces mixed salad greens

For the vinaigrette, process the red peppers in a blender or food processor until puréed. The purée should measure 3/4 cup. Add the olive oil, vinegar, cilantro, salt, black pepper, sugar and red pepper. Process until blended.

For the goat cheese, slice the goat cheese with dental floss. Chill, covered, in the freezer. Coat the slices with the flour. Chill, covered, in the freezer. Dip the slices in the eggs. Chill, covered, in the freezer. Coat the slices with the bread crumbs. Chill, covered, in the freezer.

Sauté the cheese slices in hot olive oil in a skillet for 30 seconds per side. Freeze for 40 minutes or until firm. You may prepare up to this point 2 weeks in advance. Store the frozen cheese slices in a sealable plastic bag in the freezer. Arrange the frozen slices in a single layer in a baking dish. Bake at 400 degrees for 10 minutes before serving.

For the salad, divide the salad greens evenly among serving plates. Arrange the warm goat cheese on top of each serving. Drizzle with the vinaigrette. Serve immediately.

Serves 4 to 6

Botanical Ice Bowls

Try this idea for a beautiful addition to your next buffet. The bowls are easy to make and can be made weeks in advance. All you need are assorted flowers or herbs, 2 glass bowls with a size difference of 1 to 2 inches, water, and masking tape. Start by placing a few flowers or herbs in the bottom of the bigger bowl. Place the smaller bowl inside the large bowl, center, and slowly fill the space between the two with water. Add more flowers or herbs, using a skewer to push them down into the space. Secure the smaller bowl in the center of the larger bowl, using a strip of masking tape across the edges of both bowls to ensure that it stays centered. Carefully place the bowls in the freezer and freeze for at least 8 hours.

Mustard Greens with Grapefruit

If you like mustard greens, try kale or collard greens.

Lime Dressing
    3 tablespoons finely chopped shallots
    2 tablespoons fresh lime juice
    3 tablespoons olive oil
    1/2 teaspoon sugar
    1/2 teaspoon salt

Salad
    5 cups young mustard greens, trimmed and
        cut into 1/2-inch pieces
    2/3 cup dates, chopped
    Salt to taste
    Sections of 2 pink grapefruit or
        red grapefruit
    Pomegranate seeds

For the dressing, combine the shallots and lime juice in a bowl and mix well. Let stand for 5 minutes. Whisk in the olive oil, sugar and salt.

For the salad, toss the mustard greens with the dates in a large bowl. Add the dressing and salt just before serving and toss to coat. Divide the salad evenly among 4 serving plates. Top with the grapefruit sections and sprinkle with pomegranate seeds.

The dressing, grapefruit sections and mustard greens may be prepared up to 4 hours in advance and stored, covered, in the refrigerator. Cover the greens with a damp paper towel and plastic wrap.

Serves 4

Pacific Flavors Salad

Pacific Flavors Dressing

- 1/3 cup fresh orange juice
- 1/3 cup balsamic vinegar
- 1/3 cup olive oil (not extra-virgin)
- 3 tablespoons minced fresh cilantro
- 3 tablespoons minced fresh mint
- 2 tablespoons lite soy sauce
- 2 tablespoons minced fresh gingerroot
- 2 teaspoons minced or grated orange zest
- 1/2 teaspoon Asian chili sauce

Salad

- 1/3 cup pine nuts
- 2 fresh papayas or the equivalent from a jar
- 2 ounces rice sticks
- 2 cups flavorless cooking oil
- 4 to 6 cups baby salad greens
- 1 whole nutmeg

For the dressing, combine the orange juice, balsamic vinegar, olive oil, cilantro, mint, soy sauce, gingerroot, orange zest and chili sauce in a jar with a tight-fitting lid. Shake to mix. Chill in the refrigerator. The dressing may be prepared up to 8 hours in advance and stored in the refrigerator.

For the salad, spread the pine nuts on a baking sheet. Toast at 325 degrees for 8 minutes or until light brown. Let stand until cool. Peel the papayas with a potato peeler. Cut into halves. Discard the seeds and cut the pulp into 1/2-inch pieces. Chill, covered, in the refrigerator.

Place the rice sticks in a large paper bag and seal. Pound the bag to break the rice sticks into small bundles. Heat the oil in a 10-inch sauté pan over medium-high heat. The oil has reached the correct temperature when a rice stick plunged into the oil expands immediately. Add a small bundle of rice sticks to the hot oil. Cook for 3 seconds or until they expand. Turn immediately with tongs and cook for 3 seconds longer. Remove the rice sticks to paper towels to drain. Repeat the process with the remaining bundles of rice sticks. Store in a paper bag at room temperature.

To assemble, toss the papayas and salad greens in a large bowl. Whisk the dressing and pour over the salad. Toss to mix. Fold in the crisp rice sticks, keeping them in as large pieces as possible. Divide the salad evenly among salad or dinner plates. Sprinkle with the pine nuts. Grate the nutmeg lightly over each salad serving using a nutmeg grater or cheese grater. Serve immediately.

Serves 4 to 6

Vases

Transform empty mineral water, wine, olive oil, and other colored glass bottles into vases. Assemble them in clusters and place single-stemmed flowers, such as cosmos, in each.

Roasted Beet, Caraway and Red Cabbage Slaw

8 medium beets, trimmed
2/3 cup apple cider vinegar
1/3 cup sugar
3 tablespoons stone-ground mustard
2 teaspoons caraway seeds
3/4 cup canola oil
Salt and freshly ground pepper to taste
10 cups thinly sliced red cabbage
    (1 small head)
3/4 cup finely chopped red onion
3 large carrots, coarsely grated
1/4 cup fresh dill weed, snipped

Wrap the beets tightly with foil. Bake at 400 degrees for 1 1/4 hours or until tender. Let stand until cool. Peel the beets and coarsely grate. Whisk the vinegar, sugar, stone-ground mustard and caraway seeds in a bowl. Add the canola oil gradually, whisking constantly. Season with salt and pepper.

Toss the beets, cabbage, onion and carrots in a bowl. Drizzle with the oil and vinegar mixture and toss to coat. Fold in the dill weed.

Serves 10 to 12

Tofu Coleslaw

4 cups thinly sliced green cabbage
3/4 cup grated carrot
3/4 cup finely chopped celery
1 cup (6 ounces) reduced-fat firm or silken
    tofu, drained
1/4 cup mayonnaise or reduced-fat mayonnaise
4 teaspoons rice vinegar
2 teaspoons prepared mustard
1 teaspoon sugar
1/2 teaspoon salt
2 garlic cloves
1/4 cup chopped fresh parsley

Toss the cabbage, carrot and celery in a large salad bowl. Combine the tofu, mayonnaise, vinegar, prepared mustard, sugar, salt and garlic in a blender or food processor. Process until smooth, scraping the side of the bowl occasionally. Add the parsley. Pulse once.

Add the tofu mixture to the cabbage mixture and toss to coat. Chill, covered, until serving time.

Raisins, chopped apples and/or nuts may be added for variety.

Serves 4 to 6

Spinach and Berries Salad with Dill

(Cover Recipe)

To remove berry stains, rub them with a wedge of lemon.

Red Wine Vinaigrette
- 1/2 cup olive oil
- 1/4 cup red wine vinegar
- 1/4 cup sugar
- 2 garlic cloves, crushed
- 1/4 teaspoon salt
- 1/4 teaspoon pepper
- 1/4 teaspoon dry mustard
- 1/4 teaspoon onion powder

Salad
- 1 cup slivered almonds
- 1 pound baby spinach leaves, trimmed
- 1 pound baby butterhead lettuce
- 1 bunch green onions, chopped
- 1/2 pint fresh strawberries, sliced
- 1/2 pint fresh raspberries
- 1/2 pint fresh blueberries
- 1/4 cup chopped fresh dill weed

For the vinaigrette, combine the olive oil, vinegar, sugar, garlic, salt, pepper, dry mustard and onion powder in a jar with a tight-fitting lid. Shake to mix. Chill until serving time.

For the salad, spread the almonds on a baking sheet. Toast at 350 degrees for 5 to 7 minutes or until golden brown, stirring after 3 to 4 minutes. Let stand until cool. Toss the almonds, spinach, lettuce, green onions, strawberries, raspberries, blueberries and dill weed in a large salad bowl. Add the vinaigrette just before serving and toss to coat.

Wine recommendation, Pinot Gris, Oak Knoll from Oregon.

Serves 8 to 10

Centerpiece Height

Large arrangements of flowers or objects d'art are captivating—unless they obstruct the view between you and the person across the table. Keep centerpieces under 12 inches tall.

Spinach Salad with Grilled Chicken and Mango Chutney

Cut spinach with a stainless steel knife. A carbon steel blade will cause discoloration.

Mango Chutney Dressing
    $1/2$ cup balsamic vinegar
    $1/2$ cup olive oil
    3 tablespoons mango chutney
    $1^1/2$ teaspoons honey
    1 teaspoon Dijon mustard
    $1/2$ teaspoon curry powder
    Salt and pepper to taste

Salad
    8 cups trimmed fresh spinach leaves,
        torn into bite-size pieces
    8 ounces grilled chicken or turkey,
        cut into strips
    $3/4$ cup chopped red onion
    1 cup cashews, toasted and coarsely
        chopped

For the dressing, combine the balsamic vinegar, olive oil, chutney, honey, Dijon mustard and curry powder in a food processor. Process until puréed. Season with salt and pepper.

For the salad, toss the spinach, chicken and onion in a salad bowl. Drizzle with the dressing and sprinkle with the cashews.

Serves 4 to 6

Cactus Pointers

- Cactus pads are called nopales and are known as "the fruit of the desert."
- When nopales are cooked they have the texture of a sautéed bell pepper.
- Nopales can be found fresh at specialty markets and canned in the Mexican food section of grocery stores.
- Select nopales that are firm and the size of your hand.

Spinach Salad with Crisp Red Chiles

Salad

  6 dried large red Anaheim chiles
  1/4 cup olive oil
  1 pound fresh whole or chopped cactus pads
      (nopales), or 1 1/2 cups drained canned
      chopped cactus
  2 quarts water
  1 pound fresh spinach, trimmed, torn, chilled
  4 ounces watercress, trimmed, torn, chilled
  1 large red onion, thinly sliced
  1 cup sliced radishes
  1 pound queso asadero or mozzarella cheese,
      cut into 1/2-inch cubes
  2 ripe large avocados

Cider Dressing

  2/3 cup cider vinegar
  1 tablespoon soy sauce
  1 garlic clove, minced
  1/4 teaspoon pepper

For the salad, wipe the chiles with a damp tea towel. Cut the chiles crosswise into thin strips, discarding the seeds and stems. Combine the chiles and olive oil in a skillet. Cook over low heat for 2 to 3 minutes or until the chiles are crisp, stirring constantly. Remove the chiles to a bowl with a slotted spoon, reserving the oil for the dressing. Secure the fresh cactus pad with tongs and use a knife to scrape off any spines or prickly hairs; wear gloves to protect hands. Trim around the edge of each pad if the skin is tough. Cut the cactus into 1/2-inch squares.

Bring the water to a boil in a 3- or 4-quart saucepan over high heat. Add the cactus; reduce the heat. Simmer for 5 minutes or until the cactus is barely tender when pierced with a fork. Drain the cactus and rinse to remove any mucilaginous coating. Do not cook canned cactus.

Layer the spinach, watercress, cactus, onion, radishes and cheese 1/2 at a time in a large salad bowl. You may store, covered, in the refrigerator for up to 4 hours at this point. Slice the avocados just before serving. Arrange the avocado slices and Anaheim chiles over the top of the salad.

For the dressing, whisk the vinegar, soy sauce, garlic, pepper and reserved chili oil in a bowl. Drizzle the dressing over the salad and toss gently to coat. Serve immediately.

Serves 4

Summer Orange Salad with Rhubarb Salsa

Ginger Dressing
> 3 tablespoons rice wine vinegar
> 2 tablespoons finely minced candied ginger
> 1 tablespoon shredded orange zest

Rhubarb Salsa
> 3/4 cup finely chopped rhubarb
> 2 tablespoons sugar
> 3/4 cup finely chopped jicama
> 6 large radishes, finely chopped

Salad
> 6 large butterhead lettuce leaves, chilled
> 3 large oranges, peeled and white pith
>   removed

For the dressing, combine the vinegar, ginger and orange zest in a jar with a tight-fitting lid. Shake to mix.

For the salsa, combine the rhubarb and sugar in a bowl and mix well. Let stand for 30 minutes or until juices form. Stir in the dressing, jicama and radishes.

For the salad, line each salad plate with a lettuce leaf. Thinly slice the oranges crosswise and arrange equal portions of the slices on the prepared plates. Spoon the salsa over the oranges. Serve immediately.

Serves 6

Front Range Steak Salad

> 1 pound fresh thin green beans, trimmed
> Salt to taste
> 6 cups arugula
> 4 cups cherry tomatoes, cut into halves
> 1 1/4 cups pitted kalamata olives, cut into
>   halves
> 1/2 cup plus 1 tablespoon olive oil
> 6 tablespoons balsamic vinegar
> 3 (8- to 9-ounce) New York strip steaks
> Pepper to taste
> 1 1/2 cups (6 ounces) crumbled bleu cheese

Cook the green beans in a saucepan of boiling salted water for 4 minutes or until tender-crisp; drain. Plunge the beans into a bowl of ice water to stop the cooking process; drain. Combine the green beans, arugula, tomatoes and olives in a large bowl and mix gently.

Whisk 1/2 cup of the olive oil and the balsamic vinegar in a small bowl. Brush the steaks with the remaining 1 tablespoon olive oil. Grill the steaks over medium-high heat for 4 minutes per side for medium-rare or to the desired degree of doneness. Slice the steaks crosswise into thin strips.

Toss the green bean mixture with enough of the olive oil mixture to coat. Season with salt and pepper. Divide the salad equally among 6 serving plates. Top each salad with equal portions of the steak strips and sprinkle with the cheese.

Serves 6

Ham, Gruyère and Cabbage Salad

Roquefort Dressing
1/2 cup red wine vinegar
1 tablespoon coarse-grain mustard
1 large garlic clove, minced
1 1/2 cups olive oil
1/3 cup crumbled Roquefort cheese,
    at room temperature

Salad
1 1/2 to 2 pounds cabbage, shredded
12 ounces baked ham, cut into
    1/4×3/4-inch strips
12 ounces Gruyère cheese, cut into
    1/4×3/4-inch julienne strips
6 tablespoons minced fresh parsley
Salt and pepper to taste
1 head Bibb lettuce, separated into leaves
1 or 2 truffles, grated (optional)

For the dressing, whisk the vinegar, the mustard and garlic in a bowl. Add the olive oil gradually, whisking constantly until mixed. Add the cheese and stir until smooth. You may prepare the dressing up to 1 day in advance and store, covered, in the refrigerator. Stir before serving.

For the salad, combine the cabbage, ham, cheese, 4 tablespoons of the parsley and the dressing in a bowl and mix well. Season with salt and pepper. Line a serving platter with the lettuce. Mound the salad in the center of the lettuce. Sprinkle with the remaining 2 tablespoons parsley and the truffles. Serve immediately. For a drier consistency use 2 pounds of cabbage.

Serves 12 to 14

Pecan Chicken and Wild Rice

Dressing
1/2 cup rice vinegar
1/3 cup vegetable oil
2 large garlic cloves, minced
1 tablespoon Dijon mustard
1/2 teaspoon each salt and pepper
1/4 teaspoon sugar

Salad
1 cup wild rice
4 cups chicken stock
Juice of 1 lemon
2 whole chicken breasts, cooked
1 bunch green onions, minced
6 to 8 ounces snow peas, trimmed
2 ripe avocados, chopped
1 cup pecan pieces, toasted

For the dressing, combine the vinegar, oil, garlic, Dijon mustard, salt, pepper and sugar in a jar with a tight-fitting lid. Shake to mix.

For the salad, combine the wild rice, stock and lemon juice in a saucepan. Bring to a boil; reduce the heat. Simmer, covered, for 1 hour or until tender; drain. Chop the chicken into bite-size pieces, discarding the skin and bones. Combine the dressing, rice, chicken, green onions and snow peas in a bowl 2 hours prior to serving and mix well. Chill, covered, in the refrigerator. Add the avocados and pecans just before serving and mix gently.

Serves 6 to 8

Grilled Salmon and Pear Salad

Balsamic Vinaigrette

3/4 cup olive oil

1/4 cup balsamic vinegar

2 tablespoons lemon juice

2 tablespoons honey

1 teaspoon salt

1/2 teaspoon pepper

Salad

1/3 cup hazelnuts

4 salmon fillets

4 cups baby salad greens

2 ripe Bartlett pears, thinly sliced

For the vinaigrette, whisk the olive oil, balsamic vinegar, lemon juice, honey, salt and pepper in a bowl until blended.

For the salad, spread the hazelnuts in a single layer on a baking sheet. Toast at 275 degrees for 20 to 30 minutes or until light brown, stirring occasionally. Let stand until cool.

Drizzle each fillet with 1 1/2 teaspoons of the vinaigrette. Grill the fillets over hot coals for 8 to 12 minutes or just until the salmon flakes easily, turning once. Toss the salad greens with some of the remaining vinaigrette in a bowl. Mound the salad greens on a large platter. Top with the pears, warm salmon and hazelnuts. Drizzle the remaining vinaigrette over the salmon.

Serves 4

Cranberry Lemon Tuna Salad

2 (12-ounce) cans water-pack white tuna, drained
3/4 cup lite mayonnaise
3 tablespoons lemon juice
2/3 cup finely chopped red onion
1 cup (heaping) dried cranberries

Mash the tuna with the mayonnaise in a bowl until smooth. Stir in the lemon juice, onion and cranberries. Chill, covered, for 2 hours or longer to allow the cranberries to soften.

Serves 4 to 6

Tuna, White Bean and Roasted Pepper Salad with Creamy Dijon Dressing

Creamy Dijon Dressing
1/4 cup mayonnaise
1/4 cup olive oil
3 tablespoons Dijon mustard
2 tablespoons Champagne vinegar or white wine vinegar
Salt and pepper to taste

Salad
Italian salad dressing
4 (4- to 8-ounce) tuna fillets
5 cups mixed baby salad greens
1 (15-ounce) can small white beans, drained and rinsed
2/3 cup chopped drained oil-pack roasted red peppers
1/3 cup chopped red onion
2/3 cup pitted kalamata olives or other brine-cured black olives, cut into halves

For the dressing, whisk the mayonnaise, olive oil, Dijon mustard and vinegar in a bowl until blended. Season with salt and pepper. You may prepare up to 1 day in advance and store, covered, in the refrigerator.

For the salad, drizzle Italian salad dressing over the tuna in a shallow dish, turning to coat. Marinate in the refrigerator for 30 minutes, turning once or twice. Grill the tuna over hot coals until the fillets flake easily.

Toss the salad greens with just enough of the Dijon dressing to coat. Mound the salad greens on 4 serving plates. Toss the beans, roasted peppers and onion in a bowl with just enough of the Dijon dressing to coat. Top the salad greens with equal portions of the bean mixture and tuna. Sprinkle with the olives. Serve at room temperature. Allow approximately 4 ounces of tuna per serving for a side salad and approximately 8 ounces of tuna per serving for an entrée.

Serves 4

Japanese Shrimp Salad

Wasabi paste and pickled ginger are located in the fish and/or deli section of most large supermarkets.

4 quarts water

1 1/2 pounds medium shrimp (51- to 60-count)

8 whole black peppercorns

2 thick slices lemon

1 bay leaf

1/2 cup seasoned rice vinegar

2 to 3 teaspoons wasabi paste

1/2 cup pickled ginger, chopped

1/3 cup chopped green onions (white and tender green parts)

4 teaspoons sesame oil

Coarsely ground pepper to taste

4 whole radicchio leaves

Avocado slices

Toasted sesame seeds

Bring the water to a rolling boil in a stockpot. Rinse the shrimp in cold water several times; do not peel. Add the shrimp, peppercorns, lemon slices and bay leaf to the boiling water. Return the water to a boil. Boil for 2 to 3 minutes. Plunge the shrimp into a bowl of ice water to stop the cooking process and allow to cool; drain.

Pour the vinegar into a large bowl. Whisk in 2 teaspoons of the wasabi paste until smooth. Stir in the ginger, green onions and sesame oil. Peel the shrimp and cut into bite-size pieces if desired; this depends on the size of the shrimp. Add the shrimp to the vinegar mixture and mix well. Stir in the ground pepper. Taste and add the remaining 1 teaspoon wasabi paste if desired. Chill, covered, for 20 minutes to 2 hours to allow the salad to chill and the flavors to blend.

Spoon equal portions of the salad into each whole radicchio leaf and place on a serving plate. Top each salad with avocado slices and sprinkle with sesame seeds. Serve with additional wasabi paste for those who like it hot.

Serve this salad as a very light lunch or as a first course. Chop the shrimp into smaller pieces and spread the shrimp mixture in endive spears for an eloquent hors d'oeuvre. Do not prepare more than 2 hours in advance as the shrimp tend to become mushy.

Serves 4

Napkin Rings

Use braided raffia or ribbon—wire-edged ribbon for best effect—to make your own napkin rings. It is very simple and is a most effective way of linking together the assorted decorative elements of your table.

Irish Mist Salad Dressing

1/4 cup Dijon mustard
1/4 cup Irish Mist Liqueur
3 tablespoons red wine vinegar
3 tablespoons honey
6 tablespoons canola oil

Whisk the Dijon mustard, liqueur, vinegar and honey in a bowl until blended. Add the canola oil gradually, whisking constantly. Store, covered, in the refrigerator.

Makes (about) 1 1/4 cups

Easy Balsamic Salad Dressing

1/2 cup balsamic vinegar
1/2 cup olive oil
2 tablespoons chopped fresh dill weed
4 garlic cloves, crushed
Juice of 1 lemon
Freshly ground pepper to taste

Combine the balsamic vinegar, olive oil, dill weed, garlic, lemon juice and pepper in a jar with a tight-fitting lid and seal tightly. Shake to mix.

Makes (about) 1 1/4 cups

Asian Sesame Dressing

1/3 cup sugar
1/3 cup canola oil
1/3 cup white vinegar
1/4 cup toasted sesame seeds
1/8 to 1/4 teaspoon red pepper flakes

Combine the sugar, canola oil, vinegar, sesame seeds and red pepper flakes in a jar with a tight-fitting lid and seal tightly. Shake to mix.

Makes (about) 1 cup

To make a smooth vinaigrette, combine the ingredients in a jar with a tight-fitting lid and add 1 ice cube. Shake vigorously, then discard the ice cube.

contents CONTENTS

62 Spicy Carrot Soup with Red Curry

63 Baked Potato Soup

64 Curry Pumpkin Soup

65 Chilled Sorrel Soup

65 Creamy Autumn Vegetable Soup

66 Farmer's Market Soup

67 Thai One On Soup

68 Chicken Tortilla Soup

69 Mile-High Chili over Rice

70 Scallop Dumplings in Asian Broth

71 Leek and Sautéed Shrimp Soup

72 Après Ski Stew

72 Irish Lamb and Barley Stew

73 Seafood Stew with Basil and Tomatoes

74 Cuban Shrimp Stew

76 Venison Steak Sandwiches

76 Viejo Turkey and Chutney Sandwiches

77 Lemon Tarragon Chicken Salad Sandwiches

78 Elegant Chicken and Brie Croissants

80 Open-Face Smoked Salmon Sandwiches with
    Goat Cheese

81 Open-Face Tuna Melt

81 Southwestern Shrimp Sandwiches

82 Country Picnic Loaf

83 Greek Pitas

SOUPS AND SANDWICHES

Spicy Carrot Soup with Red Curry

1 tablespoon canola oil
4 carrots, thickly sliced (about 2 cups)
2 thin slices fresh gingerroot
1 medium onion, finely chopped
4 cups chicken broth
2 cups water
1/2 cup unsweetened coconut milk
1/2 teaspoon (or more) red curry paste
3 carrots, julienned (about 1 1/2 cups)
Salt and freshly ground pepper to taste
4 teaspoons unsweetened coconut milk
1 scallion, julienned
1 tablespoon chopped fresh cilantro leaves
1 teaspoon minced candied ginger

Heat the canola oil in a large saucepan. Stir in the sliced carrots and gingerroot. Cook over medium-high heat for 6 to 8 minutes or until the carrots are tender-crisp and light brown, stirring constantly. Add the onion and mix well.

Cook for 2 minutes or until the onion is tender, stirring constantly. Stir in the broth, water, 1/2 cup coconut milk and curry paste. Bring to a boil; reduce the heat. Simmer, covered, for 25 minutes or until the carrots are tender.

Strain the liquid into another saucepan, reserving the solids. Discard the gingerroot. Transfer the solids to a blender. Add 2 cups of the reserved liquid to the blender. Process until puréed. Return the purée to the saucepan. Stir in the julienned carrots. Simmer for 5 minutes or until the carrots are tender, stirring occasionally. Season with salt and pepper.

Ladle the soup into bowls. Swirl 1 teaspoon of the coconut milk into each serving. Sprinkle with the scallion, cilantro and candied ginger. May also serve chilled.

Add chopped cooked chicken breast or chopped steamed shrimp for variety or prepare with vegetable stock and tofu for a vegetarian soup.

Makes 4 (2-cup) servings

Coconut Milk

Coconut milk is the liquid pressed from the coconut pulp. It is used in many Asian dishes. Coconut cream is made by chilling coconut milk, then skimming off the creamy surface.

Baked Potato Soup

3 (14-ounce) cans chicken broth
1/4 cup plus 1 tablespoon instant potato flakes
1/2 cup (1 stick) butter
1/2 cup flour
3 1/2 cups milk
1/4 teaspoon garlic powder
1/4 teaspoon white pepper
1/4 teaspoon sugar
Salt and black pepper to taste
4 large baking potatoes with skins, baked,
    cooled, cubed
1/4 cup thinly sliced green onions
1/4 cup crumbled crisp-cooked bacon or
    bacon bits
1/2 cup (2 ounces) shredded Cheddar cheese
Sour cream

Combine the broth and potato flakes in a bowl and mix well. Heat the butter in a large saucepan over medium heat until melted. Stir in the flour. Cook until the mixture is light brown, stirring constantly. Add the milk gradually, stirring constantly.

Cook until bubbly and thickened, stirring constantly. Stir in the potato flake mixture, garlic powder, white pepper, sugar, salt and black pepper. Simmer for 20 minutes, stirring occasionally. Add the baked potatoes and mix gently.

Simmer until of the desired consistency, stirring occasionally. Ladle into soup bowls. Sprinkle each serving with green onions, bacon and cheese. Top with a dollop of sour cream.

Serves 6 to 8

Accompaniments and
Garnishes for Soup

• Chopped or whole herbs
• Roasted nuts, chopped
• Thinly sliced sauteed baby mushrooms
• Cooked polenta, cut into tiny shapes
• Ribbons of carrots or cucumber
• Dry-roasted spice seeds such as cumin
• Herb butter, chilled and cut into an attractive shape

Curry Pumpkin Soup

Consider serving this soup in a hollowed-out pumpkin. It adds a nice autumn look to your table.

1 cup chopped onion
1 garlic clove, crushed
1/4 cup (1/2 stick) butter
1 teaspoon curry powder
1/2 teaspoon salt
1/4 teaspoon coriander
1/4 teaspoon crushed red pepper flakes
3 cups chicken broth
1 (15-ounce) can pumpkin
1 cup half-and-half or fat-free half-and-half
Sour cream
Chopped fresh chives
Toasted pumpkin seeds

Sauté the onion and garlic in the butter in a saucepan until the onion is tender. Stir in the curry powder, salt, coriander and red pepper flakes. Cook for 1 minute, stirring occasionally. Add the broth and mix well. Bring to a gentle boil.

Boil for 15 to 20 minutes, stirring occasionally. Stir in the pumpkin and half-and-half. Cook for 5 minutes, stirring occasionally.

Process the soup in batches in a blender until creamy. Ladle the warm soup into bowls. Top each serving with a dollop of sour cream and sprinkle with chives and/or toasted pumpkin seeds.

Serves 6 to 8

Chilled Sorrel Soup

Sorrel is a tart member of the buckwheat family. It has leaves shaped like spinach and has a nice lemony flavor. Sorrel is located with other fresh herbs in the grocery store.

1 medium yellow onion, chopped
3 tablespoons butter
30 sorrel leaves, chopped (about 2 bunches)
6 cups chicken stock or reduced-sodium reduced-fat chicken stock
1 teaspoon sugar
1 cup sour cream or reduced-fat sour cream
Chopped fresh dill weed

Sauté the onion in the butter in a saucepan until tender. Stir in the sorrel. Cook for 3 to 5 minutes or until the leaves are limp and olive green in color, stirring frequently. Add the stock and sugar and mix well.

Simmer for 30 minutes, stirring occasionally. Chill, covered, in the refrigerator. Pour the soup into a blender or food processor. Add the sour cream. Process until smooth. Chill until ready to serve. Ladle into soup bowls. Sprinkle each serving with chopped dill weed.

Serves 6

Creamy Autumn Vegetable Soup

1/2 cup chopped yellow onion
6 green onions, chopped (white and tender green parts)
1 garlic clove, minced (optional)
1/4 cup (1/2 stick) butter or margarine
4 (8-ounce) zucchini, sliced
3 medium carrots, sliced
1 (14-ounce) can chicken broth or reduced-sodium fat-free chicken broth
1 1/2 cups water
1/2 cup half-and-half or fat-free half-and-half
1 teaspoon salt
1/4 teaspoon coarsely ground pepper
3/4 cup loosely packed fresh basil leaves, chopped

Cook the yellow onion, green onions and garlic in the butter in a 4-quart saucepan over medium heat for 8 minutes or until the onion and green onions are tender but not brown, stirring frequently. Stir in the zucchini and carrots. Add the broth and water and mix well. Bring to a boil over high heat; reduce the heat to low.

Simmer, covered, for 15 minutes or until the vegetables are tender, stirring occasionally. Process the soup in batches in a food processor until slightly chunky. Return the soup to the saucepan. Stir in the half-and-half, salt and pepper. Cook just until heated through, stirring frequently. Stir in the basil just before serving. Ladle into soup bowls.

Makes 8 (1-cup) servings

Farmer's Market Soup

The bright taste of this soup comes from "sweating" fresh whole vegetables and fruit to capture every bit of their flavor. And while it tastes rich, the only "cream" in this soup refers to how the ingredients are puréed. If using a blender, remove the cap from the lid to allow the steam to escape.

1 medium Granny Smith apple
1/4 cup (1/2 stick) butter or margarine
3/4 cup chopped red onion
1/4 cup chopped shallots
1 medium tomato, cut into quarters
3 ribs celery with leaves, cut into
    2-inch pieces
1/3 cup dry sherry
1/2 teaspoon nutmeg
1/2 teaspoon ground ginger
2 cups chicken broth
1/2 teaspoon salt
Freshly ground pepper to taste
Apple slices
Snipped fresh chives
Chopped fresh cilantro

Cut the Granny Smith apple into quarters, leaving the peel and core intact. Discard the seeds. Heat the butter in a nonstick Dutch oven over medium-low heat until melted. Stir in the onion and shallots.

Cook until the onion is tender and golden brown. Arrange the apple quarters, tomato and celery in one layer over the onion mixture so that each piece touches the bottom of the stockpot. Pour the sherry over the top. Sprinkle with the nutmeg and ginger.

Dampen 2 sheets of waxed paper with cold water. Arrange the waxed paper over the fruit and vegetable mixture, making sure the waxed paper reaches to the edge of the Dutch oven. This will create a seal that will capture the steam and help the vegetables and fruit to "sweat" in their own juices. Simmer, covered, for 1 hour. If not using a nonstick pan, check underneath the waxed paper periodically to make sure the mixture is not sticking.

Discard the waxed paper and add the broth, salt and pepper to the fruit and vegetable mixture. Cook for 2 to 3 minutes, stirring occasionally. Remove from the heat. Process the soup in batches in a food processor or blender until puréed. Press the purée through a sieve into a clean saucepan. Reheat the soup, stirring occasionally. Taste and adjust the seasonings. Ladle into soup bowls. Top each serving with apple slices and sprinkle with chives and cilantro.

Makes 4 (1-cup) servings

Thai One On Soup

1 (14-ounce) can unsweetened coconut milk
2 cups chopped chicken breast
2 tablespoons fish sauce
1 tablespoon grated fresh gingerroot
1 (15-ounce) can straw mushrooms, drained
3/4 cup water
2 tablespoons lime juice
10 Thai chile peppers, sliced lengthwise, or
    1 large jalapeño chile, seeded and
    chopped
1 (4- to 6-inch) stalk lemon grass, thinly
    sliced horizontally
2 tablespoons Asian chili oil
1 teaspoon sugar
Chopped fresh cilantro

Shake the can of coconut milk. Pour half of the coconut milk into a large saucepan. Bring to a boil; reduce the heat to medium. Stir in the chicken, fish sauce and gingerroot. Stir-fry for 3 to 4 minutes or until the chicken is cooked through. Cut any large mushrooms into halves lengthwise. Add the remaining coconut milk, water and mushrooms to the saucepan.

Bring to a boil. Stir in the lime juice, Thai chile peppers, lemon grass, chili oil and sugar. Simmer for 5 minutes, stirring occasionally. Ladle into soup bowls. Sprinkle with cilantro.

Makes 6 (1-cup) servings

Lemon Grass

The stalk of the lemon grass has a floral, lemon-lime flavor that is one of the hallmarks of many Asian dishes. Look for stalks that have thick, firm heavy bulbs and tightly bound green leaves. Thinly chop or slice the inner core; crush the slices with the back of a knife to release their aroma and oils. Use lemon grass raw or cooked in marinades, salads, curries, and soups.

Chicken Tortilla Soup

4 corn tortillas
Salt to taste
6 cups chicken broth
2 cups tomato juice
1 (14-ounce) can diced tomatoes
1 (8-ounce) can tomato sauce
1 carrot, julienned
5 jalapeño chiles, chopped, or
    1 (4-ounce) can chopped green chiles
1/2 cup chopped red onion
1/2 cup fresh cilantro, chopped
1/4 cup fresh basil, chopped
3 garlic cloves, minced
1 tablespoon chili powder
1 teaspoon cumin
1 teaspoon garlic powder
4 boneless skinless chicken breasts,
    grilled and thinly sliced
12 ounces Monterey Jack cheese, shredded
1/2 avocado, sliced
1/2 fresh tomato, chopped
2 tablespoons lime juice

Cut the tortillas into 1/2×3-inch strips and sprinkle with salt. Arrange the tortilla strips in a single layer on a baking sheet. Bake at 375 degrees until light brown and crisp. Let stand until cool.

Combine the broth, tomato juice, undrained canned tomatoes, tomato sauce and carrot in a large saucepan and mix well. Simmer for 10 minutes, stirring occasionally. Stir in the jalapeño chiles, onion, cilantro, basil, garlic, chili powder, cumin and garlic powder. Simmer for 5 minutes longer, stirring occasionally.

Ladle the soup into heated soup bowls. Add equal portions of the chicken, tortilla strips and cheese to each bowl. Top each serving with the sliced avocado and chopped fresh tomato. Drizzle with the lime juice.

Makes 8 to 10 servings

The idea of entertaining has shifted recently, and people are focusing on smaller, more intimate gatherings at home. It is important that we continue to connect with friends and family and let that be the focus. Be creative with your menu and place settings, and realize that there is no one way to do anything. Allow for mistakes and "go with the flow."

Mile-High Chili over Rice

1 (15-ounce) can whole kernel corn, drained
12 ounces smoked turkey kielbasa, cut into
    1/2-inch pieces
11/4 cups mild, medium or hot salsa
1 cup (1-inch pieces) red bell pepper
1 cup (1-inch pieces) yellow bell pepper
1 tablespoon chili powder
2 cups hot cooked long grain rice
1/4 cup sour cream, lite sour cream or
    fat-free sour cream
1/4 cup crushed baked tortilla chips
1/4 cup chopped fresh cilantro
1/4 cup chopped green onions

Combine the corn, kielbasa, salsa, bell peppers and chili powder in a slow cooker and mix well. Cook, covered, on Low for 8 hours, stirring occasionally.

To serve, spoon 1/2 cup of the rice into each chili bowl. Ladle 1 cup of the chili over the rice in each bowl. Top each serving with 1 tablespoon of the sour cream and 1 tablespoon each of the chips, cilantro and green onions.

Makes 4 (1-cup) servings

Cilantro

Cilantro is the bright green leaves and stems of the coriander plant. Cilantro, which is also known as Chinese parsley, has a lively pungent fragrance. It is widely used in Asian, Caribbean, and Latin American cooking. Cilantro can be found year-round in most supermarkets and is sold in bunches. Choose leaves with a bright color and no sign of wilting. Just before using cilantro, wash and pat dry with paper towels. Both the leaves and stems can be used in fresh or cooked dishes.

Scallop Dumplings in Asian Broth

Dumplings

12 ounces sea scallops
1 egg white
1 tablespoon soy sauce
1 scallion, coarsely chopped
2 teaspoons minced fresh gingerroot
2 teaspoons vegetable oil
1 1/2 teaspoons sesame oil
1/2 teaspoon kosher salt
1/4 teaspoon chopped garlic
1/2 (or more) jalapeño chile, minced

Broth

3 (14-ounce) cans reduced-sodium chicken broth
2 (3-inch) strips lemon zest
2 (3-inch) strips lime zest
3 large garlic cloves, minced
2 teaspoons soy sauce
2 teaspoons minced fresh gingerroot
Freshly ground pepper to taste
Juice of 1/2 lime
1 teaspoon sesame oil
3 cups thinly sliced napa cabbage
16 snow peas, cut diagonally into 1-inch pieces
1 medium carrot, julienned
Fresh cilantro leaves
Hot Asian chili paste

For the dumplings, reserve 3 whole scallops. Cut the remaining scallops into halves. Combine the scallop halves, egg white, soy sauce, scallion, gingerroot, vegetable oil, sesame oil, salt, garlic and jalapeño chile in a food processor. Pulse to the consistency of a coarse paste. Scrape the paste into a bowl. Chop the reserved sea scallops and fold into the paste. Chill, covered, in the refrigerator. The dumpling mixture may be prepared in advance and stored, covered, in the refrigerator.

For the broth, combine the broth, lemon zest, lime zest, garlic, soy sauce and gingerroot in a large saucepan. Season with pepper. Simmer, covered, for 20 minutes. Remove from the heat. Strain the broth into a bowl, discarding the solids. Return the broth to the saucepan. Stir in the lime juice and sesame oil. Bring to a simmer.

Drop the dumpling mixture by small tablespoonfuls into the simmering broth, adjusting the temperature so that the broth continues to simmer as the dumplings are added. As the dumplings begin to rise to the top, add the cabbage, snow peas and carrot. Simmer, covered, over low heat for 2 to 4 minutes or until the dumplings and vegetables are cooked through. Ladle into soup bowls. Top with cilantro and/or chili paste.

Makes 8 (1-cup) servings

Swirl a bit of cream or pesto into puréed soup to create a design on the soup's surface.

Leek and Sautéed Shrimp Soup

1/4 cup fresh parsley

1/4 cup olive oil

1 garlic clove

18 medium shrimp, peeled, deveined, cut
    lengthwise into halves

6 tablespoons butter

5 medium leeks (pale green and white parts
    only), chopped (about 3 cups)

1 (8-ounce) russet potato, peeled and
    chopped (about 1 1/2 cups)

2 garlic cloves, chopped

1/4 teaspoon crumbled saffron threads

5 cups reduced-sodium chicken broth

2 tablespoons whipping cream

Salt and pepper to taste

1 small bunch chives, cut into 1-inch pieces

Combine the parsley, olive oil and 1 garlic clove in a food processor. Process until the parsley is coarsely chopped. Spoon the parsley mixture into a medium bowl. Add the shrimp and toss to coat. Chill, covered, in the refrigerator.

Heat the butter in a large heavy saucepan over medium-high heat. Sauté the leeks in the butter for 5 minutes or until tender. Stir in the potato, 2 garlic cloves and the saffron.

Sauté for 2 minutes. Add the broth and mix well. Bring to a boil; reduce the heat to medium-low. Simmer, covered, for 30 minutes. Cool slightly. Process the soup in batches in a blender until puréed. Return the purée to the saucepan. Stir in the whipping cream. Season with salt and pepper. Simmer just until heated through, stirring frequently.

Sauté the shrimp mixture in a heavy skillet over medium heat for 3 minutes or until the shrimp are opaque in the center. Ladle the soup into bowls. Top each serving with 6 shrimp halves. Sprinkle with the chives.

Serves 6

Soup Croutons

For a nice addition to soups, sauté small cubes or thin decoratively shaped slices of bread in butter or olive oil with herbs. Dust them with freshly grated Parmesan cheese while still hot. Serve the croutons in a small dish on the side. That way, the croutons will stay crisp until the last moment.

Après Ski Stew

1 pound round steak, trimmed and cubed
1 tablespoon vegetable oil
1/4 cup (1/2 stick) butter or margarine
1/4 cup flour
2 (14-ounce) cans beef broth or beef
    consommé
1/2 cup chopped carrots
1/2 cup chopped onion
1/2 cup chopped celery
1 medium russet potato, peeled and chopped,
    or 1 (16-ounce) package frozen soup
    vegetables with potatoes
3/4 teaspoon Kitchen Bouquet
1/4 teaspoon pepper
4 fresh tomatoes, seeded and chopped, or
    1 (14-ounce) can undrained diced
    tomatoes

Brown the beef on all sides in the oil in a skillet; drain. Melt the butter in a saucepan. Stir in the flour. Cook until smooth and bubbly, stirring constantly. Stir in the broth gradually. Cook until thickened, stirring constantly.

Add the carrots, onion, celery, potato, Kitchen Bouquet and pepper to the broth mixture and mix well. Bring to a boil; reduce the heat. Simmer for 5 minutes, stirring occasionally. Add the beef and tomatoes and mix gently. Simmer, covered, for 10 minutes or to the desired consistency, stirring occasionally. Taste and adjust the seasonings. Ladle the stew into bowls. You may substitute 1 cup dry red wine for 1 cup of the broth.

Makes 6 (1-cup) servings

Irish Lamb and Barley Stew

1 1/4 pounds boneless lean lamb,
    cut into 1-inch cubes
2 (14-ounce) cans beef broth
1 cup water
2 cups coarsely chopped cabbage
1 cup chopped carrots
1 cup chopped onion
1 cup chopped peeled rutabaga
1/3 cup quick-cooking barley
1 teaspoon thyme
1/2 teaspoon salt
1/4 teaspoon garlic powder
1/4 teaspoon allspice
1/4 teaspoon pepper
1 bay leaf
1 1/2 tablespoons cornstarch
Chopped fresh parsley

Brown the lamb in a Dutch oven coated with nonstick cooking spray over medium heat for 5 minutes, stirring frequently. Add the broth, water, cabbage, carrots, onion, rutabaga, barley, thyme, salt, garlic powder, allspice, pepper and bay leaf and mix well. Bring to a boil; reduce the heat to low.

Simmer for 20 minutes or until the lamb is tender, stirring occasionally. Discard the bay leaf. Stir in the cornstarch. Bring to a boil, stirring frequently. Cook until thickened, stirring constantly. Ladle into bowls. Sprinkle with parsley.

Serves 4 to 6

Seafood Stew with Basil and Tomatoes

2 (6-ounce) cans chopped clams
1/4 cup olive oil
1 1/4 cups chopped onions
2 tablespoons chopped garlic
4 teaspoons oregano
1 1/2 teaspoons fennel seeds
2 1/2 cups canned crushed tomatoes
    with purée
2 1/2 cups bottled clam juice or homemade
    seafood stock
1 cup dry white wine
1 pound large shrimp, peeled and deveined
1 (6-ounce) can lump crab meat, drained
    and rinsed
1/2 cup fresh basil, chopped
Cayenne pepper to taste
Salt and black pepper to taste

Drain the clams, reserving the liquid. Rinse the clams and drain. Heat the olive oil in a Dutch oven over medium heat. Sauté the onions, garlic, oregano and fennel seeds in the hot olive oil for 8 minutes or until the onions are tender. Stir in the reserved clam liquid, tomatoes, clam juice and wine. Bring to a boil. Boil for 15 to 30 minutes or until the liquid is reduced by half, stirring frequently.

Add the clams, shrimp and crab meat to the stew mixture and mix well. Simmer for 2 minutes, stirring occasionally. Stir in the basil. Simmer for 2 minutes longer or just until the shrimp turn pink. Season with cayenne pepper, salt and black pepper. Ladle into bowls. Serve with a tossed green salad and warm crusty bread. You may prepare up to 1 day in advance, adding the clams, shrimp, crab meat and basil just before serving.

Serves 4

Chair Style

Mismatched chairs give the dining table a certain whimsy. The back of the chair is the first thing guests see when they enter the dining room. Hang little herb bouquets or tassels on the chair backs or make place cards and adhere them to the backs of the chairs. Try hanging each place setting's napkin on the backs of the chairs instead of placing them in the expected spot next to the plate.

Cuban Shrimp Stew

Shrimp

3 tablespoons fresh lime juice
2 garlic cloves, minced
1/4 teaspoon oregano
1/4 teaspoon cumin
1 1/2 pounds fresh large shrimp, peeled and
   deveined
Salt and pepper to taste

Stew

3 tablespoons olive oil
2 cups chopped onions
1/3 cup julienned red bell pepper
1/3 cup julienned green bell pepper
1/3 cup julienned yellow bell pepper
2 ribs celery, finely chopped
2 tablespoons chopped fresh parsley
4 garlic cloves, minced
1/2 teaspoon cayenne pepper, or to taste
1/2 teaspoon oregano
1/2 teaspoon cumin
1 bay leaf
2/3 cup tomato paste
1 1/2 cups dry white wine
3/4 cup water
1/8 teaspoon Worcestershire sauce
Salt and black pepper to taste
2 tablespoons chopped fresh parsley

For the shrimp, combine the lime juice, garlic, oregano and cumin in a bowl and mix well. Add the shrimp and toss to coat. Sprinkle with salt and pepper. Marinate, covered, in the refrigerator for 30 minutes or for up to 4 hours, stirring occasionally.

For the stew, heat the olive oil in a large heavy saucepan or Dutch oven over medium-high heat. Sauté the onions, bell peppers, celery, 2 tablespoons parsley, garlic, cayenne pepper, oregano, cumin and bay leaf in the hot olive oil for 5 minutes or just until the onions begin to brown. Stir in the tomato paste. Sauté for 1 minute longer.

Add the wine and water to the vegetable mixture and mix well. Simmer for 5 minutes or until slightly thickened, stirring frequently. Stir in the undrained shrimp. Simmer for 6 minutes or until the shrimp turn pink, stirring occasionally. Discard the bay leaf. Stir in the Worcestershire sauce. Season with salt and black pepper. Ladle the stew into a serving bowl. Sprinkle with 2 tablespoons parsley. You may serve over hot cooked rice if desired.

Serves 4

Meals of Many Condiments

Use various different sizes of terra-cotta plant saucers for a "meal with many condiments." It is not only cost effective but makes an in-sync table with style.

Venison Steak Sandwiches

1 pound venison, elk, beef or pork loin steak
3/4 cup red wine (Merlot)
3 tablespoons chopped gherkins
2 tablespoons minced yellow onion
1 tablespoon stone-ground mustard
5 tablespoons mayonnaise
Salt and pepper to taste
8 (1/2-inch-thick) slices olive bread
8 thick tomato slices (about 2 tomatoes)
Nasturtiums or arugula

Place the venison in a shallow nonreactive dish. Pour 1/2 cup of the wine over the venison and turn to coat. Marinate, covered, in the refrigerator for 12 to 24 hours, turning every few hours; drain. Cut the venison into cubes.

Sauté the venison in the remaining 1/4 cup wine in a skillet over medium heat for 5 to 10 minutes or until cooked through. Cool slightly. Combine the venison, pickles, onion, mustard and mayonnaise in a bowl and mix well. Season with salt and pepper.

Toast the bread if desired. Spread 1 side of 4 slices of the bread with the venison mixture. Top each with 2 tomato slices, nasturtiums or arugula. Top with the remaining bread slices. Cut the sandwiches into halves and serve immediately. Decrease the marinating time for beef or pork to 1 to 4 hours.

Makes 4 sandwiches

Viejo Turkey and Chutney Sandwiches

8 slices cranberry walnut bread
8 leaves butterhead lettuce
6 ounces smoked Gouda cheese, sliced
12 ounces roasted turkey breast, sliced
2 pears, thinly sliced
Salt and pepper to taste
4 to 6 tablespoons mango chutney

Arrange 1 bread slice on a work surface. Layer with 2 of the lettuce leaves, 2 or 3 slices of the cheese, 3 ounces of the turkey and 4 or 5 of the pear slices. Sprinkle with salt and pepper. Spread another slice of the bread with 1 to 1 1/2 tablespoons of the chutney and place chutney side down over the prepared layers. Cut into halves. Repeat the process with the remaining bread, lettuce, cheese, turkey, pears, salt, pepper and chutney. Serve immediately. You may substitute 4 sliced croissants for the cranberry walnut bread, leftover turkey for the turkey breast and cranberry sauce for the chutney.

Makes 4 sandwiches

Lemon Tarragon Chicken Salad Sandwiches

Salt to taste
1 pound boneless skinless chicken breasts
   (about 3)
3/4 cup finely chopped celery
1/4 cup finely chopped green onions
1/4 cup chopped red bell pepper
2 tablespoons chopped fresh tarragon
2 tablespoons fresh lemon juice
1 teaspoon lemon zest
1/2 cup mayonnaise
Pepper to taste
8 slices Jewish rye bread or bread of
   your choice
3 tablespoons mayonnaise
1 medium tomato, cut into 4 slices
2 cups thinly sliced romaine

Bring a large saucepan of salted water to a boil over high heat. Add the chicken; reduce the heat to medium-low. Simmer, covered, for 15 to 20 minutes or until the chicken is cooked through; drain. Let stand until cool. Cut the chicken into 1/4-inch pieces.

Combine the celery, green onions, bell pepper, tarragon, lemon juice and lemon zest in a bowl and mix well. Add 1/2 cup mayonnaise and stir until mixed. Stir in the chicken. Season with salt and pepper.

Arrange 4 of the bread slices on a work surface. Spread 1 side of each slice with 1/4 of the 3 tablespoons mayonnaise and 1/4 of the chicken mixture. Layer each with a tomato slice and 1/2 cup lettuce. Top with the remaining bread slices. Cut each sandwich into halves and serve immediately. You may prepare the chicken filling up to 4 hours in advance and store, covered, in the refrigerator.

Makes 4 sandwiches

Sandwich Ideas

- Smoked turkey, cranberry relish, and watercress on challah or brioche
- Ripe tomatoes, fresh mozzarella, and pesto on a hard roll
- Scrambled eggs, smoked salmon, and sliced red onion on a croissant
- Sharp Cheddar and red apple slices on an English muffin — grilled open-face under a broiler
- Cream cheese, currants, chopped pecans on cinnamon toast
- Thinly sliced roast pork with apple butter on walnut raisin bread
- Monterey Jack cheese and jalapeño chutney on toasted sourdough bread
- Thinly sliced shrimp, cucumber, and radishes with dill butter on pumpernickel bread

Elegant Chicken and Brie Croissants

Walnut Vinaigrette

    2 teaspoons extra-virgin olive oil
    1 teaspoon balsamic vinegar
    1/8 teaspoon kosher salt
    1/3 cup walnuts, toasted, coarsely chopped

Sandwiches

    1 teaspoon olive oil
    2 cups (about 1 pound) cherry tomatoes, cut
        into halves
    2 tablespoons balsamic vinegar
    1 tablespoon chopped fresh thyme
    1/4 teaspoon kosher salt
    1/8 teaspoon pepper
    2 cups trimmed fresh spinach leaves
    1/4 cup reduced-fat mayonnaise
    1 tablespoon stone-ground Dijon mustard
    1 garlic clove, minced
    6 croissants, cut lengthwise into halves and
        lightly toasted
    3 ounces Brie cheese, sliced
    2 cups shredded cooked chicken breasts
    1/2 cup golden raisins

For the vinaigrette, whisk the olive oil, balsamic vinegar and salt in a bowl. Stir in the walnuts.

For the sandwiches, heat the olive oil in a large nonstick ovenproof skillet over medium-high heat. Stir in the tomatoes. Cook for 4 minutes, stirring once. Remove from the heat. Stir in the balsamic vinegar. Sprinkle with the thyme, salt and pepper. Bake at 300 degrees for 15 minutes. Remove the tomatoes to a bowl using a slotted spoon. Cover to keep warm.

Toss the spinach with the vinaigrette in a bowl until coated. Combine the mayonnaise, Dijon mustard and garlic in a bowl and mix well. Spread the mayonnaise mixture over the cut sides of the croissants. Spoon the tomatoes evenly over the bottom half of each croissant. Layer the sliced cheese, chicken, raisins and spinach over the tomatoes. Top with the remaining croissant halves.

You may substitute sun-dried tomatoes for the cherry tomatoes and any sliced bread for the croissants.

Wine recommendation, California Chardonnay. Two nice examples, Byington Sonoma Chardonnay or Chateau St. Jean Chardonnay also from Sonoma, California.

Makes 6 sandwiches

Open-Face Smoked Salmon Sandwiches with Goat Cheese

This serves twelve or more as an appetizer. Cut bread slices into halves, or use toasted crackers instead of bread. Increase the number of lemon slices to match the number of appetizer servings.

8 ounces mild goat cheese, such as
    Montrachet, softened
6 tablespoons minced arugula
2 tablespoons olive oil
2 teaspoons minced fresh chives
Freshly ground pepper to taste
1 pound thinly sliced smoked salmon
    (lox-style)
3 tablespoons olive oil
2 tablespoons fresh lemon juice
1/4 cup minced arugula
4 teaspoons minced fresh chives
12 slices sourdough bread, Swedish rye or
    egg bread
12 thin lemon slices
Arugula leaves

Combine the cheese, 6 tablespoons minced arugula, 2 tablespoons olive oil and 2 teaspoons chives in a bowl and mix well. Season generously with freshly ground pepper. Chill, covered, for up to 1 day in advance.

Arrange the salmon in a single layer on a large plate. Drizzle with 3 tablespoons olive oil and the lemon juice. Sprinkle with 1/4 cup minced arugula, 4 teaspoons chives and a generous amount of freshly ground pepper. Chill, covered, in the refrigerator for up to 4 hours.

Toast the bread slices just before serving. Spread 1 side of each bread slice with the goat cheese mixture and top with the salmon. Make a cut in each lemon slice from the center to the edge and twist. Top each sandwich with 1 lemon twist. Arrange each sandwich open-face on a bed of arugula leaves on a serving plate.

Makes 6 (2-sandwich) servings

Garlic

If you have a head of garlic that is sprouting, don't throw it out. Separate the cloves and plant them close together in a pot or your garden. The young shoots that will soon appear are garlic chives. They are mild with a faint garlic taste—perfect for eggs, salads, and sandwiches.

Open-Face Tuna Melt

1 (7-ounce) can water-pack artichoke hearts, drained and coarsely chopped
1 (6-ounce) can water-pack albacore tuna, lightly drained and flaked
1/2 cup sliced green onions (about 3)
1 tablespoon fresh lemon juice
2 teaspoons olive oil
1/2 teaspoon oregano
1/8 teaspoon black pepper
1/8 teaspoon cayenne pepper
2 English muffins, split, toasted
4 slices provolone cheese

Combine the artichokes, tuna, green onions, lemon juice, olive oil, oregano, black pepper and cayenne pepper in a bowl and mix well. Spread the cut sides of the muffins with the tuna mixture. Top each with a slice of cheese.

Arrange the muffins on a baking sheet. Broil 5 inches from the heat source for 4 to 5 minutes or until golden brown. Double the recipe for a crowd.

Serves 4

Southwestern Shrimp Sandwiches

1 1/2 cups (about 10 ounces) peeled cooked Bay shrimp
1 cup fresh or frozen corn kernels
1 cup chopped red bell pepper
2 tablespoons chopped fresh cilantro
2 tablespoons finely chopped green onions
4 teaspoons fresh lime juice
1 teaspoon grated lime zest
1 jalapeño chile, finely chopped
2 tablespoons mayonnaise
Salt and pepper to taste
6 (3- or 4-inch) egg bread rolls or croissants, split horizontally into halves
1 avocado, sliced

Combine the shrimp, corn, bell pepper, cilantro, green onions, lime juice, lime zest and jalapeño chile in a bowl and mix well. Stir in the mayonnaise. Season with salt and pepper.

Hollow out each roll half slightly. Spoon the shrimp salad into the rolls. Top each with avocado slices. Serve immediately.

Serves 6

Country Picnic Loaf

This is a great hearty picnic sandwich that can be transported without refrigeration. Vegetables can be varied according to taste. The meat should be cured to deter spoilage. Do not substitute mayonnaise or a mayonnaise-based spread for the pesto.

1 small to medium round loaf crusty
    sheepherder bread
5 to 7 ounces pesto
6 to 8 ounces thinly sliced prosciutto
8 ounces thinly sliced provolone cheese or
    Monterey Jack cheese
5 to 6 ounces roasted red bell peppers
1 (4-ounce) can sliced olives, drained
1 large ripe tomato, sliced
Salt and pepper to taste
8 to 10 fresh basil leaves, torn into bite-size
    pieces

Cut a large circle in the top of the bread approximately 1 inch from the edge to create a lid. Reserve the lid. Remove the bread from the lid and center of the loaf carefully, creating a bread shell. Spread about 2/3 to 3/4 of the pesto over the inside of the shell, covering completely. Spread the remaining pesto on the underside of the lid.

Layer 1/2 of the prosciutto over the bottom of the bread shell, tucking securely into the side. Top with 1/2 of the cheese, the bell peppers, olives and tomato slices. Sprinkle with salt, pepper and basil. Layer with the remaining cheese and remaining prosciutto, again tucking securely into the side of the shell. Replace the lid, matching cut marks to make a tight seal. Wrap the loaf securely in plastic wrap and then in foil to seal in additional flavor.

Store in a cool dry place until serving time. Do not chill. The sandwich should be prepared 6 to 8 hours in advance and served at room temperature.

Serves 4 to 8

Spread bread with butter or cream cheese to keep wet ingredients from making the bread soggy.

Greek Pitas

Lemon Dressing
    1/4 cup olive oil
    Juice of 1 lemon
    1 large garlic clove, minced

Filling and Assembly
    6 cups baby spinach leaves
    2 cups chopped fresh tomatoes
    1 1/2 cups thinly sliced peeled cucumber
    1 cup (4 ounces) crumbled feta cheese
    1/3 cup chopped kalamata olives
    16 fresh basil leaves, thinly sliced
    4 (5- to 6-inch) pita bread rounds,
       cut crosswise into halves, toasted

For the dressing, whisk the olive oil, lemon juice and garlic in a small bowl.

For the filling, combine the spinach, tomatoes, cucumber, cheese, olives and basil in a bowl and mix gently. Add the dressing and toss gently to coat. Spoon the filling into the pita halves and serve immediately.

Makes 4 sandwiches

CONTENTS

86 The Best Focaccia Ever
87 Hazelnut Chocolate Breakfast Bread
88 Bakery Shoppe Blueberry Bread
88 Rhubarb Sweet Bread
90 Cinnamon Streusel Buns
91 English Crumpets
92 High Country Herb Rolls
93 Parmesan Sesame Biscuits
94 Sweet Fruit Scones
94 Cranberry Orange Preserves
96 Puffy Pear Pancake
97 Wheat Germ Pancakes
98 Lemon Poppy Seed Waffles with Raspberry Sauce
100 Baked French Toast with Cardamom and Marmalade
100 Bubbly Cinnamon Toast
101 Strawberry Patch Soup
101 Scrambled Eggs with Smoked Salmon and Chives
102 Savory Baked Eggs and Asparagus
103 Chile Rellenos Soufflé with Sage Cheese
104 Apple Sausage Quiche
104 Artichoke Tart
105 Pesto and Prosciutto Breakfast Strata
106 Spanish Frittata with Fruit Salsa
108 Goldilock's Goodness
108 Sweet Potato Hash Browns
109 Fresh Pineapple in Cinnamon Syrup
109 Christmas Oranges

BREADS AND BRUNCH

The Best Focaccia Ever

1 envelope dry yeast
1¹/₂ cups warm (110 to 115 degrees) water
3 to 4 cups bread flour
1¹/₂ teaspoons finely ground sea salt
2 tablespoons lard or shortening
5 to 6 tablespoons extra-virgin olive oil
1 teaspoon coarse sea salt, or to taste
¹/₄ cup finely chopped fresh herbs, or to taste

Dissolve the yeast in the warm water in a bowl
and mix well. Combine 3 cups of the bread flour
and 1¹/₂ teaspoons finely ground sea salt in a bowl
and mix well. Drop the lard by teaspoonfuls into
the flour mixture. Rub the lard into the flour with
your fingers until the consistency of fine cornmeal.
The mixture should feel silky to the touch.

Make a well in the center of the flour mixture.
Add the yeast mixture to the well and stir with a
wooden spoon until mixed. Switch to mixing with
hands until a very soft dough forms, adding
additional bread flour if the dough is too moist.
Do not knead the dough. Let rise, covered, in a
warm place for 1 hour or until doubled in bulk.

Brush the bottom of a 10×15-inch baking pan with
3 tablespoons of the olive oil. Pat the dough over
the bottom of the prepared baking pan. Turn the
dough so the olive oil coats both sides. Let rise for
45 minutes or until doubled in bulk.

Dimple the dough with your fingers, creating little
nooks and crannies over the dough surface. Drizzle
with the remaining 2 to 3 tablespoons olive oil.
Sprinkle with 1 teaspoon coarse sea salt and fresh
herbs. Place the baking pan on the lower oven
rack. Bake at 450 degrees for 15 minutes or until
the top is light golden brown and the bottom has a
nice crust. Cool briefly on a wire rack. Serve or
wrap the warm bread in foil, where it will stay
fresh and warm for hours. To serve, cut into fifteen
3×3-inch pieces or serve whole and allow the guests
to tear their own pieces for a more "rustica" feel.

You may omit the chopped herbs and sprinkle with
1 cup chopped marinated artichokes, sun-dried
tomatoes, kalamata olives or freshly grated
Parmesan cheese.

Serves 15

Hazelnut Chocolate Breakfast Bread

Hazelnut Topping

    1/4 cup sugar
    1 teaspoon cinnamon
    1/2 cup hazelnuts, finely chopped
    1/2 cup double chocolate chips (Ghirardelli)

Bread

    2 cups flour
    1 teaspoon baking soda
    1 teaspoon baking powder
    1/4 teaspoon salt
    1 cup sour cream or reduced-fat sour cream
    1 teaspoon almond extract
    1 teaspoon vanilla extract
    1/2 cup (1 stick) butter, softened
    1 cup sugar
    2 eggs, beaten

For the topping, combine the sugar and cinnamon in a small bowl and mix well. Stir in the hazelnuts and chocolate chips.

For the bread, sift the flour, baking soda, baking powder and salt together. Combine the sour cream and flavorings in a bowl and mix well. Beat the butter and sugar in a mixing bowl until creamy. Add the eggs and mix well. Add the dry ingredients alternately with the sour cream mixture to the creamed mixture, stirring well after each addition.

Spoon 1/2 of the batter into a greased 5×9-inch loaf pan. Sprinkle with 1/2 of the topping mixture. Top with the remaining batter and remaining topping. Bake at 350 degrees for 1 hour or until the loaf is brown and the chocolate is melted. Cool in the pan on a wire rack for 15 to 20 minutes. Remove the loaf to a wire rack. Slice and serve warm for gooey bread or let stand until room temperature.

Makes 1 loaf (10 to 12 slices)

If you bake a lot, save
time greasing and flouring pans
by whisking together 1/2 cup each
of flour, vegetable oil and solid vegetable
shortening until smooth. Brush the mixture
onto baking pans to substitute for greasing and
flouring. Refrigerate the mixture in a covered container
for up to 4 months.

Bakery Shoppe Blueberry Bread

2¹/4 cups flour
1 tablespoon baking powder
1 cup sugar
¹/2 cup shortening
2 eggs
1 teaspoon vanilla extract
²/3 cup milk
2 cups fresh or thawed frozen blueberries
²/3 cup sugar
²/3 cup flour
¹/2 cup (1 stick) butter
¹/2 teaspoon almond extract
¹/2 cup slivered almonds
Confectioners' sugar to taste

Mix 2¹/4 cups flour and baking powder in a bowl. Beat 1 cup sugar and shortening in a mixing bowl until light and fluffy. Beat in the eggs and vanilla until blended. Add the dry ingredients alternately with the milk, mixing well after each addition.

Spoon the batter into 2 greased and lightly floured round baking pans. Sprinkle with the blueberries. Mix ²/3 cup sugar and ²/3 cup flour in a bowl. Cut in the butter and flavoring until crumbly. Sprinkle the crumb mixture over the blueberries. Top with the almonds. Bake at 350 degrees for 45 minutes or until a wooden pick inserted in the center comes out clean. Cool in the pans on a wire rack. Sprinkle with confectioners' sugar. Remove the bread to a plate. Cut into 8 wedges.

Makes 2 loaves (16 slices)

Rhubarb Sweet Bread

1 teaspoon baking soda
1 cup buttermilk
1¹/2 cups packed brown sugar
²/3 cup vegetable oil
1 egg, beaten
1 teaspoon vanilla extract
1 teaspoon salt
2¹/2 cups flour
1¹/2 cups sliced fresh or frozen rhubarb
¹/2 cup chopped walnuts or pecans (optional)
¹/2 cup sugar
1 tablespoon butter, softened

Dissolve the baking soda in the buttermilk in a small bowl. Combine the brown sugar, oil, egg, vanilla and salt in a large bowl and mix well. Stir in the buttermilk mixture. Add the flour gradually and stir just until moistened. Fold in the rhubarb and walnuts. Spoon the batter into 2 greased and lightly floured 4×9-inch or 4×10-inch loaf pans. Mix the sugar and butter in a bowl until crumbly. Sprinkle the crumb mixture over the batter. Bake at 325 degrees for 50 to 55 minutes or until a wooden pick inserted in the center comes out clean. Cool in the pans on a wire rack for 10 minutes. Remove the loaves from the pans and cool on a wire rack. Serve with whipped butter or vanilla ice cream if desired.

Makes 2 loaves (34 slices)

Cinnamon Streusel Buns

Streusel

2 1/2 cups packed brown sugar
4 3/4 teaspoons cinnamon
2 cups pecans, toasted, chopped
3/4 cup (1 1/2 sticks) butter, melted

Buns

2 teaspoons dry yeast
1/2 cup lukewarm (85 to 95 degrees) water
1 1/2 cups lukewarm milk
1/2 cup (1 stick) butter, melted
1/2 cup sugar
1 1/4 teaspoons salt
2 eggs, beaten
5 1/2 cups (about) flour

For the streusel, combine the brown sugar and cinnamon in a bowl and mix well. Stir in the pecans. Add the butter and mix well.

For the buns, dissolve the yeast in the lukewarm water in a bowl and mix well. Whisk in the lukewarm milk, butter, sugar and salt. Add the eggs and mix well. Add the flour 1/2 cup at a time until a smooth but very sticky dough forms, stirring constantly with a wooden spoon. Place the dough in a buttered bowl, turning to coat. Chill, covered with plastic wrap, for 8 to 10 hours; do not punch the dough down.

Reserve 2 cups of the streusel. Sprinkle the remaining streusel over the bottom of a buttered 10×15-inch baking dish. Turn the dough onto a generously floured work surface. Scrape the bowl if the dough sticks; do not punch the dough down. Sprinkle the dough lightly with additional flour and roll into a 14-inch square. Sprinkle the square with the reserved streusel, leaving a 3/4-inch border on all sides. Roll as for a jelly roll, enclosing streusel completely.

Cut the roll crosswise into halves. Cut each half crosswise into seven 1-inch rounds. Arrange the rounds cut side down and evenly spaced in the prepared baking dish; the rounds will not cover the streusel completely. Let rise, loosely covered with plastic wrap, in a warm place for 45 minutes or until the rounds are puffed and almost touching.

Arrange the baking dish on the center oven rack. Bake at 400 degrees for 10 minutes. Reduce the oven temperature to 375 degrees. Bake for 20 minutes longer or until the buns are golden brown. Remove from the oven. Place a large baking sheet over the baking dish immediately and invert the buns onto the baking sheet. Let stand for 30 minutes or longer before serving. The dough is much easier to handle if prepared 1 day in advance and stored, covered, in the refrigerator.

Makes 14 buns

English Crumpets

1¹/4 cups milk
6 tablespoons water
1 tablespoon dry yeast
1 teaspoon sugar
1¹/2 cups bread flour
1 teaspoon salt
Butter

Heat the milk and water in a saucepan to 110 to 115 degrees, "hand hot." Do not allow the mixture to boil. Remove from the heat. Stir in the yeast and sugar. Let stand for 10 to 15 minutes or until frothy.

Sift the bread flour and salt into a 2-quart bowl and mix well. Make a well in the center of the flour mixture. Pour the milk mixture into the well. Whisk until the batter is smooth and the consistency of pancake batter. Let rise, covered, in a warm dry draft-free environment for 30 minutes or until doubled in bulk.

Brush a hot griddle and egg cooking rings or English muffin rings with butter. Spoon 2 tablespoons of the batter into each ring; the batter will spread to the edge of the rings. Cook over medium heat for 2 minutes or until bubbles appear on the top and edge of the rings. Lift the rings off each crumpet with a fork and knife and turn the crumpet with a spatula. Cook for 1 to 2 minutes longer or until both sides are golden brown. Serve with clotted cream, jam or butter.

Makes 14 crumpets

Bread Spreads
Creamy butter and sweet preserves are meant to be together, but they're usually not applied until they hit the toast. Blended together and cut into colorful little pats, they spread on in one neat layer. Combine 1/2 cup (1 stick) of softened unsalted butter and 1/2 cup plus 2 tablespoons of best quality jam or preserves; combine thoroughly with a rubber spatula. Wrap in waxed paper, forming an inch cylinder; tie ends. Keep refrigerated for up to 2 weeks, or frozen for up to 1 month. Slice off pats and serve with toast, muffins, or pancakes.

High Country Herb Rolls

1/2 cup all-purpose flour
2 tablespoons sugar
4 teaspoons dry yeast
1/2 cup lukewarm water
1/4 cup (1/2 stick) butter, softened
3 tablespoons molasses
2 tablespoons onion flakes
1 teaspoon salt
1 garlic clove, finely minced
1 cup milk, scalded
3 cups all-purpose flour
1 cup whole wheat flour
1 egg, lightly beaten
1 tablespoon oregano
1 tablespoon marjoram
1 tablespoon sage
1 egg
1 teaspoon water

Combine 1/2 cup all-purpose flour, sugar and yeast in a nonreactive bowl and mix well. Stir in the lukewarm water. Proof, covered with plastic wrap, for 12 to 15 minutes or until bubbly.

Combine the butter, molasses, onion flakes, salt and garlic in a bowl and mix well. Pour the hot milk over the molasses mixture and mix well. Let stand until lukewarm. Add the yeast mixture, 3 cups all-purpose flour, the whole wheat flour, 1 lightly beaten egg, oregano, marjoram and sage to the molasses mixture. Mix by hand or with an electric mixer fitted with a dough hook; this is a no-knead dough. Let rise for 1 hour or until doubled in bulk.

Punch the dough down and cut into 16 equal pieces. Shape into "flower rolls" by rolling each piece into a 7-inch-long strip and tying into a loose knot. Tuck the ends of each strip under and arrange on greased baking sheets, 8 per sheet. Let rise, covered with greased plastic wrap or a tea towel, for 30 minutes.

Whisk 1 egg and 1 teaspoon water in a bowl. Brush the egg wash over the rolls. Bake at 350 degrees for 20 to 30 minutes or until golden brown. Serve warm with butter. Store the rolls in an airtight container. They will stay soft and fresh for several days.

Makes 16 rolls

Parmesan Sesame Biscuits

2 cups flour
1 tablespoon baking powder
1/4 teaspoon cayenne pepper, or to taste
2 tablespoons butter, chilled
1 1/2 cups (6 ounces) grated Parmesan cheese
    or finely shredded Cheddar cheese
1 tablespoon sesame seeds, lightly toasted
1 to 1 1/4 cups buttermilk

Sift the flour, baking powder and cayenne pepper into a bowl and mix well. Cut in the butter using a pastry cutter or 2 knives until crumbly. Add the cheese and sesame seeds and mix gently. Stir in 1 cup of the buttermilk. Add the remaining 1/4 cup buttermilk gradually if the dough is too stiff.

Knead the dough 6 times on a lightly floured surface. Roll 1/2 inch thick and cut into rounds with a 2 1/2-inch biscuit cutter or floured glass. Arrange the rounds on a greased baking sheet. Bake at 425 degrees for 12 to 15 minutes or until light brown. Serve warm with butter. Great with eggs, soup, chili or pasta.

Makes 10 to 12 biscuits

Cherry Bruschetta

This is a 10-minute recipe that will enliven a brunch! Stir together 1 cup coarsely chopped, pitted light or dark cherries and 2 tablespoons jalapeño jelly. Mound the mixture on slices of French bread or leaves of butterhead lettuce. Top with a small amount of crumbled bleu cheese and sprinkle with slivered almonds.

Sweet Fruit Scones

2 cups flour
1/3 cup sugar
1 tablespoon baking powder
1/2 teaspoon salt
1/2 cup dried cranberries or miniature
    chocolate chips
2 teaspoons grated orange zest
3/4 to 11/4 cups half-and-half
1/4 cup half-and-half
Cinnamon-sugar to taste

Combine the flour, sugar, baking powder and salt in a large bowl and mix well. Stir in the cranberries and orange zest. Add 3/4 to 11/4 cups half-and-half gradually, mixing constantly until the dough is moistened and forms a ball; knead gently if necessary.

Place the dough on a lightly floured surface. Pat gently into a 1-inch-thick circle. Place the circle on a greased baking sheet. Brush the top with 1/4 cup half-and-half and sprinkle with cinnamon-sugar. Score into 8 equal wedges. Bake at 425 degrees for 12 to 15 minutes or until light brown. Cut into wedges and serve warm.

Makes 8 scones

Cranberry Orange Preserves

3/4 cup orange juice
1/2 cup sugar
2 cups fresh cranberries
2 cups orange marmalade
3/4 cup dried cranberries
3/4 tablespoon grated orange zest
3/4 tablespoon grated lemon zest
1/4 teaspoon ground cloves

Combine the orange juice and sugar in a medium saucepan and mix well. Cook over medium heat until the sugar dissolves, stirring frequently. Stir in the fresh cranberries, marmalade, dried cranberries, orange zest, lemon zest and cloves. Bring to a gentle boil; reduce the heat to medium-low.

Simmer for 20 minutes or until the mixture is reduced to 3 cups, stirring occasionally. Let stand until cool. Chill, covered, in the refrigerator. You may prepare up to 1 week in advance and store, covered, in the refrigerator.

Makes 3 cups

Puffy Pear Pancake

The subtle anise flavor makes this pretty pear pancake so tasty!

2 tablespoons butter
1 teaspoon anise seeds
3 ripe large Bartlett pears or Anjou pears, cut
    lengthwise into halves
5 egg whites
1/2 teaspoon cream of tartar
1/2 cup sugar
5 egg yolks
1/4 cup flour
1/2 teaspoon vanilla extract

Combine the butter and anise seeds in an ovenproof 10-inch skillet. Cook over medium heat until the butter melts, stirring frequently. Add the pears. Cook for 10 minutes or until the pears are light brown on both sides, turning occasionally. Remove from the heat. Space the pears evenly in the skillet and cover to keep warm.

Beat the egg whites and cream of tartar in a mixing bowl at high speed until foamy. Add the sugar gradually, beating constantly until stiff peaks form. Beat the egg yolks in a mixing bowl with the unwashed beaters until the volume doubles. Add the flour and vanilla to the egg yolks and beat until mixed. Fold 1/4 of the egg whites into the egg yolk mixture. Fold the egg yolk mixture into the remaining egg whites.

Pour the egg mixture over the warm pears, pushing the batter between the pears with a spatula. Cook over medium heat for 10 minutes or until the pancake is dark golden brown on the bottom. Bake at 300 degrees for 15 minutes or until puffy and the top is dark golden brown and set.

Run a sharp knife around the edge of the skillet to loosen the pancake. Invert the pancake onto a serving plate. Cut into 6 wedges and serve immediately.

Serves 6

The most luminous ice cubes are made from bottled water. The coldest ice is cracked, because it can cover more surface area in a glass or cup than chunky ice cubes can; bartenders prefer it for expert chilling of glasses and shaking startlingly cold drinks.

Wheat Germ Pancakes

Pancakes can be served with fruit syrup, maple syrup, or clear honey and topped with thick yogurt, cream, or crème fraîche.

3 cups all-purpose flour or whole wheat flour
1¹/3 cups nonfat dry milk powder
¹/3 cup sugar
¹/3 cup wheat germ
1 tablespoon baking powder
1 teaspoon salt
3 eggs, beaten
¹/4 cup vegetable oil
4 cups water

Combine the flour, milk powder, sugar, wheat germ, baking powder and salt in a 3-quart bowl and mix well. Add the eggs and oil and stir just until moistened. Add 2 cups of the water ¹/2 cup at a time until the ingredients are well moistened; the batter will be thick for pancakes. Do not overmix. Chill, covered, for 8 to 10 hours.

Add the remaining 2 cups water ¹/2 cup at a time until the batter is of the desired consistency, mixing well after each addition. The more water added the thinner the pancakes. Drop the batter by ¹/4 cupfuls onto a hot greased griddle. Cook over medium heat until bubbles appear around the edges of the pancakes and the underside is golden brown; turn. Cook until golden brown. Serve immediately with whipped butter and warm maple syrup. Add 1 mashed banana to the batter just before cooking for a tropical treat.

Serves 4 to 6

Try a yogurt bar at your next brunch. Present bowls of plain and fruited yogurts alongside a selection of your favorite toppings such as dried fruit, chopped nuts, granola, coconut, and melon balls.

Lemon Poppy Seed Waffles with Raspberry Sauce

Raspberry Sauce

1 pound fresh or drained thawed frozen
    raspberries
1/2 cup orange juice
1/2 cup sugar
1 tablespoon cornstarch
2 tablespoons orange juice
1 tablespoon lemon juice

Waffles

1 1/2 cups flour
6 tablespoons sugar
2 tablespoons poppy seeds
1 1/2 teaspoons baking powder
1 1/4 cups buttermilk
1/4 cup (1/2 stick) butter, melted
3 eggs
1 tablespoon grated lemon zest

For the sauce, combine the raspberries, 1/2 cup orange juice and sugar in a medium saucepan. Bring to a gentle boil, stirring occasionally; reduce the heat. Simmer over medium-low heat for 15 minutes or until the mixture is reduced to 2 cups, stirring occasionally.

Dissolve the cornstarch in 2 tablespoons orange juice in a small bowl and mix well. Stir the cornstarch mixture into the raspberry mixture. Add the lemon juice and mix well. Bring to a boil, stirring constantly; reduce the heat.

Simmer for 1 to 2 minutes or until thickened, stirring frequently. Cool slightly before serving. The sauce may be prepared up to 2 days in advance and stored, covered, in the refrigerator. Reheat before serving.

For the waffles, mix the flour, sugar, poppy seeds and baking powder in a bowl. Whisk the buttermilk, butter, eggs and lemon zest in a bowl until mixed. Add the buttermilk mixture to the flour mixture and stir just until moistened. Let stand for 15 to 20 minutes.

Pour half the batter onto a hot waffle iron. Bake for 5 to 7 minutes or until golden brown on both sides. Repeat with the remaining batter. Serve immediately with the warm sauce.

Serves 4

Baked French Toast with Cardamom and Marmalade

1 1/4 cups orange marmalade
10 (1-inch) slices challah or egg bread
1 1/4 cups milk
3/4 cup whipping cream
1/2 cup sugar
3 egg yolks
3 eggs
1 1/4 teaspoons cardamom
1 teaspoon grated orange zest
1 teaspoon grated lemon zest
Confectioners' sugar to taste

Grease a 10×15-inch baking dish. Spread the marmalade on 1 side of each bread slice. Cut the slices diagonally into halves to form triangles. Arrange the triangles marmalade side up crosswise and slightly overlapping in the prepared baking dish.

Whisk the milk, whipping cream, sugar, egg yolks, eggs, cardamom, orange zest and lemon zest in a bowl. Pour the milk mixture over the prepared layer. Chill, covered, for at least 1 hour or for up to 10 hours. Bake, uncovered, at 350 degrees for 50 minutes or until puffed and golden brown. Sprinkle with confectioners' sugar and serve immediately.

Serves 10

Bubbly Cinnamon Toast

1 cup packed brown sugar
1/2 cup (1 stick) butter, softened
2 teaspoons evaporated milk or evaporated
    skim milk
1 teaspoon cinnamon
1/2 teaspoon lemon juice
1 loaf English muffin bread, cut into
    3/4-inch slices

Combine the brown sugar, butter, evaporated milk, cinnamon and lemon juice in a bowl and mix well. Spread the butter mixture 1/4 inch thick on 1 side of each bread slice.

Arrange the slices butter side up on a baking sheet. Bake at 350 degrees for 10 to 12 minutes or until bubbly and set. Serve immediately. The butter mixture may be stored, covered, in the refrigerator for 2 weeks.

Serves 6 to 8

Strawberry Patch Soup

Using large shallow soup bowls helps the strawberries stay "afloat."

1 cup fresh or frozen strawberries, cut into
    halves
1/2 cup sugar
1/2 cup sour cream
1/2 cup whipping cream
1/2 cup burgundy
3/4 cup seltzer water
Fresh mint leaves
Sour cream
Sliced strawberries

Combine 1 cup strawberry halves, sugar, 1/2 cup sour cream, whipping cream, wine and seltzer water in a blender. Process until smooth. Pour into a bowl. Chill, covered, for 3 hours or longer.

Ladle the soup into bowls or cantaloupe halves. Garnish each serving with mint leaves, additional sour cream and sliced strawberries.

Makes 6 cups

Scrambled Eggs with Smoked Salmon and Chives

8 eggs
3 tablespoons chopped fresh chives
3 tablespoons milk
5 tablespoons butter
1 medium onion, finely chopped
6 ounces thinly sliced smoked salmon, cut into
    strips
Salt and pepper to taste
2 tablespoons chopped fresh chives

Whisk the eggs, 3 tablespoons chives and the milk in a bowl until well mixed. Heat the butter in a large heavy skillet over medium heat. Sauté the onion in the butter for 15 minutes or until golden brown. Stir in the egg mixture.

Cook for 4 minutes or until the eggs are almost set, stirring occasionally. Stir in the salmon gently. Cook for 1 minute longer or until the eggs are cooked through but still moist. Season with salt and pepper. Spoon the eggs onto a heated platter. Sprinkle with 2 tablespoons chives. Serve immediately.

Serves 4

Savory Baked Eggs and Asparagus

Serve with mimosas, a colorful fresh fruit plate, and breakfast bread for an elegant Sunday brunch.

Cheese Sauce

1/4 cup (1/2 stick) butter
1/4 cup flour
1 cup milk
1 1/4 cups chicken broth
1/4 cup sherry
2 cups (8 ounces) shredded extra-sharp
  Cheddar cheese
2 teaspoons dry mustard
1/2 teaspoon Worcestershire sauce
1/2 teaspoon Tabasco sauce
1/2 teaspoon salt
1/4 teaspoon marjoram
1/4 teaspoon tarragon
1/8 teaspoon freshly ground pepper

Baked Eggs

1 pound fresh asparagus, sliced diagonally
  into 3/4-inch pieces
3 cups cornflakes, lightly crushed
2 tablespoons butter, melted
4 ounces fresh mushrooms, coarsely chopped
  or sliced
3 or 4 green onions, sliced
2 tablespoons butter, melted
6 hard-cooked eggs, cut into halves
6 slices crisp-cooked bacon, crumbled
1 (2-ounce) jar diced pimento, drained

For the sauce, heat the butter in a saucepan over medium-high heat. Add the flour gradually, whisking constantly. Cook for 1 minute, stirring constantly. Remove from the heat. Whisk in the milk until smooth. Return to the heat. Stir in the broth and sherry.

Bring almost to a boil, stirring frequently. Add the cheese gradually, stirring constantly. Cook until the cheese melts, stirring constantly; reduce the heat to low. Stir in the dry mustard, Worcestershire sauce, Tabasco sauce, salt, marjoram, tarragon and pepper. Remove from the heat. Cover to keep warm.

For the eggs, blanch the asparagus in boiling water in a saucepan for 2 minutes; drain. Combine the cornflake crumbs and 2 tablespoons butter in a bowl and mix well. Sauté the cornflake mixture in a small skillet until light brown. Sauté the mushrooms and green onions in 2 tablespoons butter in a small skillet until all the liquid evaporates.

Spoon 3 tablespoons of the cornflake crumbs into each of six 2-cup ramekins. Place 2 egg halves over the crumbs in each ramekin. Arrange the asparagus, bacon, pimento and mushroom mixture over and around the egg halves. Spoon enough of the warm sauce over the layers to cover completely. Sprinkle with the remaining cornflake crumbs. Bake at 350 degrees for 20 minutes or until bubbly. You may prepare 1 day in advance and store, covered, in the refrigerator, allowing for additional baking time.

Serves 6

Chile Rellenos Soufflé with Sage Cheese

Sage Cheese

    8 ounces cream cheese, softened

    4 ounces chèvre, softened

    3 tablespoons minced green onions

    2 tablespoons finely chopped fresh sage

    1 egg

    1 garlic clove, minced

    Salt and pepper to taste

Soufflé

    2 (7-ounce) cans whole green chiles, drained

    8 eggs

    2 cups milk

    1/2 cup flour

    1/4 cup grated Parmesan cheese

    Salsa, green chile sauce or pico de gallo

For the cheese, combine the cream cheese, chèvre, green onions, sage, egg, garlic, salt and pepper in a mixing bowl. Beat until mixed, scraping the bowl occasionally.

For the soufflé, cut the chiles lengthwise into halves and pat dry. Spread 1 to 2 tablespoons of the cheese on the cut side of half the chiles. Top with the remaining chile halves. Arrange the chiles in a single layer in a greased 21/2- to 3-quart baking dish.

Combine the eggs, milk, flour and Parmesan cheese in a food processor or blender. Process until smooth. Pour the egg mixture over the chiles. Bake at 375 degrees for 45 minutes or until light brown. Serve immediately with salsa, green chile sauce or pico de gallo.

Serves 8

Fruit Arrangement

An oval terra-cotta bowl brimming with fruit, a few candles, and a few simple flowers is an impressive decoration for a festive buffet.

Apple Sausage Quiche

2 (9-inch) pie shells
8 ounces reduced-fat bulk pork sausage
1 cup milk
3 eggs, lightly beaten
1/2 cup reduced-fat mayonnaise
2 tablespoons flour
2 cups (8 ounces) shredded Cheddar cheese
1 large or 2 small Granny Smith apples or
    Jonathan apples, peeled and chopped

Prick the bottom and sides of the pie shells with a fork. Bake at 400 degrees for 6 minutes. Remove the pie shells from the oven. Maintain the oven temperature.

Brown the sausage in a skillet, stirring until crumbly; drain. Mix the milk, eggs, mayonnaise and flour in a bowl. Stir in the sausage, cheese and apple. Spoon the sausage mixture into the prepared pie shells. Bake for 40 to 45 minutes or until light brown. You may freeze the cooked quiches for future use. Reheat the frozen quiches at 350 degrees for 30 to 35 minutes.

Serves 12 to 16

Artichoke Tart

1 (11-ounce) package frozen artichokes
3/4 cup whipping cream
3/4 cup milk
3/4 cup (3 ounces) shredded Swiss cheese
3/4 cup (3 ounces) grated Parmesan cheese
3 eggs, beaten
1 teaspoon salt
1 teaspoon thyme
1/8 teaspoon cayenne pepper
1 (10-inch) deep-dish pie shell, frozen

Cook the artichokes using package directions; drain. Combine the whipping cream, milk, Swiss cheese, Parmesan cheese, eggs, salt, thyme and cayenne pepper in a bowl and mix well.

Pour the egg mixture into the frozen pie shell. Arrange the artichokes on top of the egg mixture. Bake at 375 degrees for 45 minutes or until a knife inserted in the center comes out clean. Let stand for 10 minutes before serving.

Serves 8

When there's finally time to relax on the weekend, give breakfast the attention you give other meals. Brew some coffee or tea, and savor this casual time with friends and family.

Pesto and Prosciutto Breakfast Strata

1 1/2 cups milk

1/2 cup dry white wine

1 loaf dry French bread, cut into 1/2-inch slices

8 ounces prosciutto, thinly sliced

1/3 cup fresh dill weed, snipped

3 tablespoons olive oil

1 pound smoked Gouda cheese, shredded

3 ripe tomatoes, cut into 1/8-inch slices

1/2 cup basil pesto

6 eggs, beaten

Salt and pepper to taste

1 cup whipping cream

Mix the milk and wine in a shallow dish. Dip the bread slices in the milk mixture until coated. Squeeze the slices gently to release any excess liquid; do not tear.

Layer the bread slices slightly overlapping, prosciutto, dill weed, olive oil, cheese, tomatoes and pesto 1/2 at a time in a 9×13-inch baking pan sprayed with nonstick cooking spray. Beat the eggs, salt and pepper in a mixing bowl until blended. Pour the egg mixture evenly over the prepared layers. Chill, covered with plastic wrap, for 8 to 10 hours.

Let stand at room temperature for 30 to 45 minutes. Drizzle the whipping cream over the top. Bake at 350 degrees for 50 minutes or until puffy and golden brown. Serve immediately.

Serves 6 to 8

Omelette Filling Ideas

- Bacon, avocado, and Brie
- Caramelized onion, ham, and Gruyère
- Bacon, apple, and Stilton
- Feta, spinach, and tomato
- Sour cream and chutney
- Ricotta and strawberry
- Asparagus and Parmesan
- Zucchini, red onion, goat cheese, and mint
- Fresh fig, prosciutto, and asiago
- Salmon, dill, and orange
- Leek, sun-dried tomato, and Brie

Spanish Frittata with Fruit Salsa

Frittata

8 ounces cheese-onion bread, cheese-jalapeño
    bread or any savory bread, cut into
    1/2-inch cubes
9 eggs
2 cups whole milk, reduced-fat milk or
    nonfat milk
1 (7-ounce) can diced green chiles, drained
1 cup (4 ounces) shredded Monterey Jack
    cheese
1 cup (4 ounces) shredded Cheddar cheese
1/2 cup (1/4-inch pieces) onion
1/4 cup (1/4-inch pieces) seeded fresh
    Anaheim chiles
1/4 cup fresh cilantro, finely chopped
3/4 teaspoon salt
Sprigs of fresh cilantro
Sliced avocado

Fruit Salsa

1 firm ripe mango, peeled and coarsely
    chopped
3 or 4 Roma tomatoes, coarsely chopped
1/2 cup thinly sliced green onions
1/2 cup fresh cilantro, chopped
3 tablespoons lime juice
2 tablespoons minced fresh Anaheim chiles
1 garlic clove, crushed
Salt to taste

For the frittata, spread the bread cubes evenly in a buttered 9×13-inch baking dish. Whisk the eggs and milk in a bowl just until blended. Stir in the green chiles, Monterey Jack cheese, Cheddar cheese, onion, Anaheim chiles, 1/4 cup chopped cilantro and salt. Pour the egg mixture evenly over the bread cubes. You may chill, covered, at this point for 8 to 10 hours before baking.

Bake at 350 degrees for 45 minutes or until the center barely moves when shaken gently and the top is light brown. Top each serving with sprigs of cilantro and sliced avocado.

For the salsa, combine the mango, tomatoes, green onions, cilantro, lime juice, Anaheim chiles, garlic and salt in a nonreactive bowl and mix gently. Serve with the frittata.

Serves 8

Goldilock's Goodness

Perfect for a snowy Colorado ski weekend.

3 cups water
1/4 teaspoon salt
1 2/3 cups 4-grain hot cereal
2/3 cup raisins
1/4 cup maple syrup
1/4 cup walnuts, chopped
2 tablespoons molasses
2 tablespoons brown sugar
1/2 teaspoon cinnamon
1/2 teaspoon ginger
1/4 teaspoon nutmeg
1 cup milk

Bring the water and salt to a boil in a large heavy saucepan; reduce the heat to medium-low. Stir in the cereal. Cook for 5 minutes, stirring frequently. Add the raisins, maple syrup, walnuts, molasses, brown sugar, cinnamon, ginger and nutmeg and mix well. Spoon the cereal mixture into a 2-quart baking dish sprayed with nonstick cooking spray. Bake, covered, at 375 degrees for 45 minutes or until bubbly. Serve immediately with the milk and additional maple syrup.

Serves 6

Sweet Potato Hash Browns

Salt to taste
2 large sweet potatoes (about 2 pounds),
   peeled and cut into 3/4-inch pieces
6 tablespoons olive oil
1 medium yellow or sweet onion,
   cut into 1/3-inch pieces
2 tablespoons coarsely chopped fresh parsley
Freshly ground pepper to taste

Bring a 6-quart stockpot of salted water to a boil. Add the sweet potatoes. Cook for 7 to 8 minutes or until tender. Drain and rinse with cold water. Chill for 1 hour or until cold.

Heat the olive oil in a large skillet over medium heat. Sauté the onion in the hot olive oil for 20 minutes or until tender and golden brown. Remove the onion to a bowl with a slotted spoon, reserving the pan drippings. Add the chilled sweet potatoes to the reserved pan drippings. Cook for 8 to 10 minutes or until golden brown, stirring occasionally. Add the onion to the sweet potatoes and mix well.

Cook for 2 minutes longer, stirring frequently. Remove from the heat. Stir in the parsley, salt and pepper. Serve immediately with eggs of any style if desired.

For a spicier flavor, substitute 1/8 teaspoon cayenne pepper for the freshly ground black pepper.

Serves 4

Fresh Pineapple in Cinnamon Syrup

1²/3 cups water

³/4 cup sugar

3 cinnamon sticks, broken into halves

4 (¹/4-inch-thick) slices fresh gingerroot

2 (¹/4-inch-thick) slices lemon, seeds removed

1 (4- to 4¹/2-pound) pineapple, peeled and
    cut lengthwise into 8 wedges

1 tablespoon sugar

¹/4 teaspoon cinnamon

Combine the water, ³/4 cup sugar, cinnamon sticks, gingerroot and lemon slices in a heavy saucepan. Cook over medium heat until the sugar dissolves, stirring occasionally. Bring the syrup to a gentle boil; reduce the heat. Simmer, covered, over low heat for 10 minutes to blend the flavors, stirring occasionally. Cut the pineapple wedges crosswise into ³/4-inch pieces and add to the syrup. Simmer for 3 to 5 minutes or until the pineapple begins to turn translucent; do not overcook. Discard the cinnamon sticks, gingerroot and lemon slices.

Spoon the pineapple and syrup into a bowl. Chill, covered, for 2 hours or longer. Sprinkle with a mixture of 1 tablespoon sugar and cinnamon just before serving. You may prepare up to 2 days in advance and store, covered, in the refrigerator. Sprinkle with the cinnamon-sugar mixture just before serving.

Serves 6

Christmas Oranges

¹/4 cup dried cranberries

¹/2 cup AlizE (passion fruit liqueur) or orange
    juice

4 large navel oranges

Combine the cranberries and liqueur in a small bowl and mix well. Let stand at room temperature for 30 minutes.

Peel the oranges and separate the sections by cutting a slice off the top and bottom of the oranges. Cut the peel and white pith away from the pulp, working from the top to the bottom. Follow the shape of the orange as you cut, working over a bowl to catch the juice. Cut between the membranes to remove each section. Add the undrained cranberries to the orange sections and juice and mix gently. Chill, covered, for 2 to 10 hours.

Serves 4 to 6

CONTENTS

112   Raspberry Asparagus
113   Roasted Asparagus and Portobello Mushrooms
113   Hearty Baked Beans
114   Balsamic-Glazed Beets
114   Baked Bok Choy with Gruyère Cheese
115   Asperation Inspiration
115   Sautéed Brussels Sprouts
115   Roasted Carrots
116   Edamame and Cherry Medley
116   Corn Cheese Boats
117   Eggplant Stacks
117   Greens with Orange and Ginger
118   Grilled Peppers Stuffed with Goat Cheese
119   Tuscan Green Beans
119   Boursin Potatoes
120   Herb and Garlic Cheese Stuffed Potatoes
121   Roasted Red Potatoes with Artichokes
122   Spinach and Leek Sauté
122   Grilled Yellow Squash
123   Acorn Squash Apple Rings
124   Mashed Sweet Potatoes Brûlée
124   Zesty Spring Vegetable Medley
125   Roasted Root Vegetables
126   Wild Mushroom and Bleu Cheese Bread Pudding
126   Orzo with Spinach and Taleggio
127   Rice Pilaf with Almonds and Dried Mangoes
128   Orange Curry Couscous

VEGETABLES
AND SIDES

Raspberry Asparagus

Asparagus is most tender when the stalks are apple green and the tips have a purple tinge.

1½ pounds fresh asparagus spears
2 tablespoons raspberry vinegar
1 teaspoon Dijon mustard
¾ teaspoon salt
3 tablespoons safflower oil
3 tablespoons olive oil
¼ cup fresh raspberries
¼ cup coarsely chopped pecans, toasted

Snap off the woody ends of the asparagus spears and cut the spears approximately the same length. Peel the ends about 1 inch. Steam the asparagus until tender-crisp; drain.

Whisk the raspberry vinegar, Dijon mustard and salt in a bowl. Whisk in the safflower oil and olive oil until blended. Add the raspberries and mash lightly. Spoon the vinaigrette over the asparagus on a serving platter. Sprinkle with the pecans.

Serves 4

Roasted Asparagus and Portobello Mushrooms

2 leeks, thickly sliced lengthwise
1/4 cup walnut oil
2 or 3 large portobello mushrooms, stems
    removed and thickly sliced
2 bunches fresh asparagus spears, trimmed
3 to 4 teaspoons balsamic vinegar
1 teaspoon coarsely ground salt
1 teaspoon freshly ground pepper
1/2 teaspoon herbes de Provence

Toss the leeks with 1/3 of the walnut oil in a large roasting pan. Spread the leeks in the pan. Roast at 450 degrees for 5 to 10 minutes, stirring occasionally. Toss the mushrooms with 1/2 of the remaining walnut oil and add to the roasting pan. Roast for 5 to 10 minutes, stirring occasionally.

Toss the asparagus with the remaining walnut oil and add to the roasting pan. Drizzle the balsamic vinegar over the vegetables and sprinkle with the salt and pepper. Roast for 10 to 15 minutes longer or until the vegetables are tender-crisp, stirring occasionally. Sprinkle with the herbes de Provence and toss. Serve hot or at room temperature.

Serves 8

Hearty Baked Beans

1 pound ground beef
8 ounces bacon, chopped
1 onion, chopped
1 (3-pound) can baked beans
1 (14-ounce) can kidney beans, drained
1 (14-ounce) can black beans, drained
1 (14-ounce) can stewed tomatoes, drained
    and chopped
1 cup packed brown sugar
1/2 cup ketchup
2 tablespoons molasses
2 tablespoons dry mustard
1 teaspoon vinegar
1 teaspoon cayenne pepper
1/2 teaspoon each salt and black pepper

Brown the ground beef with the bacon and onion in a skillet, stirring until the ground beef is crumbly; drain. Combine the ground beef mixture, beans, tomatoes, brown sugar, ketchup, molasses, dry mustard, vinegar, cayenne pepper, salt and black pepper in a bowl and mix well.

Spoon the bean mixture into a baking pan. Bake, covered, at 350 degrees for 1 hour; remove cover. Bake for 1 hour longer or until bubbly. Serve immediately.

Serves 8 to 10

Balsamic-Glazed Beets

3 1/2 pounds fresh beets (4 pounds beets if
    greens attached)
Salt to taste
3 tablespoons balsamic vinegar
2 tablespoons maple syrup
1 tablespoon olive oil
Pepper to taste
1 1/2 teaspoons minced fresh thyme
Orange zest to taste

Trim the beets, leaving about 1 inch of the stems.
Combine the beets and salt in a large saucepan.
Add enough water to cover by 1 inch. Bring to a
boil; reduce the heat. Simmer, covered, for 35 to
45 minutes or until tender. Drain the beets in a
colander and let stand until cool enough to handle.
Slip off the skins and stems.

Cut the beets lengthwise into slender wedges. The
beets may be prepared up to this point 2 days in
advance and stored, covered, in the refrigerator.
Bring the beets to room temperature before
proceeding with the recipe.

Combine the balsamic vinegar, maple syrup and
olive oil in a large skillet and mix well. Add the
beets, salt and pepper and mix gently. Cook over
medium heat until the beets are glazed and heated
through, stirring frequently. Sprinkle with 1/2 of
the thyme and orange zest and toss gently. Spoon
the beets into a serving bowl. Sprinkle with the
remaining thyme.

Serves 8

Baked Bok Choy with Gruyère Cheese

1 1/2 pounds bok choy
1 cup chicken broth
1 tablespoon butter
1 1/2 tablespoons flour
2 teaspoons Dijon mustard
1 cup (about 2 ounces) shredded Gruyère
    cheese
Salt to taste
3 to 4 drops of Tabasco sauce or any hot
    pepper sauce

Cut the bok choy stalks into 1/2-inch slices and
coarsely chop the leaves. Combine the sliced bok
choy and broth in a shallow baking dish. Bake,
covered, at 400 degrees for 35 minutes. Stir in the
chopped bok choy leaves. Bake for 10 minutes
longer or until the leaves wilt.

Heat the butter in a small saucepan. Add the flour
gradually, stirring constantly. Cook over medium
heat for 1 minute, stirring constantly. Whisk in the
Dijon mustard. Add the liquid from the bok choy
and mix well. Increase the heat to high.

Cook until thickened, stirring constantly. Stir in
the cheese. Cook until the cheese melts, stirring
constantly. Add the salt and Tabasco sauce and mix
well. Fold the cheese sauce into the bok choy. Bake
for 10 minutes longer or until bubbly.

Serves 4

Asperation Inspiration

3 cups chopped asperation or broccolini
1/4 cup sake
1 1/2 tablespoons soy sauce
2 1/2 teaspoons honey
2 teaspoons sesame oil
2 to 3 tablespoons sesame seeds, toasted
   if desired

Steam the asperation until tender-crisp; drain. Combine the sake, soy sauce, honey and sesame oil in a serving bowl and mix well. Add the asperation and toss to coat. Sprinkle with the sesame seeds. You may substitute broccoli or asparagus for the asperation and add water chestnuts and unsalted cashews for a different twist.

Serves 4

Sautéed Brussels Sprouts

1 pound fresh brussels sprouts, trimmed and
   cut into halves
1 tablespoon walnut oil
Salt and pepper to taste

Sauté the brussels sprouts in the walnut oil in a skillet until brown and tender. Season with salt and pepper. Spoon the brussels sprouts into a serving bowl and serve immediately.

Serves 4

Roasted Carrots

12 carrots
3 tablespoons olive oil
1 1/4 teaspoons kosher salt
1/2 teaspoon freshly ground pepper
2 tablespoons minced fresh dill weed or
   flat-leaf parsley

Cut any thick carrots lengthwise into halves; otherwise leave whole. Cut the carrots diagonally into 1 1/2-inch slices. Toss the carrots with the olive oil, salt and pepper in a bowl.

Arrange the carrots in a single layer on a baking sheet. Roast at 400 degrees for 20 minutes, stirring occasionally. Toss the carrots with the dill weed in a serving bowl. Taste and adjust the seasonings. Serve immediately.

Serves 4 to 6

Edamame and Cherry Medley

3 tablespoons vegetable oil
1 cup shiitake mushroom caps, coarsely
    chopped
1 tablespoon minced fresh gingerroot
5 garlic cloves, minced
1 jalapeño chile, seeded and minced
2 cups fresh or thawed frozen shelled edamame
1 cup frozen whole kernel corn
1/2 cup milk
1 tablespoon rice vinegar
1 cup dried cherries
1/4 teaspoon salt
1/8 teaspoon white pepper
Endive spears
2 tablespoons black sesame seeds, toasted

Heat the oil in a large nonstick skillet over medium-high heat. Stir-fry the mushrooms, gingerroot, garlic and jalapeño chile in the hot oil for 2 minutes. Add the edamame. Stir-fry for 1 minute. Add the corn, milk and vinegar and mix well.

Cook for 3 minutes or until the liquid almost evaporates, stirring frequently. Remove from the heat. Stir in the cherries, salt and white pepper. Spoon the edamame mixture into the center of a large serving platter. Arrange endive spears around the outer edge of the mixture. Sprinkle with the black sesame seeds.

Serves 8

Corn Cheese Boats

6 ears of fresh corn
1 tablespoon unsalted butter
1/4 red onion, finely chopped
2 jalapeño chiles, finely chopped
1 tablespoon chopped fresh cilantro
8 ounces Cheddar cheese, shredded
1 tomato, seeded and chopped
2 tablespoons mayonnaise

Remove the husks from the corn by pulling 1 strip of husk off and discarding. Pull the remaining husks back, pulling the corn toward you and snapping the ear off at the base. Remove the silk and husks, reserving the husks. Cut the kernels off the corn cobs into a bowl using a sharp knife. Heat the unsalted butter in a skillet. Stir in the onion, jalapeño chiles and cilantro. Sauté for 2 minutes. Add the corn and mix well. Sauté for 10 minutes. Remove from the heat. Stir in the cheese, tomato and mayonnaise.

Spoon the corn mixture into the husks and arrange the stuffed husks on a broiler rack in a broiler pan. Broil for 2 to 3 minutes. Serve immediately. You may prepare in advance and store, covered, in the refrigerator. Bake at 350 degrees for 10 minutes and then broil for 2 to 3 minutes.

Serves 6

Eggplant Stacks

1 (1- to 1½-pound) eggplant
1 teaspoon kosher salt
4 tablespoons sun-dried tomato pesto or basil
  pesto
1½ cups (6 ounces) shredded Monterey Jack
  cheese
4 tablespoons grated Parmesan cheese

Peel the eggplant in alternating strips to create a zebra effect. Cut the eggplant crosswise into 12 slices, ⅓ inch thick. Sprinkle both sides of the slices with the salt. Arrange the eggplant in a single layer on paper towels. Top with additional paper towels. Let stand for 30 minutes and pat dry.

Arrange 4 of the slices in a single layer in an oiled baking pan, spreading each slice with 1 teaspoon of the pesto and sprinkling with 2 tablespoons of the Monterey Jack cheese. Repeat the stacking process twice, creating 3 layers. Sprinkle 1 tablespoon of the Parmesan cheese on each eggplant stack. Bake on the middle oven rack at 375 degrees for 30 to 35 minutes or until the eggplant is tender. Serve immediately.

Serves 4

Greens with Orange and Ginger

9 to 10 ounces trimmed greens (kale, collard
  greens, chard or spinach), cut into
  ½-inch strips
1 tablespoon unsalted butter
1 tablespoon olive oil
2 garlic cloves, minced
1 tablespoon chopped fresh gingerroot
⅓ cup thawed frozen orange juice
  concentrate
½ teaspoon coarse salt

Pile the greens in a large nonstick skillet. Cook over high heat for 4 minutes or until the greens wilt, gently turning with tongs. Drain the greens in a colander.

Wipe the skillet clean with a paper towel. Heat the unsalted butter and olive oil in the skillet over medium-low heat. Stir in the garlic and gingerroot. Sauté for 2 minutes or until tender and fragrant. Add the orange juice concentrate and mix well.

Cook over high heat for no longer than 1 minute to reduce the liquid to a glaze consistency, stirring constantly. Reduce the heat to low. Add the greens and salt and toss to coat. Serve immediately.

Serves 4

Grilled Peppers Stuffed with Goat Cheese

1 medium yellow bell pepper
1 medium red bell pepper
2 ounces soft goat cheese (chèvre)
1/2 cup (2 ounces) shredded Monterey Jack
    cheese
2 tablespoons snipped fresh chives
2 tablespoons snipped fresh basil

Cut the bell peppers lengthwise into halves, discarding the stem ends, seeds and membranes. Combine the bell peppers with a small amount of water in a saucepan. Bring to a boil. Boil for 2 minutes. Drain cut side down on paper towels.

Combine the goat cheese, Monterey Jack cheese, chives and basil in a bowl and mix well. Spoon about 2 tablespoons of the cheese mixture into each bell pepper half. Fold an 18×24-inch sheet of foil in half to make a 12×18-inch rectangle. Arrange the bell pepper halves inside the foil. Bring up 2 opposite sides of the foil and seal with a double fold. Fold the remaining ends to completely enclose the bell peppers, allowing space for steam to build.

Arrange the foil packet on a grill rack. Grill over medium to medium-hot coals for 5 to 6 minutes or until the bell peppers are tender-crisp and the cheese melts. To serve, cut each half into 2 wedges. Serve warm.

Serves 8

Tuscan Green Beans

6 quarts water
1 pound fresh green beans, trimmed and
    cut into 2-inch pieces
1/3 cup olive oil
1/3 cup sliced onion
2 garlic cloves, minced
1 medium tomato, chopped
1 1/2 tablespoons chopped fresh rosemary
1 teaspoon salt
1 teaspoon freshly ground pepper

Bring the water to a boil in a stockpot. Add the beans; reduce the heat. Simmer for 4 minutes or until tender-crisp; drain.

Heat the olive oil in a large skillet or sauté pan. Stir in the onion. Cook over medium-high heat until tender, stirring frequently. Stir in the garlic; reduce the heat to medium-low. Add the beans and mix well. Stir in the tomato and rosemary.

Simmer, covered, for 6 minutes, stirring occasionally. Season with the salt and pepper. Serve hot or at room temperature. Excellent with grilled tuna or chicken.

Serves 4

Boursin Potatoes

1 tablespoon butter
2 cups whipping cream
5 ounces boursin
3 pounds medium red potatoes, thinly sliced
1 teaspoon salt
1 teaspoon freshly ground pepper

Coat the bottom and sides of a 9×13-inch baking dish with the butter. Heat the whipping cream and cheese in a saucepan over medium heat until blended, stirring frequently. Remove from the heat.

Layer the potatoes, salt, pepper and cheese sauce 1/2 at a time in the prepared baking dish, arranging the potato slices so they are slightly overlapping. Bake, covered, at 400 degrees for 30 minutes; remove the cover. Bake for 30 minutes longer.

Serves 8

Haricots Verts

These slender delicate French green beans are truly special. They cook in a minute, turn a deep emerald green, and they will never ever taste like canned beans.

Herb and Garlic Cheese Stuffed Potatoes

16 new red potatoes
7 tablespoons butter, softened
2 cups chopped green cabbage
1/2 cup chopped onion
6 ounces cream cheese, softened
2 tablespoons sour cream
3 ounces Gruyère cheese, shredded
3 tablespoons minced fresh parsley
3 large scallions, minced
2 tablespoons minced fresh basil, or
    2 teaspoons dried basil
1 large garlic clove, minced
1 teaspoon salt
1/2 teaspoon freshly ground pepper
Minced fresh chives, minced scallions or
    fresh basil leaves

Arrange the potatoes on a baking sheet. Bake at 400 degrees for 1 hour or until tender. Cool slightly. Cut the potatoes crosswise into halves. Scoop out the pulp carefully, leaving 1/4-inch shells. Mash the pulp in a bowl with 5 tablespoons of the butter.

Heat the remaining 2 tablespoons butter in a heavy skillet over high heat. Add the cabbage and onion to the melted butter and mix well. Cook for 8 minutes or until the vegetables are brown, stirring frequently. Add the cabbage mixture to the mashed potatoes and mix well.

Beat the cream cheese and sour cream in a mixing bowl until fluffy. Add the Gruyère cheese, parsley, 3 minced scallions, minced basil and garlic. Beat until mixed. Add 2/3 of the cheese mixture to the potato mixture and mix well. Season with the salt and pepper. Spoon the cheese mixture into the potato shells. Press 2 potato shells together to form a whole potato.

Arrange the potatoes on their sides in a large buttered baking dish. Spoon a dollop of the remaining cheese mixture on each potato. Chill, covered, for 1 hour or for up to 2 days. Bake at 325 degrees for 20 minutes or until heated through. Top with minced fresh chives, minced scallions or fresh basil leaves before serving.

Serves 8

Roasted Potatoes

Peel 1 1/2 pounds Yukon gold potatoes and cut into thin slices. Toss with 2 tablespoons olive oil, 2 teaspoons chopped fresh thyme leaves and coarse salt and freshly ground pepper to taste in a bowl. Brush a large-rimmed baking sheet with 1 to 2 tablespoons olive oil and arrange the potato slices on the baking sheet, overlapping them slightly. Roast at 400 degrees for 30 minutes or until golden brown and crisp.

Roasted Red Potatoes with Artichokes

2 pounds small red potatoes, cut into quarters
2 tablespoons olive oil
2 tablespoons chopped fresh thyme
1/4 teaspoon pepper
2 (14-ounce) cans artichokes, drained and
  cut into halves
1 yellow onion, cut into 1- to 2-inch pieces
1/2 cup (2 ounces) crumbled feta cheese
Paprika to taste

Line a 9×13-inch baking pan with foil. Spray with nonstick cooking spray. Combine the potatoes, olive oil, thyme and pepper in a sealable plastic bag and seal tightly. Turn to coat. Pour the potato mixture into the prepared baking pan.

Roast at 425 degrees for 45 to 50 minutes or until the potatoes are tender, stirring occasionally and adding the artichokes and onion during the last 20 minutes of the baking process. Toss the potato mixture with the feta cheese in a serving bowl. Sprinkle with paprika. Serve immediately.

May substitute coarsely chopped peeled taro root for the potatoes.

Serves 8

Variations on Classic Mashers

- Subtle flavors — Cooked cubed celery root (celeriac) with potatoes.
- Venetian — Instead of milk, yogurt, or cream, try mascarpone and Italian sweet cheese.
- Vegan — Substitute a splash of olive oil and vegetable broth for the dairy. Or try oat milk, which boosts the creamy texture.

Spinach and Leek Sauté

1 or 2 leeks
1 tablespoon olive oil
1 red bell pepper, sliced (optional)
8 ounces bok choy, chopped (optional)
10 ounces baby spinach, trimmed
Salt and pepper to taste
1 tablespoon balsamic vinegar

Slice the leek lengthwise into halves. Trim the root end and most of the green end of the leek. Rinse to remove the grit and coarsely chop (see page 245). Sauté the leek in the olive oil in a skillet for 5 to 10 minutes or until tender and light brown. Add the bell pepper and bok choy and mix well.

Sauté for 2 minutes if adding the bell pepper. Sauté for 2 to 5 minutes if adding the bell pepper and bok choy. Stir in the spinach. Cook until the spinach is evenly wilted, tossing every 1 to 2 minutes. Season with salt and pepper. Drizzle with the balsamic vinegar just before serving.

Serves 4

Grilled Yellow Squash

6 yellow squash, cut lengthwise into halves
6 Roma tomatoes
1/2 cup olive oil
3 to 4 tablespoons chopped fresh basil
3 garlic cloves, minced
1 teaspoon salt
1 teaspoon pepper

Starting approximately 2 to 3 inches below the neck of each squash half, cut lengthwise 4 or 5 times to create a fan. Cut the tomatoes lengthwise into 4 or 5 slices and place the slices between the slits. Fan out the slices and thread with wooden skewers. Arrange the fans in a single layer in a dish.

Combine the olive oil, basil, garlic, salt and pepper in a bowl and mix well. Pour the olive oil mixture over the squash. Marinate, covered, at room temperature for 1 to 5 hours. Grill over medium-hot coals for 8 to 12 minutes or to the desired degree of crispness. Serve warm or cold.

Serves 12

Acorn Squash Apple Rings

1 tablespoon butter
1 large yellow onion, chopped
1 tablespoon curry powder, or to taste
2 Granny Smith apples, peeled and chopped
    (about 2⅓ cups)
⅔ cup apple cider
½ cup dried cranberries or cherries
⅛ teaspoon nutmeg (optional)
Salt and pepper to taste
5 tablespoons butter
1½ teaspoons curry powder, or to taste
2 medium acorn squash, seeded and cut into
    1-inch-thick rings

Heat 1 tablespoon butter in a large heavy skillet over medium heat. Sauté the onion in the butter for 12 minutes or until tender. Stir in 1 tablespoon curry powder. Sauté for 1 minute. Add the apples, apple cider and cranberries and mix well.

Sauté for 6 minutes or until the liquid evaporates. Stir in the nutmeg, salt and pepper. You may prepare up to this point 1 day in advance and store, covered, in the refrigerator.

Heat 5 tablespoons butter and 1½ teaspoons curry powder in a small skillet over medium heat until the butter melts, stirring occasionally. Brush 2 large baking sheets with sides with some of the curry butter. Arrange the squash rings in a single layer on the prepared baking sheets. Sprinkle with salt and pepper. Spoon some of the apple mixture into the center of each ring. Drizzle with the remaining curry butter.

Bake, covered with foil, at 350 degrees for 40 minutes or until the squash is tender when pierced with a skewer. Serve immediately.

May substitute pears for the apples and pear nectar for the apple cider for a slightly less sweet dish.

Serves 8

Roasted Sweet Potatoes with Garlic

Slice 2 medium sweet potatoes into rounds. Toss with 1½ tablespoons olive oil, 2 thinly sliced large garlic cloves and salt and pepper to taste in a bowl. Spread on a baking sheet and roast at 475 degrees for 30 minutes or until crisp, stirring occasionally.

Mashed Sweet Potatoes Brûlée

6 cups hot mashed cooked orange or red
    garnet sweet potatoes (about 4 pounds)
3/4 cup milk
1 tablespoon butter, softened
1/2 teaspoon salt
1/4 teaspoon cinnamon
1/4 teaspoon nutmeg
1/4 teaspoon ginger
1/2 cup packed brown sugar
1/2 cup chopped pecans

Combine the sweet potatoes, milk, butter, salt, cinnamon, nutmeg and ginger in a bowl and mix well. Spoon the sweet potato mixture into an 11×17-inch baking dish sprayed with nonstick cooking spray. Sprinkle the brown sugar and pecans over the top. Broil for 2 to 5 minutes or until the brown sugar melts. Serve immediately.

Serves 12

Zesty Spring Vegetable Medley

3 pounds fava beans, shelled, or 1 pound
    frozen fordhook lima beans
1 tablespoon olive oil
1/2 teaspoon unsalted butter
4 shallots, thinly sliced crosswise
1 pound sugar snap peas, trimmed and
    strings removed
Salt to taste
1 tablespoon olive oil
2 1/2 teaspoons unsalted butter
1 pound asparagus, trimmed and cut
    diagonally into 1/2-inch slices
1 tablespoon fresh lemon juice
Zest of 1 lemon
Pepper to taste

Blanch the fava beans in a small amount of boiling water in a saucepan for 1 minute; drain. Remove the outer skins of the beans if desired.

Heat 1 tablespoon olive oil and 1/2 teaspoon unsalted butter in a large skillet until foamy. Sauté the shallots in the olive oil mixture for 2 minutes or until tender. Remove the shallots to a bowl with a slotted spoon, reserving the pan drippings. Sauté the sugar snap peas and salt in the reserved pan drippings until tender-crisp. Remove the sugar snap peas to the bowl containing the shallots, using a slotted spoon and reserving the pan drippings.

Heat 1 tablespoon olive oil and 2 1/2 teaspoons unsalted butter with the reserved pan drippings. Sauté the asparagus and salt in the olive oil mixture until tender-crisp. Stir in the fava beans. Sauté for 2 minutes. Add the shallot mixture, lemon juice, lemon zest, salt and pepper. Sauté just until heated through. Add julienned or sliced carrots for variety.

Serves 6

Roasted Root Vegetables

8 ounces fresh beets

2 1/2 tablespoons olive oil

8 ounces carrots, cut diagonally into
    3/4- to 1-inch pieces

8 ounces fennel, cut diagonally into
    3/4- to 1-inch pieces

8 ounces parsnips, cut diagonally into
    3/4- to 1-inch pieces

8 ounces turnips or rutabagas, cut diagonally
    into 3/4- to 1-inch pieces

2 small white onions, cut into 1-inch wedges

3 tablespoons honey

1 tablespoon chopped fresh sage

1 tablespoon chopped fresh parsley

1/2 teaspoon kosher salt

1/2 teaspoon freshly ground pepper

1 teaspoon chopped fresh sage

Trim the beets, leaving 1/2 inch of the stem. Wrap the beets in foil. Roast at 400 degrees for 70 minutes.

Pour the olive oil into a 9×13-inch baking pan. Heat over medium-high heat until the olive oil is smoking. Add the carrots, fennel, parsnips, turnips and onions to the hot olive oil and toss to coat. Roast at 400 degrees for 10 minutes. Add the honey and 1 tablespoon sage and mix well.

Roast for 60 to 70 minutes longer or until the vegetables are tender, shaking the pan every 10 to 15 minutes. Cut the beets into 3/4-inch chunks and add to the vegetable mixture. Toss the vegetables with the parsley, salt, pepper and 1 teaspoon sage just before serving.

Serves 6

Wild Mushroom and Bleu Cheese Bread Pudding

2 cups heavy cream
4 eggs
1/2 loaf focaccia, cubed (about 6 to 8 cups)
1/2 cup (2 ounces) crumbled bleu cheese
1 1/2 teaspoons chopped fresh thyme
1 teaspoon chopped fresh rosemary
1 andouille sausage, cooked and chopped
1/2 cup chopped cremini mushrooms
1/2 cup chopped portobello mushrooms
1/2 cup chopped shiitake mushrooms
1/2 medium yellow onion, chopped
1 tablespoon salt
1 teaspoon pepper

Whisk the heavy cream and eggs in a large bowl until blended. Add just enough of the bread cubes so only a small portion of liquid is left. Stir in the cheese, thyme and rosemary.

Sauté the sausage, mushrooms and onion in a skillet or sauté pan until the mushrooms and onion are tender-crisp. Add the mushroom mixture to the bread mixture and mix well. Stir in the salt and pepper.

Spoon the mushroom mixture into ramekins or a large baking pan sprayed with nonstick cooking spray. Cook in a water bath at 350 degrees for 40 to 45 minutes or until set; the texture should be spongy. Serve with grilled meats.

For a milder flavor, substitute a mixture of 1/4 cup crumbled bleu cheese and 1/4 cup crumbled goat cheese for the 1/2 cup bleu cheese.

Serves 8

Orzo with Spinach and Taleggio

Taleggio is an Italian semisoft cheese. Its mildly piquant flavor sharpens with age.

1 cup orzo
10 ounces fresh spinach or thawed frozen
    spinach
5 ounces Taleggio cheese, rind removed and
    cut into small pieces
Salt and freshly ground pepper to taste

Cook the pasta for 10 minutes using package directions. Add the spinach and mix well. Cook for 2 to 3 minutes. Drain in a colander.

Spoon the pasta mixture into a 9×11-inch baking pan. Stir in the cheese, salt and pepper. Bake at 400 degrees for 8 minutes. Serve immediately.

For a milder flavor, substitute Camembert cheese or Brie cheese for the Taleggio cheese.

Serves 4

Rice Pilaf with Almonds and Dried Mangoes

1/2 cup whole almonds

4 cups water

1 cup wild rice

1 tablespoon unsalted butter

1 small onion, finely chopped

2 ribs celery, finely chopped

2 teaspoons herbes de Provence

1 teaspoon salt

1/2 teaspoon freshly ground pepper

1 cup brown rice

2 cups chicken broth

8 dried mangoes, finely chopped

1 cup fresh flat-leaf parsley, finely chopped

Spread the almonds in a single layer on a baking sheet. Toast at 350 degrees for 10 minutes or just until the almonds begin to smell fragrant; coarsely chop. Bring the water to a boil in a saucepan. Stir in the wild rice; reduce the heat. Simmer for 45 minutes or until the rice is tender but not split; drain. Cover to keep warm.

Heat the unsalted butter in a saucepan. Stir in the onion. Cook for 3 minutes, stirring frequently. Stir in the celery, herbes de Provence, salt and pepper. Add the brown rice and mix well. Cook for 3 to 4 minutes or until the rice begins to turn translucent, stirring occasionally. Stir in the broth. Bring to a boil; reduce the heat.

Simmer, covered, for 20 minutes. Remove from the heat. Mix the wild rice and brown rice mixture in a serving bowl. Stir in the almonds, mangoes and parsley.

May substitute chopped dried apricots, pears or papayas for the mangoes for variety. Can be used as a stuffing for Cornish game hens.

Serves 6

Sugar Snap Peas with Toasted Sesame Seeds

Steam two 8-ounce packages sugar snap peas for 3 minutes or until tender-crisp. Combine with 1 teaspoon toasted sesame seeds and 1 teaspoon sesame oil in a bowl. Season with salt and toss to coat well.

Orange Curry Couscous

Orange Curry Dressing

- 1 cup seasoned rice vinegar
- 2 tablespoons minced garlic
- 2 tablespoons grated orange zest
- 1 tablespoon sugar or honey
- 2 teaspoons cinnamon
- 2 teaspoons curry powder
- 1/2 teaspoon salt
- 2 cups canola oil

Couscous

- 2 cups water
- 1 1/2 cups couscous
- 1 cup fresh parsley, minced
- 1 cup chopped green onions
- 1 cup almonds, toasted and chopped
- 1 cup currants
- 1/2 cup frozen peas, thawed
- 1/2 teaspoon salt

For the dressing, process the vinegar, garlic, orange zest, sugar, cinnamon, curry powder and salt in a blender for 1 minute. Add the canola oil gradually, processing constantly until blended. Store, covered, in the refrigerator for up to 2 weeks.

For the couscous, bring the water to a boil in a saucepan. Stir in the couscous. Remove from the heat. Let stand, covered, for 10 minutes. Spoon the couscous into a serving bowl. Let stand until cool. Add 1 1/2 cups of the dressing, parsley, green onions, almonds, currants, peas and salt and mix well. Add additional dressing if the mixture is too dry.

Serves 8

Fried Parsley

Heat a small amount of oil in a skillet until almost smoking. Add 1 bunch of Italian or curly parsley a small amount at a time. Cook until the parsley turns a bright green; remove with a slotted spoon and drain on paper towels. Sprinkle with grated cheese and serve at once. This makes a great hors d'oeuvre, garnish or side dish.

contents

132 Cornish Game Hens with Tamarind Glaze

134 Grilled Rosemary Chicken in Herb Vinaigrette

134 Roasted Chicken with Vegetables

135 Feta-Stuffed Chicken

136 Tarragon Chicken (Poulet à l'Estragon)

137 Braised Chicken with Shallots and Pancetta

138 Chicken with Figs and Artichoke Hearts

138 Mango Chili Chicken

139 Lemon Chicken with Rosemary Orzo

140 Cinnamon-Cured Smoked Chicken with
Cherry Barbecue Sauce

141 Crispy Pan-Fried Chicken with Summer Sauce

142 Green Olive Enchiladas

144 Ginger Chicken and Vegetable Stir-Fry

145 Sticky Glazed Coconut Chicken and Coconut Basil Rice

146 Sautéed Chicken Paprika

146 Brown Sugar–Rubbed Turkey Breast

147 Roasted Turkey Breast with Sage Corn Bread Crust

148 Seared Duck Breasts with Two Sauces

POULTRY

Cornish Game Hens with Tamarind Glaze

Turmeric is a spice that is related to ginger and gives food a golden color and slightly pungent flavor.

Roasted Spice Mixture
1 teaspoon fennel seeds
1 teaspoon cumin
1/2 teaspoon each cardamom, coriander,
    cinnamon and red pepper flakes

Marinade
1 cup plain yogurt
8 garlic cloves, chopped
1 (3-inch) piece fresh gingerroot, minced
1 tablespoon paprika
2 teaspoons kosher salt
1 teaspoon cayenne pepper
1/2 teaspoon turmeric

Cornish Game Hens
4 frozen Cornish game hens, thawed and
    cleaned

For the spice mixture, combine the fennel seeds, cumin, cardamom, coriander, cinnamon and red pepper flakes in a nonstick skillet and mix well. Cook over medium heat until the spices are fragrant and begin to change color, stirring constantly. Grind the spice mixture in a miniature food processor or clean coffee grinder or crush with a mortar and pestle.

For the marinade, mix the spice mixture, yogurt, garlic, gingerroot, paprika, salt, cayenne pepper and turmeric in a nonreactive bowl.

For the game hens, pat the game hens dry with paper towels. Cut along both sides of the backbone of each hen with kitchen shears, discarding the backbone. Place the hens breast side up and spread open on a work surface. Push down on the hen with the heel of your hand to flatten. Cut through the breast of the hen to split. Pierce the hen on both sides with the tip of a sharp knife. Arrange the hen halves in a large glass dish. Coat each half with some of the marinade. Marinate, covered, in the refrigerator for 2 to 10 hours.

Tamarind Water

Place 1 pound shelled tamarind in a heatproof bowl and cover with 4 cups hot water. Let stand overnight. Strain, discarding the fruit. Stir in sugar to taste until dissolved. Place in bottles and chill in the refrigerator for up to 2 days. Serve chilled.

Tamarind Balls

Combine 1/2 cup tamarind pulp with 1 cup packed brown sugar or superfine sugar in a bowl and knead until well mixed. Shape into 1/2-inch balls and roll in additional sugar to coat. Store in an airtight container.

Tamarind Glaze

    3 tablespoons tamarind pulp

    1 cup hot water

    2 teaspoons brown sugar

    2 teaspoons finely grated fresh gingerroot

    2 teaspoons fresh lemon juice

    1 teaspoon salt

    1 teaspoon cumin

    1/2 teaspoon ground fennel seeds

    1/8 teaspoon chili powder

For the glaze, if only tamarind pods are available, peel the hard shell. Peel the pulp off the seeds; the seeds are large and come out easily. Combine the tamarind pulp in a heatproof glass bowl with the hot water. Knead the pulp to break it up and dissolve the solids. Strain through a sieve into a bowl, pushing the pulp through with your fingers. Stir in the brown sugar, gingerroot, lemon juice, salt, cumin, fennel seeds and chili powder. Store, covered, in the refrigerator until needed.

To grill the hens, preheat the grill on high. Turn off 1 burner or move the coals to the outer edge of the rack. Turn the remaining burners to medium. Shake the excess marinade off the hens, reserving the remaining marinade. Arrange the hens breast side up over the burner that is off. Grill for 50 to 60 minutes or until a meat thermometer registers 165 degrees, basting every 20 minutes with the reserved marinade. Rotate the hens around the indirect heat each time the basting process takes place; do not flip. Pour a small amount of the glaze into a dish. Brush the hens with some of the glaze. Remove the hens to a platter and tent with foil. Let rest for 10 minutes. Drizzle the remaining glaze over the hens and serve immediately.

You may serve with basmati rice and grilled eggplant, cauliflower, onions and/or tomatoes.

Serves 4 to 6

Grilled Rosemary Chicken in Herb Vinaigrette

Herb Vinaigrette

1/4 cup dry white wine
1/4 cup rice vinegar
1 tablespoon Dijon mustard
1 1/2 teaspoons Worcestershire sauce
1 garlic clove, minced
1/4 cup olive oil
1/4 cup canola oil
Salt and pepper to taste
3 tablespoons chopped fresh rosemary
3 tablespoons chopped fresh marjoram

Chicken

1 (3-pound) chicken, butterflied

For the vinaigrette, process the wine, vinegar, Dijon mustard, Worcestershire sauce and garlic in a blender or food processor until blended. Add the olive oil and canola oil gradually, processing constantly until thickened. Season with salt and pepper. Add the rosemary and marjoram. Process just until blended.

For the chicken, pierce the chicken with a sharp knife and arrange in a shallow dish. Pour the vinaigrette over the chicken, turning to coat. Marinate, covered, in the refrigerator for 6 to 8 hours, turning occasionally; drain. Grill the chicken over medium-hot coals until cooked through, turning occasionally. Serve with a lighter-style Chardonnay such as a Banrock Station from Australia.

Serves 6

Roasted Chicken with Vegetables

2 tablespoons butter, softened
2 teaspoons paprika
2 teaspoons freshly ground pepper
1 teaspoon salt
1 (4- to 5-pound) chicken
40 baby carrots
12 cippolini, or 40 pearl onions
2 ribs celery, cut into 1-inch pieces
5 garlic cloves
2 cups dry white wine

Mix the butter, paprika, pepper and salt in a bowl. Pat the chicken dry with paper towels. Loosen the skin of the chicken carefully and place 1/2 of the butter mixture beneath the skin. Rub the remaining butter mixture over the outer surface of the chicken.

Place the chicken, carrots, cippolini, celery and garlic in a roasting pan. Roast at 425 degrees for 40 to 50 minutes or until the chicken is brown and crisp and a meat thermometer registers 180 degrees. Remove the chicken and vegetables to a serving platter, reserving the pan juices in the roasting pan. Let chicken rest for 10 minutes before carving. Add the wine to the reserved pan juices and mix well. Heat over high heat until the liquid is reduced by 1/2, stirring frequently and adding any collected juices from the chicken to the sauce. Serve carved chicken with roasted vegetables and pan juices on a platter.

Serves 4

Feta-Stuffed Chicken

3 ounces feta cheese, crumbled

1/4 cup julienned marinated sun-dried
    tomatoes (optional)

1 1/2 teaspoons unsalted butter

1/2 teaspoon minced dried rosemary

Freshly ground pepper to taste

1 (3 1/2- to 4-pound) chicken, back removed
    and cut into quarters

Coarse salt to taste

1 tablespoon olive oil

1/2 cup dry white wine

1/2 cup reduced-sodium chicken broth

18 small unpitted olives, such as picholine,
    kalamata or catalan

1 tablespoon unsalted butter

Mash the cheese, sun-dried tomatoes, 1 1/2 teaspoons unsalted butter, rosemary and pepper in a bowl with a fork until mixed. Push the feta stuffing gently under the skin and spread evenly over the surface of the chicken except the wings; do not tear the skin. Sprinkle with salt and pepper.

Heat a deep ovenproof 10-inch skillet over medium heat for 2 minutes or until very hot. Add the olive oil to the hot skillet. Sear the chicken quarters skin side down for 4 minutes per side or until golden brown. Place the chicken on a plate. Drain the skillet. Deglaze the skillet with the wine and broth, stirring to dislodge any browned bits on the bottom of the skillet.

Return the chicken skin side up to the skillet. Add the olives. Bake at 350 degrees for 40 minutes or until the juices run clear when the chicken is pierced with a fork. Remove the chicken and olives to a heated platter with a slotted spoon, reserving the pan juices.

Bring the reserved pan juices to a boil over high heat. Boil for 4 minutes or until thickened and reduced by 1/2, stirring frequently. Whisk in 1 tablespoon unsalted butter. Pour over the chicken. You may serve with bow tie pasta, rice or couscous, as the juices are delicious.

You may substitute 3 pounds chicken parts or 4 chicken breasts for the whole chicken.

Serves 4

Poultry Tips

- To prepare poultry for cooking, rinse the poultry and allow to drain thoroughly. Carefully pat dry, inside and out, with a linen cloth or paper towels.
- When cooking poultry that has been cut into pieces, remember that white meat cooks more quickly than dark.

Tarragon Chicken (Poulet à l'Estragon)

1 (3¹/₂-pound) chicken, cut into 8 pieces
Salt and freshly ground pepper to taste
2 tablespoons butter
1 tablespoon extra-virgin olive oil
8 sprigs of fresh tarragon
1 cup white wine
1¹/₂ teaspoons dried tarragon
3 cups rich veal stock, beef stock or
　　chicken stock
1 tablespoon butter

Season the chicken with salt and pepper. Heat 2 tablespoons butter and olive oil in a large skillet over medium-high heat. Arrange the chicken pieces skin side down in the skillet. Cook for 5 minutes or until brown; do not turn. Turn the chicken and add 4 of the tarragon sprigs. Reduce the heat to medium. Cook, covered, for 10 to 15 minutes or until the juices run clear when the chicken is pierced with a sharp knife.

Blanch 2 sprigs of the tarragon in a saucepan of boiling water over high heat for 5 seconds. Drain and set aside. Chop the leaves of the remaining 2 sprigs of tarragon, discarding the stalks.

Remove the chicken to an ovenproof platter, discarding the tarragon in the skillet. Keep warm in a 200-degree oven. Drain the skillet. Heat the skillet over medium-high heat. Add the wine and 1¹/₂ teaspoons dried tarragon. Cook for 1 minute, stirring to release any browned bits on the bottom of the skillet. Stir in the stock. Bring to a boil.

Boil for 30 minutes or until the liquid is reduced to 2 cups and thickened, stirring occasionally. Strain the sauce into a bowl, discarding the solids. Return the sauce to the skillet and heat over medium heat. Whisk in 1 tablespoon butter and the reserved chopped fresh tarragon. Return the chicken and any accumulated juices to the skillet and baste the chicken with the sauce.

To serve, sprinkle with the blanched fresh tarragon.

Try a French Chablis with this French-inspired dish.

Serves 4 to 6

Polynesian Chicken Burgers

Season ground chicken with teriyaki sauce, white pepper, green onions, grated ginger, and chili flakes. Add enough Japanese panko crumbs to bind. Shape into patties and grill. While burgers are grilling, sauté pineapple rings in teriyaki sauce in a skillet and then grill for 2 minutes on each side. Serve on a toasted sesame seed bun.

Braised Chicken with Shallots and Pancetta

6 slices bacon or pancetta, cut into
    1/4-inch strips
1 (31/2-pound) chicken, cut into 8 pieces
Salt and pepper to taste
1 pound shallots, thinly sliced
4 ounces cremini mushrooms, thinly sliced
1 head garlic, separated into cloves
1 cup mushroom stock or chicken stock
1/4 cup red balsamic vinegar

Fry the bacon in a 12-inch deep heavy skillet over medium-low heat for 8 minutes or until brown and crisp. Remove the bacon to paper towels to drain, reserving the bacon drippings. Season the chicken with salt and pepper.

Arrange 1/2 of the chicken pieces skin side down in the skillet with the reserved bacon drippings. Cook over medium-high heat until brown on all sides, turning after 8 minutes. Remove the chicken with tongs to a platter. Repeat the browning process with the remaining chicken pieces and remaining bacon drippings.

Drain all but 2 tablespoons of the bacon drippings from the skillet. Stir the shallots and mushrooms into the remaining bacon drippings. Cook, covered, over medium-low heat for 10 minutes or until tender and light golden brown, stirring occasionally; remove the lid. Cook for 10 minutes longer or until deep golden brown, stirring frequently. Stir in the garlic and stock. Bring to a boil.

Boil for 1 minute, stirring constantly. Return the chicken to the skillet, turning the pieces to coat. Arrange skin side up in the skillet. Simmer, covered, for 30 minutes or until the chicken is cooked through and the garlic is tender. Remove the chicken with tongs to a serving bowl, reserving the pan juices. Cover to keep warm.

Add the balsamic vinegar to the reserved pan juices and mix well. Bring to a boil. Boil until slightly thickened and of a sauce consistency, stirring frequently and mashing the garlic with the back of a spoon. Season with salt and pepper. Pour the sauce over the chicken. Sprinkle with the bacon.

Serves 4

Front Range Buffalo Chicken Burger

Season ground chicken with prepared buffalo wing sauce, a dash of celery salt, and finely chopped celery. Add enough Japanese panko crumbs to bind. Shape into patties and grill. Top with bleu cheese. Serve on a toasted roll with lettuce and tomato.

Chicken with Figs and Artichoke Hearts

1 1/2 cups dry white wine
3 tablespoons tomato paste
3 tablespoons minced garlic
3 tablespoons brown sugar
1 1/2 teaspoons oregano
1 1/2 teaspoons kosher salt
1 1/2 teaspoons poultry seasoning
1 1/2 teaspoons chicken base
1 1/2 cups drained marinated artichoke hearts
1 cup pitted dried plums
1 cup dried figs, cut into halves
3 tablespoons drained rinsed capers
2 pounds boneless skinless chicken breasts
2 tablespoons sour cream

Combine the wine, tomato paste, garlic, brown sugar, oregano, salt, poultry seasoning and chicken base in a bowl and mix well. Stir in the artichoke hearts, dried plums, figs and capers. Arrange the chicken in a single layer in a baking dish. Spoon the wine mixture over the chicken, turning to coat.

Marinate, covered, in the refrigerator for 2 to 10 hours, turning occasionally. Bake at 350 degrees for 1 hour. Remove the chicken with a slotted spoon to a serving platter. Stir the sour cream into the sauce and pour over the chicken. Serve immediately.

Serves 4 to 6

Mango Chili Chicken

1/3 cup mango chutney
2 teaspoons hot chili garlic sauce
1 1/2 teaspoons black bean sauce
2 teaspoons vegetable oil
1 small dried hot chile pepper (optional)
1 pound boneless skinless chicken breasts, cut into 3/4- to 1-inch pieces
1 teaspoon minced fresh gingerroot
1 teaspoon minced garlic
1 red bell pepper, cut into 1- to 2-inch strips
5 fresh asparagus spears, cut into 1-inch pieces (optional)
1 mango, peeled and julienned
2 cups hot cooked rice

Combine the chutney, garlic sauce and bean sauce in a bowl and mix well. Heat the oil in a large wok or large nonstick skillet over medium-high heat. Add the chile pepper. Stir-fry for 10 seconds; be sure the area is well ventilated. Add the chicken, gingerroot and garlic.

Stir-fry for 3 to 4 minutes or until the chicken is cooked through. Push the chicken to the side of the wok. Add the bell pepper and asparagus. Stir-fry for 1 minute. Stir in the chutney mixture. Stir-fry just until heated through. Top with the mango and serve with the rice.

You may substitute 1 cup sugar snap peas for the fresh asparagus.

Serves 4

Lemon Chicken with Rosemary Orzo

2 medium zucchini
3 plum tomatoes
1 tablespoon olive oil
1 pound boneless skinless chicken breasts,
    cut into 1-inch strips
1 teaspoon paprika
1¹/3 cups orzo
1 large shallot, minced
2 or 3 garlic cloves, chopped
1 (14-ounce) can chicken broth
1 medium green bell pepper, chopped
²/3 cup dry white wine
2 tablespoons lemon juice
2 tablespoons capers
1¹/2 tablespoons chopped fresh rosemary, or
    1¹/2 teaspoons dried rosemary
¹/2 teaspoon salt
Paprika to taste

Cut the zucchini lengthwise into quarters; cut each
quarter crosswise into slices. Cut the tomatoes
into quarters and slice. Heat the olive oil in a large
skillet over medium-high heat. Add the chicken
and 1 teaspoon paprika and mix well.

Stir-fry for 3 to 4 minutes or until the chicken is
brown. Stir in the orzo, shallot and garlic. Stir-fry
for 1 minute or until light brown. Stir in the broth
and cover. Bring to a boil; reduce the heat.

Simmer for 5 to 8 minutes or until the orzo is al
dente and most of the liquid has been absorbed.
Fold in the zucchini, tomatoes, bell pepper and
wine. Simmer, covered, for 5 minutes or until the
vegetables are tender-crisp and the pasta is tender;
do not overcook the vegetables. Stir in the lemon
juice, capers, rosemary and salt and sprinkle with
paprika to taste just before serving.

Serves 4

Cinnamon-Cured Smoked Chicken with Cherry Barbecue Sauce

Cherry Barbecue Sauce

1 cup canned reduced-sodium chicken broth
1/3 cup cherry preserves
1/3 cup fresh orange juice
1/4 cup fresh lemon juice
1/2 teaspoon grated lemon zest
1/2 teaspoon grated orange zest
1/2 teaspoon cinnamon
1/2 teaspoon ground cloves
1/2 cup ruby port
2 teaspoons cornstarch
1/4 cup orange marmalade
1 tablespoon chili sauce
1/8 teaspoon red pepper flakes
Salt and black pepper to taste

Chicken

4 cups water
1/4 cup coarse salt
1/4 cup packed dark brown sugar
4 boneless skinless chicken breasts
    (about 1 1/2 pounds)
1 small onion, thinly sliced
2 thin lemon slices
2 thin orange slices
1/2 teaspoon cinnamon
2 cups cherry or apple wood chips

For the sauce, combine the broth, preserves, orange juice, lemon juice, lemon zest, orange zest, cinnamon and cloves in a medium heavy saucepan and mix well. Bring to a boil over medium-high heat. Boil for 8 minutes or until the mixture is reduced to 1 1/2 cups, stirring occasionally.

Whisk the port and cornstarch in a small bowl until blended. Whisk the port mixture, marmalade and chili sauce into the broth mixture. Bring to a simmer over medium heat, whisking constantly. Simmer for 5 minutes or until the flavors blend and the sauce is slightly thickened, whisking frequently. Season with the red pepper flakes, salt and black pepper. Serve warm or at room temperature. You may prepare up to 1 day in advance and store, covered, in the refrigerator. Reheat over low heat or bring to room temperature before serving.

For the chicken, whisk the water, salt and brown sugar in a large bowl until the brown sugar dissolves. Add the chicken, onion, lemon slices, orange slices and cinnamon. Marinate, covered with plastic wrap, in the refrigerator for 1 to 3 hours; do not marinate longer than 3 hours.

Combine the wood chips with enough water to cover in a bowl. Let stand for 1 hour; drain. Preheat the grill on medium heat. Place the wood chips in a 6×8-inch foil packet; do not seal top. Place the packet on the coals 5 minutes before the grilling process begins and cover the grill. Drain the chicken, discarding the marinade. Grill the chicken for 8 minutes per side or until cooked through. Remove the chicken to a serving platter. Serve with the sauce.

Serves 4

Crispy Pan-Fried Chicken with Summer Sauce

Panko are special Japanese bread crumbs that are shaped with tiny points that stick out in all directions. They provide more crispness and taste lighter and less dense than regular bread crumbs. Find them in the Asian food section of most large grocery stores or try your local Asian market.

Summer Sauce

2 cups fresh cilantro leaves

3 garlic cloves, minced

1 jalapeño chile, seeded and finely chopped

2 tablespoons white vinegar

2 tablespoons water

1 cup mayonnaise

Chicken

4 (6-ounce) boneless skinless chicken breasts

1/2 cup flour

1/4 teaspoon salt

1/4 teaspoon freshly ground pepper

2 eggs, lightly beaten

3/4 cup panko or crushed tortilla chips

2 tablespoons vegetable oil

For the sauce, process the cilantro, garlic, jalapeño chile, vinegar and water in a blender or food processor until puréed. Pour the cilantro mixture into a bowl and whisk in the mayonnaise. Chill, covered, in the refrigerator.

For the chicken, pound the chicken 1/2 inch thick between sheets of heavy-duty plastic wrap with a meat mallet. Mix the flour, salt and pepper in a shallow dish. Coat the chicken lightly with the flour mixture; shake off the excess. Dip in the eggs and coat with the panko.

Heat the oil in a large nonstick skillet until simmering. Add the chicken. Cook over medium-high heat for 5 minutes per side or until cooked through and golden brown. Serve immediately with the sauce.

Serves 4

Colorful Marinade for Chicken

Combine 1/2 finely chopped green bell pepper, 1/2 finely chopped red bell pepper, 1/2 finely chopped yellow bell pepper, 1 finely chopped jalapeño chile, 3 crushed garlic cloves, 1/2 thinly sliced small onion, 1 teaspoon salt, 1 teaspoon grated lemon zest and 1 cup vegetable oil in a small bowl and mix well. Refrigerate, covered with foil, for 8 to 10 hours.

Green Olive Enchiladas

3 tablespoons olive oil
1 cup finely chopped onion
3 tablespoons chopped garlic
1¹/2 teaspoons oregano
1 teaspoon cumin
¹/4 teaspoon cinnamon
5 tablespoons medium-hot Mexican-style
  chili powder
3 tablespoons flour
4¹/2 cups canned reduced-sodium chicken
  broth
¹/2 ounce semisweet chocolate, chopped
Salt and pepper to taste
3 cups shredded cooked skinless chicken
8 (8-inch) flour tortillas
1 pound Monterey Jack cheese, coarsely
  shredded
1 cup drained pimento-stuffed green olives,
  sliced
1 cup finely chopped onion

Heat the olive oil in a large saucepan over medium-low heat. Add 1 cup onion, garlic, oregano, cumin and cinnamon and mix well. Cook, covered, for 10 minutes or until the onion is almost tender, stirring occasionally. Stir in the chili powder and flour. Cook for 3 minutes, stirring constantly. Whisk in the broth gradually.

Bring to a boil over medium-high heat. Boil for 35 minutes or until the mixture is reduced to 3 cups and of a sauce consistency, stirring occasionally. Remove from the heat. Whisk in the chocolate. Season with salt and pepper. Let stand until cool.

Spread ¹/3 cup of the sauce in a 9×13-inch baking dish. Combine the chicken with 1 cup of the sauce in a bowl and mix well. Arrange the tortillas on a work surface. Spoon 3 tablespoons of the cheese, 1 tablespoon of the olives, 1 tablespoon of the chopped onion and ¹/4 cup of the chicken mixture on the center of each tortilla. Roll to enclose the filling. Arrange the enchiladas seam side down in the prepared dish. You may prepare up to this point 1 day in advance and store, covered, in the refrigerator.

Spoon the remaining sauce over the enchiladas. Sprinkle with the remaining cheese. Bake, covered with foil, at 375 degrees for 20 minutes or for 30 minutes if chilled; remove the foil. Bake for 10 minutes longer or until bubbly. Let stand for 10 minutes before serving. If time is of the essence, purchase a supermarket rotisserie chicken and shred. You may adjust the spiciness of this dish by using hot Mexican-style chili powder or mild Mexican-style chili powder or a combination of the two. You may substitute a combination of Monterey Jack cheese and Cheddar cheese for the Monterey Jack cheese if desired.

Serves 8

Shredded Chicken

Chicken is best shredded by hand into bite-size pieces. Hand-shredding helps the sauce to coat and cling to the chicken because of the irregular surfaces it makes.

Ginger Chicken and Vegetable Stir-Fry

1/4 cup water

1 1/2 teaspoons cornstarch

1 pound boneless skinless chicken breasts,
    cut into 1/4-inch pieces

3 tablespoons vegetable oil

2 cups snow peas, trimmed

2 zucchini, cut lengthwise into halves and
    cut into 1/4-inch slices

1/2 red bell pepper, julienned

1 cup mushrooms, sliced

2 tablespoons minced fresh gingerroot

1 tablespoon minced garlic

1 teaspoon chili paste (optional)

3 tablespoons oyster sauce

1/4 cup chicken stock

2 tomatoes, cut into thin wedges

2 tablespoons sake or sherry

Hot cooked rice

Whisk the water and cornstarch in a bowl until blended. Add the chicken and toss to coat. Set aside.

Heat 1 1/2 tablespoons of the oil in a wok over high heat. Stir-fry the snow peas, zucchini and bell pepper in the hot oil until tender-crisp. Add the mushrooms. Stir-fry for 1 minute. Remove the vegetables with a slotted spoon to a bowl, reserving the pan drippings.

Heat the remaining 1 1/2 tablespoons oil with the reserved pan drippings. Stir-fry the gingerroot, garlic and chili paste in the hot oil for 20 seconds. Remove the chicken from the cornstarch mixture with a slotted spoon and add to the gingerroot mixture. Stir in the oyster sauce. Stir-fry until the chicken is cooked through. Stir in the stock.

Stir-fry until thickened. Add the snow pea mixture and the tomatoes to the chicken mixture. Stir-fry for 1 to 2 minutes or until heated through. Pour in the sake. Remove from the heat. Serve with hot cooked rice.

Serves 4

Make-Ahead Veggies

Slice vegetables in advance for a stir-fry. You can keep them fresh and crisp two to three days by wrapping each prepped vegetable separately in white paper towels, then refrigerating in sealable plastic bags.

Sticky Glazed Coconut Chicken and Coconut Basil Rice

Chicken

3/4 cup coconut milk, stirred

2 stalks lemon grass, tough outer leaves removed

1 tablespoon minced fresh gingerroot

1 tablespoon minced garlic

1 tablespoon sweet Asian chili sauce, or
   1 teaspoon hot chile flakes and
   2 teaspoons brown sugar

6 to 8 boneless skinless chicken breasts and
   thighs, cut into 1½-inch strips

30 bamboo skewers, soaked in water

Glaze

1½ cups rice vinegar

1 cup sugar

6 tablespoons soy sauce

2 tablespoons sweet Asian chili sauce, or
   2 teaspoons hot chile flakes and
   ¼ cup packed brown sugar

Coconut Basil Rice

1 cup jasmine rice

1½ cups water

½ cup coconut milk, stirred

6 fresh basil leaves, julienned

1 teaspoon sweet Asian chili sauce

1 teaspoon salt

1 teaspoon butter or vegetable oil

¼ cup crushed salted peanuts

For the chicken, process the coconut milk, lemon grass, gingerroot, garlic and chili sauce in a food processor until blended. Pour over the chicken in a shallow dish, turning to coat. Marinate, covered, in the refrigerator for 2 to 10 hours; drain. Thread the chicken on the bamboo skewers.

For the glaze, combine the vinegar, sugar, soy sauce and chili sauce in a nonreactive saucepan and mix well. Simmer until the mixture is reduced by ½, stirring frequently. Cover to keep warm. You may prepare up to 1 week in advance and store, covered in an airtight container, in the refrigerator. Reheat before serving.

For the rice, rinse the rice until the water runs clear. Combine the rice, 1½ cups water, coconut milk, basil, chili sauce, salt and butter in a heavy saucepan. Bring to a boil; reduce the heat to low. Cook, covered, for 20 minutes. Remove from the heat. Let stand for 5 minutes; fluff with a fork.

To serve, grill the chicken skewers over hot coals for 15 to 20 minutes or until the chicken is cooked through, turning frequently. Arrange the skewers on a serving platter. Drizzle with the warm glaze and sprinkle with the peanuts. Serve with the rice.

Serves 4 to 6

Sautéed Chicken Paprika

4 1/2 teaspoons sweet Hungarian paprika
1/2 teaspoon hot Hungarian paprika
4 to 6 boneless skinless chicken breasts
Salt and pepper to taste
1 1/4 cups (2 1/2 sticks) butter
1 large onion, thinly sliced
1/2 teaspoon sugar
1 cup dry white wine
1 cup whipping cream

Combine the sweet paprika and hot paprika in a bowl and mix well. Sprinkle 1/2 of the paprika mixture over the chicken. Season with salt and pepper.

Heat 2 tablespoons of the butter in a nonstick skillet over medium-high heat. Sauté the chicken in the melted butter for 4 minutes per side or until cooked through. Remove the chicken to a platter with a slotted spoon, reserving the pan drippings.

Reduce the heat to medium. Add the remaining butter and the onion to the reserved pan drippings. Sprinkle with the sugar. Cook, covered, for 5 minutes, stirring occasionally. Whisk in the remaining paprika mixture, the wine and whipping cream. Simmer until slightly thickened, stirring frequently. Return the chicken and any collected juices to the skillet. Simmer just until heated through, stirring frequently. Season with salt and pepper. Serve immediately with hot cooked noodles or potato pancakes.

Serves 4 to 6

Brown Sugar–Rubbed Turkey Breast

1 (3-pound) turkey breast
2 tablespoons brown sugar
1 teaspoon parsley flakes
1 teaspoon sweet paprika
1/2 teaspoon dry mustard
1/2 teaspoon garlic powder
1/2 teaspoon onion powder
1/2 teaspoon salt
1/4 teaspoon cinnamon
1/4 teaspoon pepper
1/4 teaspoon ginger

Pat the turkey with paper towels to dry. Mix the brown sugar, parsley flakes, paprika, dry mustard, garlic powder, onion powder, salt, cinnamon, pepper and ginger in a bowl. Pat the brown sugar mixture evenly over the turkey.

Arrange the turkey on a rack in a baking pan. Roast at 350 degrees for 1 hour or until a meat thermometer registers 170 degrees. Let rest before slicing.

Serves 4 to 6

Roasted Turkey Breast with Sage Corn Bread Crust

1 (2-pound) boneless skinless turkey breast
2 teaspoons salt
1/2 teaspoon pepper
1 tablespoon olive oil
1 tablespoon unsalted butter
2 garlic cloves, minced
1 cup crumbled sweet corn bread
1 teaspoon finely chopped fresh sage
Salt and pepper to taste
2 tablespoons Dijon mustard

Pat the turkey dry with paper towels. Sprinkle with 2 teaspoons salt and 1/2 teaspoon pepper. Heat the olive oil in a 10-inch nonstick skillet over high heat until hot but not smoking. Brown the turkey on all sides in the hot olive oil for 4 minutes, turning frequently. Remove the turkey to an oiled shallow baking pan, reserving the pan drippings.

Heat the unsalted butter with the reserved pan drippings. Stir in the garlic. Cook over medium heat for 30 seconds or until fragrant, stirring constantly. Remove from the heat. Stir in the corn bread and sage. Season with salt and pepper to taste.

Spread the Dijon mustard over the surface of the turkey. Pat 1/2 of the corn bread mixture over the mustard. Sprinkle with the remaining corn bread mixture. Place the baking pan on the middle oven rack.

Roast at 425 degrees for 10 minutes. Reduce the oven temperature to 375 degrees. Roast for 45 minutes longer or until a meat thermometer registers 170 degrees.

Serves 4

Cranberry Salsa Sorbet

Combine 1 (10-ounce) can whole cranberry sauce, 1 minced jalapeño chile and the juice of 1 lime in a food processor and process just until chunky. Stir in 1/4 cup chopped fresh cilantro. Spoon into a freezer container and freeze until firm. Serve with fish, chicken or pork.

Seared Duck Breasts with Two Sauces

Serve with one or both of the sauces.

Basil-Scented Kumquat Sauce

    1 pound kumquats, cut into halves (3 cups)
    4 cups water
    3 tablespoons honey
    3 tablespoons dark soy sauce
    6 fresh basil leaves
    1 (1/2-inch) piece fresh gingerroot
    1/4 cup mirin

Raspberry Port Sauce

    1 tablespoon unsalted butter
    1 shallot, minced
    1/4 cup dry white wine
    1/4 cup ruby port
    2 tablespoons seedless raspberry preserves
    1 tablespoon Dijon mustard
    1 tablespoon raspberry vinegar
    1/2 cup fresh raspberries
    1 tablespoon unsalted butter
    Salt and pepper to taste

Duck

    4 boneless duck breasts with skin
    Salt and freshly cracked pepper to taste

For the kumquat sauce, combine the kumquats, water, honey, soy sauce, basil and gingerroot in a saucepan and mix well. Bring to a boil; reduce the heat. Simmer at a low boil for 20 minutes, stirring occasionally. Strain, discarding the solids. Return the strained mixture to the saucepan. Simmer until reduced to 1 cup, stirring occasionally.

Heat the mirin in a saucepan over medium heat until reduced to 2 tablespoons; it will reduce to a syrup. Stir 1 tablespoon of the syrup into the sauce, adding more if desired. Cover to keep warm. The sauce is best if prepared 1 day in advance and stored, covered, in the refrigerator. Reheat before serving.

For the port sauce, heat 1 tablespoon unsalted butter in a medium saucepan. Add the shallot. Cook over medium heat for 2 minutes or until tender, stirring frequently. Stir in the white wine and port. Cook over medium heat for 7 minutes or until the mixture is reduced to 2 tablespoons, stirring frequently. Whisk in the preserves, Dijon mustard and vinegar. Stir in the raspberries. Cook until heated through, whisking gently to break up the raspberries. Whisk in 1 tablespoon unsalted butter. Season with salt and pepper. Cover to keep warm.

For the duck, pat the duck dry with paper towels. Make three 4-inch-long slits in each duck breast. Sprinkle all sides with salt and pepper. Heat an ovenproof skillet over medium heat. Add the duck skin side down. Sear for 3 minutes per side or until crisp and golden brown.

Bake at 400 degrees for 3 minutes for rare or 5 minutes for medium. Remove the duck to a cutting board. Let rest for 10 minutes. Slice as desired and serve with one or both of the sauces

Wine recommendation, David Bruce Central Coast Pinot Noir from California.

Serves 4

CONTENTS

152   Beef en Croûte with Cilantro Walnut Filling
154   Beef Tenderloin with Thai Green Curry Sauce
155   Mediterranean Pot Roast
156   Wine-Braised Brisket
157   Grilled Tri-Tip Roast with Cherry Tomato Relish
158   Spicy Rib-Eyes with Dueling Salsas
160   Steak Chimichurri
160   Cold Sliced Beef Sirloin with Herb Sauce
161   Lemon Grass Beef with Rice Paper
162   Spicy Thai Beef Strips
163   Southwest-Style Salisbury Steaks with Lime-Pickled Onions
164   Grilled Lamb with Roasted Olives and Onions
166   Piquant Spicy Leg of Lamb
166   Souvlaki Marinade
167   Celebrity Ribs
167   Slow-Baked Spareribs with Mango Chutney Marinade
168   Sugar-Spiced Pork Chops with Chipotle Sauce
170   Romano Sage Pork Chops
171   Pork with Dried Plums
171   Curried Pork Tenderloin
172   Chipotle Burgers with a Kick
173   Buffalo Chili

MEATS

Beef en Croûte with Cilantro Walnut Filling

Cilantro Walnut Filling

2 cups walnut halves

2³/4 bunches spinach, stems removed

3 cups fresh cilantro sprigs, stems removed

2 cups fresh flat-leaf parsley

1 cup bread crumbs

¹/2 cup honey

2 egg whites

4 garlic cloves, minced

1¹/2 teaspoons salt

1 teaspoon ground coriander seeds

1 teaspoon cumin

¹/4 teaspoon pepper

Sour Cream Pastry

1¹/4 cups (2¹/2 sticks) butter, sliced and chilled

1 teaspoon salt

1³/4 cups chilled sour cream

3¹/2 cups flour

4 to 6 tablespoons ice water (optional)

For the filling, spread the walnuts in a single layer on a baking sheet. Toast at 350 degrees for 10 to 15 minutes or until light brown. Let stand until cool. Blanch the spinach in boiling water in a saucepan for 20 seconds. Remove the spinach to a bowl of ice water with a slotted spoon to stop the cooking process. Return the water to a boil. Blanch the cilantro and parsley in the boiling water for 5 seconds. Remove the cilantro and parsley to the bowl of ice water using a slotted spoon. Drain the spinach, cilantro and parsley in a colander; press to remove any excess moisture.

Pulse the walnuts in a food processor until finely ground. Add the spinach, cilantro, parsley, bread crumbs, honey, egg whites, garlic, salt, coriander, cumin and pepper. Pulse until smooth. You may prepare up to 1 day in advance and store, covered, in the refrigerator.

For the pastry, combine the butter and salt in a food processor. Pulse until the mixture is crumbly. Add the sour cream. Pulse until mixed. Add the flour; pulse until mixed. Test the mixture by gently squeezing a small handful; when it is mixed correctly, the mixture should adhere without crumbling. If not, slowly pulse again and retest. Add small amounts of the ice water if needed. Do not overprocess the pastry or add too much water.

Divide the pastry into 4 equal portions and place on a lightly floured hard surface. Knead each portion once with the heel of your hand. Shape the portions together into a disc. Chill, covered with plastic wrap, for 1 hour or until firm. You may prepare up to 1 day in advance and store, covered, in the refrigerator.

Beef Tenderloin

    1 (4¹/2-pound) beef tenderloin, trimmed
    Salt and pepper to taste
    1 tablespoon vegetable oil
    1 egg
    1 tablespoon water

For the beef, pat the beef dry with paper towels. Cut the beef into halves and season with salt and pepper. Heat the oil in a skillet. Brown the beef on all sides 1 portion at a time in the hot oil for 2 minutes. Remove to a platter.

For the assembly, roll the pastry into a 15×19-inch rectangle a little less than ¹/4 inch thick on a lightly floured surface. Cut a 1-inch strip of the pastry from the shorter end, creating a 15×18-inch rectangle, and reserve. Spread ¹/3 of the filling lengthwise down the middle of the rectangle, forming a 2×16-inch strip. Arrange the beef end to end over the filling. Spread the beef with the remaining filling. Fold the pastry over the beef to completely enclose and seal the edges. Arrange seam side down on a baking sheet.

Brush the pastry with a mixture of the egg and water. Cut out holly leaves or the desired decorations from the reserved 1-inch pastry strip. Brush the bottoms of the decorations with the egg wash and adhere to the top; brush the tops with the egg wash. Make small slits in the top at 3-inch intervals with a sharp knife. Chill, loosely covered, for 1 to 6 hours.

Bring the beef to room temperature. Bake at 350 degrees for 55 to 60 minutes or until the pastry is golden brown and a meat thermometer registers 140 to 145 degrees for medium-rare. Let rest for 25 minutes; the beef will continue to cook. Increase the baking time 5 to 10 minutes for medium.

Wine recommendation, California Merlot. Try a Merlot from Windy Ridge, Blackstone or Beringer Napa Valley.

Serves 8

Creative Dining

Meals don't always have to be served in the dining room. Try a picnic in front of a fire in your family room on a cold winter evening. For a casual approach to a meal, a coffee table and floor pillows could be your answer. And don't forget your porch or patio, which offers a refreshing change of pace from the formal dining room. Your porch can be used for a fancy sunlit luncheon or for an elegant dinner at sunset.

Beef Tenderloin with Thai Green Curry Sauce

Thai Green Curry Sauce

1/2 cup chicken broth
2 tablespoons fish sauce
2 whole cloves
8 whole black peppercorns
1 teaspoon coriander seeds
1/2 teaspoon caraway seeds
1/2 teaspoon cumin seeds
3 garlic cloves
1 small shallot
4 whole serrano chiles, stems removed
1/2 cup fresh basil leaves
1/3 cup fresh cilantro sprigs
1/4 cup fresh mint leaves
2 tablespoons vegetable oil

Beef

1 cup hoisin sauce
3/4 cup plum sauce
1/4 cup dry sherry
1/4 cup white wine vinegar
3 tablespoons honey
2 tablespoons sesame oil
2 tablespoons dark soy sauce
1 tablespoon Asian chili sauce
1 tablespoon grated orange zest
8 garlic cloves, finely chopped
1 (3-pound) beef tenderloin, trimmed
Vegetable oil

For the sauce, combine the broth and fish sauce in a small bowl and mix well. Chill, covered, in the refrigerator. Combine the cloves, peppercorns, coriander seeds, caraway seeds and cumin seeds in a small sauté pan. Toast over high heat for 1 minute or just until the spices begin to smoke, stirring frequently. Immediately grind the spice mixture in a spice grinder to a powdery consistency.

Process the garlic, shallot and serrano chiles in a food processor until finely minced. Add the ground spice mixture, basil, cilantro and mint. Process until finely minced. Add the oil gradually, processing constantly until a paste forms. Chill, covered, for up to 8 hours.

For the beef, combine the hoisin sauce, plum sauce, sherry, vinegar, honey, sesame oil, soy sauce, chili sauce, orange zest and garlic in a shallow nonreactive dish large enough to hold the beef and mix well. Add the beef and turn to coat. Marinate, covered, in the refrigerator for 30 minutes or for up to 8 hours, turning occasionally.

Bring the beef to room temperature. Drain, reserving the marinade. Brush the grill rack with oil. Arrange the beef on the prepared rack. Grill with the lid closed for 20 minutes or until a meat thermometer registers 140 degrees, turning and brushing with the reserved marinade occasionally. Let rest for 5 minutes.

To serve, heat the chilled paste in a 10-inch sauté pan over medium heat for 30 seconds, stirring constantly. Stir the chilled broth mixture and add to the paste. Bring to a boil, stirring constantly. Remove from the heat. Cut the beef into 6 equal steaks. Drizzle some of the sauce over each steak. Serve immediately with the remaining sauce.

If a grill is not available, place the beef on a rack in a baking pan. Roast at 500 degrees for about 20 minutes or to the desired degree of doneness.

Serves 6

Mediterranean Pot Roast

Don't forget that once a roast is removed from the oven the internal temperature will continue to rise for about 20 minutes.

1 (4- to 5-pound) pot roast or other cut of
    beef from the chuck
1 teaspoon cracked pepper
2 tablespoons olive oil
1 medium onion, thinly sliced
1 cup canned tomato sauce
1/4 cup oil-pack sun-dried tomatoes, chopped
1 bay leaf
1 1/2 teaspoons thyme
2 cups beef stock
1/2 cup red wine
1/2 cup balsamic vinegar
1/4 cup kalamata olives, coarsely chopped

Sprinkle both sides of the roast with the pepper. Heat the olive oil in a Dutch oven or roasting pan over medium heat. Brown the roast on all sides in the hot olive oil for 5 to 7 minutes. Remove to a platter, reserving the pan drippings.

Add the onion, tomato sauce, sun-dried tomatoes, bay leaf and thyme to the reserved pan drippings and mix well. Cook until bubbly, stirring frequently. Return the roast to the Dutch oven and spoon some of the onion mixture over the top. Add the stock, wine and balsamic vinegar and mix well. Bring to a simmer.

Braise, covered with foil, at 300 degrees for 2 to 2 1/2 hours or until the roast is fork-tender. Remove the roast to a serving platter. Skim the fat from the sauce. Discard the bay leaf. Adjust the consistency by adding a small amount of water if needed. Slice the beef and drizzle with the sauce. Sprinkle with the olives.

The flavor is enhanced if the roast is chilled overnight to allow the flavors to meld.

Serves 4 to 6

Meat Tips

Nothing brings out the flavor of meat better than a generous sprinkling of kosher salt and freshly ground pepper.

Use the right method of cooking for a particular cut of meat. Cook tender cuts with dry heat; cook tougher cuts of meat with moist heat.

Wine-Braised Brisket

4 garlic cloves, minced
3 tablespoons vegetable oil
1 (4- to 6-pound) beef brisket (do not remove
    layer of fat from trimmed brisket)
2 or 3 large onions, coarsely chopped
1 bottle hearty red wine
2 cups water
1 teaspoon salt
1 teaspoon freshly ground pepper
White potatoes, peeled, quartered (optional)

Brown the garlic in the oil in a large roasting pan.
Add the brisket fat side down to the roasting pan.
Sear for 3 to 5 minutes; turn. Sear for 3 to 5 minutes
or until brown. Arrange the onions over and around
the brisket. Add the wine, water, salt and pepper.

Bake, covered, at 400 degrees for 30 minutes.
Reduce the oven temperature to 325 degrees. Bake
for 3 to 4 hours longer, basting occasionally with
the pan juices and adding additional water if
needed. Remove cover, increase oven temperature
to 400 degrees and bake until the juices are
reduced. Remove the brisket to a cutting board.
Cut across the grain into 1/4- to 1/2-inch slices.
Spoon the onions and some of the gravy over the
slices. Serve the remaining gravy with the brisket.

Add peeled and quartered white potatoes after
1 hour of baking if desired. Be aware that the
potatoes will absorb the gravy, but the juices are
rich enough to be diluted with added water.

The flavor is best when the brisket is allowed to
rest in the refrigerator for 2 to 3 hours before
reheating and serving. Preparing 1 to 2 days in
advance assures a full-bodied dish that guarantees
raves.

Serve with a California Cabernet Sauvignon.
Foppiano or Rodney Strong, both from Sonoma,
California, would work well.

Serves 4 to 6

Heavenly Horseradish Cream Sauce

Whip 3/4 cup whipping cream in a mixing bowl until
soft peaks form. Mix 1/2 cup mayonnaise, 1/2 cup prepared
horseradish and 2 tablespoons Dijon mustard in a small bowl.
Fold into the whipped cream. Add sugar, salt and freshly ground
pepper to taste and mix gently. Serve with beef tenderloin.

Grilled Tri-Tip Roast with Cherry Tomato Relish

Cherry Tomato Relish

1/4 cup balsamic vinegar

4 teaspoons chopped fresh oregano

1/2 cup olive oil

1/4 cup drained canned diced mild
   green chiles

5 green onions, finely chopped

4 cups cherry tomato halves

Salt and pepper to taste

Beef

6 tablespoons fresh lime juice

1/4 cup olive oil or canola oil

1/4 cup gold tequila

3 tablespoons chopped fresh cilantro

1 tablespoon finely minced garlic

2 teaspoons oregano

2 teaspoons cumin

1 1/2 teaspoons grated lime zest

2 (2-pound) beef tri-tip roasts
   (bottom sirloin)

1 teaspoon cracked pepper

1 teaspoon sea salt

For the relish, whisk the balsamic vinegar and oregano in a medium bowl. Whisk in the olive oil gradually. Stir in the green chiles and green onions. You may prepare to this point up to 6 hours in advance and store, covered, in the refrigerator. Add the tomatoes just before serving and toss to coat. Season with salt and pepper.

For the beef, combine the lime juice, olive oil, tequila, cilantro, garlic, oregano, cumin and lime zest in a bowl and mix well. Rub the beef with the pepper and salt and pierce the surface with a fork. Place the beef in a large sealable plastic bag. Pour the lime juice mixture over the beef and seal tightly. Turn to coat.

Marinate in the refrigerator for 2 to 10 hours, turning occasionally. Let stand at room temperature for 1 hour. Drain, discarding the marinade. Grill the beef over hot coals for 10 minutes per side for medium-rare. Remove the beef to a cutting board. Let rest for 10 minutes. Slice diagonally across the grain. Serve with the relish.

For variety, use as a filling for fajitas. Serve with warm flour tortillas, sautéed bell peppers and sweet onions, guacamole, sour cream and Cherry Tomato Relish. Or simply serve with a mélange of fresh sautéed vegetables and rice. Serve the leftovers as a topping for a cold beef salad or on sandwiches.

Serves 4 to 6

Spicy Rib-Eyes with Dueling Salsas

Dueling Salsas

1 ripe avocado, chopped
3 tablespoons chopped fresh cilantro
1 large shallot, finely chopped
1 large garlic clove, minced
1 tablespoon green pepper sauce
1¹/2 teaspoons fresh lime juice
1 teaspoon coarsely ground black pepper
1 teaspoon cumin
1 teaspoon coriander
¹/2 teaspoon red chile pepper
1 cup chopped tomato
1 cup chopped seeded peeled cucumber

Rib-Eyes

4 rib-eye steaks, ³/4 to 1 inch thick
8 teaspoons olive oil
¹/4 cup cumin
Salt and coarsely ground pepper to taste

For the salsas, rinse the avocado with cold water and drain. Combine the avocado, cilantro, shallot, garlic, green pepper sauce, lime juice, black pepper, cumin, coriander and red chile pepper in a bowl and mix gently. Spoon ¹/2 of the avocado mixture into another bowl. Add the tomato to 1 bowl and mix gently. Add the cucumber to the remaining bowl and mix gently. Chill, covered, for up to 4 hours.

For the steaks, rub each steak with 2 teaspoons of the olive oil. Sprinkle both sides with the cumin and rub to adhere. Sprinkle with salt and pepper. Grill the steaks over hot coals to the desired degree of doneness. Remove the steaks to dinner plates. Serve with the salsas.

Wine recommendation, Faustino Rioja VII, a Spanish red wine.

Serves 4

Every affair doesn't need to be an extravaganza. There are many styles of entertaining, including sit-down dinners, buffets, and kitchen parties. Try a wine tasting party instead of the more traditional cocktail and hors d'oeuvre, have an old-fashioned Sunday dinner instead of the traditional Saturday night meal, or invite friends for an informal patio brunch.

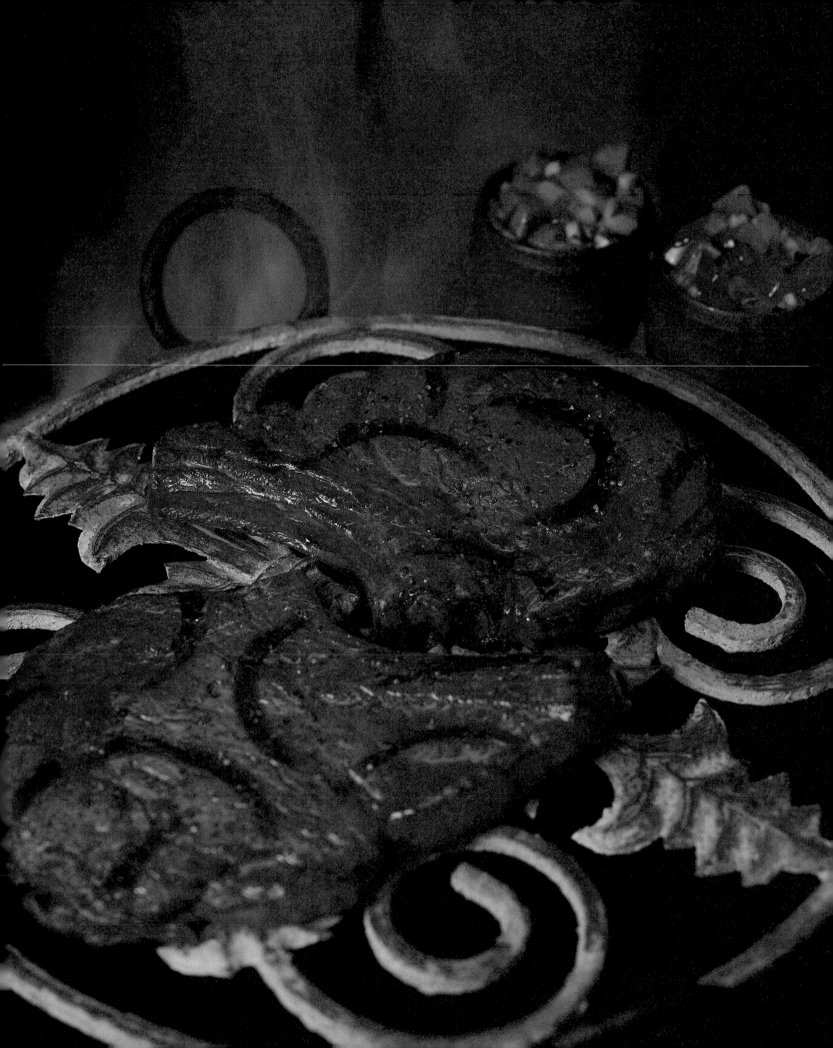

Steak Chimichurri

Chimichurri is a popular Argentine condiment, which is a thick herb sauce packed with flavor. This condiment is a pungent cross between a vinaigrette and pesto and is served over steak.

Chimichurri
    5 fresh jalapeño chiles, seeded and chopped
    1 medium plum tomato
    1/2 onion, chopped
    1/4 cup balsamic vinegar
    1/4 cup fresh parsley leaves
    1 teaspoon sugar
    1/8 teaspoon salt

Steaks
    4 boneless rib-eye steaks, 3/4 to 1 inch thick
    1/2 teaspoon coarsely ground pepper

For the chimichurri, combine the jalapeño chiles, tomato, onion, balsamic vinegar, parsley, sugar and salt in a food processor or blender. Pulse to a chunky consistency.

For the steaks, sprinkle the steaks with pepper. Grill the steaks over hot coals to the desired degree of doneness, turning once. Serve with the sauce.

Serves 4

Cold Sliced Beef Sirloin with Herb Sauce

Herb Sauce
    1 cup olive oil
    1/2 cup pine nuts
    1/4 cup coarsely chopped fresh basil
    1/4 cup coarsely chopped fresh parsley
    1/4 cup coarsely chopped fresh mint
    1/4 cup fresh lemon juice
    4 garlic cloves
    4 teaspoons Dijon mustard

Beef
    1 (3-pound) beef sirloin steak
    1/2 teaspoon salt
    1/2 teaspoon pepper

For the sauce, combine the olive oil, pine nuts, basil, parsley, mint, lemon juice, garlic and Dijon mustard in a food processor or blender. Pulse to the consistency of a coarse purée. Let stand at room temperature. You may prepare 1 day in advance and store, covered, in the refrigerator. Bring to room temperature before serving.

For the beef, sprinkle the steak with the salt and pepper. Grill the steak over medium-high heat to the desired degree of doneness. Let stand until cool and slice. Arrange the slices on a serving platter. Drizzle with the sauce or serve on the side. You may prepare up to 1 day in advance and store, covered, in the refrigerator. Let stand at room temperature for 30 minutes before slicing.

Serves 8

Lemon Grass Beef with Rice Paper

Vietnamese Dipping Sauce

2 small garlic cloves

1 teaspoon ground chili paste

1 fresh Thai Bird chile, chopped (optional)

2/3 cup hot water

1/4 cup fish sauce

1/4 cup sugar

2 tablespoons fresh lime juice with pulp

2 tablespoons shredded carrot

Beef

1 1/2 pounds top sirloin

3 tablespoons minced lemon grass

2 tablespoons vegetable oil

2 teaspoons minced garlic

1 teaspoon fish sauce

1 teaspoon sugar

1 teaspoon soy sauce

Table Salad and Assembly

1/3 pound rice noodles

1 head red leaf lettuce, leaves separated

1 cucumber, seeded and julienned

3 cups bean sprouts

10 sprigs of fresh mint

10 sprigs of fresh basil

8 ounces (6-inch-round) rice paper sheets

For the sauce, grind the garlic, chili paste and Thai Bird chile into a paste using a mortar and pestle. If mortar and pestle are not available, finely mince the garlic and chile and stir in the chili paste. Combine the garlic mixture with the hot water, fish sauce, sugar and lime juice in a bowl and mix until the sugar dissolves. Ladle the sauce into serving bowls. Sprinkle with the carrot.

For the beef, cut the beef into 1/4-inch-thick 2×4-inch slices. Combine the lemon grass, oil, garlic, fish sauce, sugar and soy sauce in a shallow dish and mix well. Add the beef and toss to coat. Marinate at room temperature for 15 minutes, turning several times.

For the salad, cook the noodles in boiling water in a saucepan for 5 minutes. Drain and rinse. Arrange the noodles, lettuce, cucumber, bean sprouts, mint and basil separately on a large platter. Place the rice papers on a platter. Heat water in a saucepan. Cover to keep warm.

To serve, grill the beef over hot coals or pan sear in a skillet to the desired degree of doneness. Remove the beef to a serving platter. Arrange the beef, table salad, rice paper and dipping sauce on the serving table. Pour the hot water into a heatproof bowl large enough to use to dip the rice papers. Guests should dip the edges of the rice papers in the hot water and turn to evenly moisten, allowing the excess water to drip off. Place the moistened wrap on a dinner plate. Arrange the beef and table salad on the wrap and roll to enclose the filling. Dip in the dipping sauce.

Wine recommendation, a dry-style Riesling. Try Claiborne & Churchill from California or Schmitt Sochne Classic Riesling from Germany.

Serves 4

Spicy Thai Beef Strips

1 pound beef flank steak or London broil
1/4 cup soy sauce
2 tablespoons Asian chili sesame oil
2 tablespoons chopped green onions
2 medium garlic cloves, minced
2 teaspoons sesame seeds, toasted
1 teaspoon rice wine vinegar
1/2 teaspoon black pepper
1/4 teaspoon cayenne pepper
1 head green leaf lettuce, separated

Freeze the flank steak for 30 to 45 minutes. Slice the partially frozen steak into thin strips using a long sharp knife with a thin blade. Arrange the slices in a shallow dish.

Combine the soy sauce, chili sesame oil, green onions, garlic, sesame seeds, vinegar, black pepper and cayenne pepper in a bowl and mix well. Pour the soy sauce mixture over the steak, turning to coat. Marinate, covered, in the refrigerator for 8 to 10 hours, stirring occasionally. Drain, reserving the marinade.

Pour the marinade into a small saucepan. Bring to a boil. Boil for 2 to 3 minutes or until slightly thickened, stirring occasionally. Grill the beef strips over medium-hot coals for 1 to 2 minutes per side for medium-rare, turning once. Arrange the beef on a serving platter. Drizzle with the warm marinade.

To serve, place 1 strip of the beef on a lettuce leaf and roll to enclose the beef.

You may thread the uncooked beef strips on bamboo skewers that have been soaked in water, weaving the skewers in and out of the beef strips to create a serpentine effect. Grill the skewers for 1 to 2 minutes per side. Spoon the warm marinade over the skewers. Serve immediately.

Serves 4

Herb Marinade for Lamb or Beef

Combine 1/4 cup freshly squeezed lemon juice, 1/2 cup soy sauce and 1/2 cup vegetable oil in a large sealable plastic bag. Add 4 puréed large garlic cloves and 2 tablespoons each minced rosemary, thyme and oregano. Add lamb or beef and marinate in the refrigerator for 6 hours or longer.

Southwest-Style Salisbury Steaks with Lime-Pickled Onions

Lime-Pickled Red Onions

1 large red onion, thinly sliced
1/4 cup fresh lime juice
2 tablespoons chopped fresh cilantro
2 teaspoons olive oil
1/2 teaspoon oregano
1/2 teaspoon salt

Salisbury Steaks

1 1/2 pounds ground sirloin
1 (4-ounce) can chopped mild green chiles
1/2 cup shredded Monterey Jack cheese
1/4 cup chopped fresh cilantro
3 tablespoons minced green onions
1 tablespoon tequila
2 teaspoons chili powder
1 teaspoon salt
1 avocado, sliced
Commercially prepared salsas

For the onions, combine the onion, lime juice, cilantro, olive oil, oregano and salt in a bowl and mix well. Let stand, covered, at room temperature for 1 to 3 hours, stirring occasionally. You may prepare up to 2 days in advance and store, covered, in the refrigerator.

For the steaks, combine the ground sirloin, green chiles, cheese, cilantro, green onions, tequila, chili powder and salt in a bowl and mix gently just until blended. Shape the ground sirloin mixture into four 3/4-inch-thick oval patties. You may prepare up to this point 1 day in advance and store, covered, in the refrigerator. Grill the patties over medium-high heat until a meat thermometer registers 160 degrees. Remove the patties to individual plates. Top each patty with sliced avocado and Lime-Pickled Red Onions. Serve immediately with assorted salsas.

Serves 4

Finger Bowl

A bowl of warm water with citrus slices for finger-dipping placed beside each setting at a barbecue is a thoughtful gesture.

Grilled Lamb with Roasted Olives and Onions

1 cup kalamata olives
2 large white onions or yellow onions,
    cut into 3/4-inch slices
2 teaspoons pepper
2 teaspoons kosher salt
1 tablespoon olive oil
1 teaspoon thyme
1 teaspoon minced garlic
1/2 teaspoon coriander
1/2 teaspoon cardamom
1/2 teaspoon cumin
1/2 teaspoon paprika
1/8 teaspoon nutmeg
1/8 teaspoon ginger
1/8 teaspoon allspice
1 (2-pound) boneless leg of lamb, butterflied
8 (1/8-inch) slices lemon

Remove the pits from the olives by lightly cracking open with the side of a knife. Arrange the olives and onion slices in a single layer on separate baking sheets. Sprinkle the olives with 1/2 teaspoon of the pepper. Sprinkle the onions with 1/2 teaspoon of the pepper and 1/2 teaspoon of the salt. Drizzle the olives and onions with the olive oil.

Roast the olives at 400 degrees for 10 minutes or until toasted. Bake the onions at 400 degrees for 15 to 30 minutes or until light brown and tender. Cover to keep warm.

Combine the remaining 1 teaspoon pepper, remaining 1 1/2 teaspoons salt, thyme, garlic, coriander, cardamom, cumin, paprika, nutmeg, ginger and allspice in a bowl and mix well. Rub the surface of the lamb with the spice mixture.

Grill the lamb over high heat for 40 to 50 minutes or until a meat thermometer registers 145 degrees for medium-rare. Let rest for 10 minutes before slicing. Grill the lemon slices for 30 seconds per side or until light brown.

To serve, toss the warm olives and warm onions in a bowl. Arrange the sliced lamb on dinner plates. Top each serving with some of the olive mixture and 2 lemon slices.

This recipe, pictured on page 165, was prepared using a Rack of Lamb.

Serves 4

Fresh Mint Vinaigrette for Lamb

Combine 2/3 cup olive oil, 1/4 cup white wine vinegar, 2 finely chopped Italian tomatoes and 1/3 cup chopped fresh mint leaves in a bowl. Add 2 teaspoons stone-ground mustard, 1/2 teaspoon sugar, 1 teaspoon salt and freshly ground pepper to taste and mix well. Serve with lamb.

Piquant Spicy Leg of Lamb

1 (3- to 4-pound) leg of lamb, butterflied
1/2 cup Dijon mustard
1/2 cup apricot preserves or peach preserves
1/4 teaspoon garlic salt

Have the butcher remove the bone and leave the leg of lamb butterflied. Buy the end of the leg with the bone down the center, closer to the foot.

Combine the Dijon mustard, preserves and garlic salt in a bowl and mix well. Arrange the lamb flat on a baking sheet. Spread the Dijon mustard mixture over both sides of the lamb. Marinate, covered with plastic wrap, in the refrigerator for up to 24 hours, turning occasionally. Grill the lamb over medium-hot coals for 20 to 30 minutes per side or to the desired degree of doneness; do not overcook. You may roast in the oven at 350 degrees for 20 minutes per pound.

Serve with a Pinot Noir, such as Cristom from Oregon.

Serves 4

Souvlaki Marinade

1 cup white wine
1/4 cup olive oil
Juice of 2 lemons
2 garlic cloves, crushed
2 bay leaves
1 teaspoon salt
1 teaspoon oregano
1/2 teaspoon rosemary
1/8 teaspoon pepper
Lemons, cut into quarters

Combine the wine, olive oil, lemon juice, garlic, bay leaves, salt, oregano, rosemary, pepper and lemon quarters in a bowl and mix well. Pour the marinade over 1-inch cubes of beef, pork, lamb or chicken in a sealable plastic bag and seal tightly. Turn to coat.

Marinate in the refrigerator for 3 to 24 hours, turning occasionally. Thread the cubes on 8-inch skewers. Grill over hot coals to the desired degree of doneness, brushing frequently with the marinade. Allow 8 ounces beef, pork, lamb or chicken per guest.

Servings variable

Celebrity Ribs

Seasoned salt to taste

1 teaspoon ground pepper

5 pounds baby back ribs or ribs of
    your choice

6 garlic cloves, chopped

2 jalapeño chiles, seeded and chopped

2 green bell peppers, sliced

2 yellow bell peppers, sliced

2 red bell peppers, sliced

2 onions, sliced

Sprinkle the seasoned salt and pepper over the surface of the ribs. Rub the garlic and jalapeño chiles over the ribs. Arrange the ribs on a sheet of foil large enough to wrap tightly around the ribs. Layer the bell peppers and onions over the ribs. Seal the foil tightly. Marinate in the refrigerator for 24 to 48 hours. Place the foil packet in a heavy baking pan and place the pan on the middle oven rack. Bake at 300 degrees for 6 to 8 hours or until tender; the meat should easily fall off the bones. Check the ribs periodically to avoid overcooking.

Serves 4 to 6

Slow-Baked Spareribs with Mango Chutney Marinade

2 racks (about 6$^{1}/_{2}$ pounds) pork spareribs

1 cup dry sherry

$^{1}/_{2}$ cup soy sauce

$^{1}/_{4}$ cup sesame oil

$^{1}/_{4}$ cup mango chutney

2 tablespoons honey

2 green onions, finely chopped

1 tablespoon finely chopped fresh gingerroot

4 large garlic cloves, minced

1 teaspoon cayenne pepper

Arrange the ribs in a large roasting pan. Whisk the sherry, soy sauce, sesame oil, chutney, honey, green onions, gingerroot, garlic and cayenne pepper in a bowl. Pour the sherry mixture over the ribs, turning to coat. Marinate, covered, in the refrigerator for 8 to 10 hours, turning once. Drain the ribs, reserving the marinade. Pour the reserved marinade into a saucepan. Bring to a boil. Remove from the heat. Position 1 oven rack in the top third of the oven and 1 oven rack in the bottom third of the oven.

Arrange each rib rack on a baking sheet with sides. Place 1 baking sheet on each oven rack. Bake at 300 degrees for about 3 hours or until tender, basting with $^{1}/_{4}$ cup of the reserved marinade every 20 minutes and covering the edges of the ribs with strips of foil if necessary to protect from burning. Cut between the bones to separate the ribs. Remove to a serving platter. Serve immediately.

Serves 4

Sugar-Spiced Pork Chops with Chipotle Sauce

Chipotle Sauce

1 cup canned solid-pack pumpkin
1 (8-ounce) jar salsa
1/4 cup shredded Parmesan cheese
1 chipotle chile (optional)
1/4 teaspoon nutmeg

Pork Chops and Assembly

2 tablespoons brown sugar
1 teaspoon cumin
1 teaspoon chili powder
1/2 teaspoon salt
1/2 teaspoon pepper
4 boneless pork chops, 1 inch thick
1 teaspoon olive oil
2 plum tomatoes, seeded and chopped
4 teaspoons chopped fresh cilantro

For the sauce, combine the pumpkin, salsa, cheese, chipotle chile and nutmeg in a saucepan and mix well. Cook over medium heat for 10 minutes or until the mixture is almost to the boiling point, stirring occasionally. Remove from the heat. Cover to keep warm.

For the pork chops, combine the brown sugar, cumin, chili powder, salt and pepper in a bowl and mix well. Sprinkle the brown sugar mixture over both sides of the pork chops. Heat the olive oil in a skillet over medium heat. Add the pork chops. Cook for 10 minutes or until cooked through, turning occasionally; drain. Toss the tomatoes and cilantro in a bowl.

To serve, spoon the sauce evenly onto 4 serving plates. Arrange 1 pork chop on each plate. Top with the tomato mixture.

Serves 4

Ancho Chile Pepper

A dried poblano chile that is used mostly in Mexican and southwest cooking, the ancho pepper has mild flavor with tones of coffee, raisins, and plums.

Romano Sage Pork Chops

1¹/₂ cups fresh crustless French bread
    crumbs
1 cup (about 3 ounces) freshly grated
    Romano cheese
1 tablespoon rubbed sage
1 teaspoon grated lemon zest
¹/₄ cup flour
Salt and pepper to taste
4 bone-in center-cut pork loin chops,
    1 inch thick
2 eggs, beaten
2 tablespoons butter
2 tablespoons olive oil
Lemon wedges (optional)
Orange wedges (optional)

Mix the bread crumbs, cheese, sage and lemon zest in a shallow dish. Place the flour on a plate and season generously with salt and pepper. Coat the pork chops on both sides with the flour mixture, shaking off the excess. Dip the pork chops in the eggs and coat both sides with the bread crumb mixture.

Heat the butter and olive oil in a large ovenproof skillet over medium-high heat. Add the pork chops to the butter mixture. Cook for 2 minutes per side or until golden brown. Bake at 425 degrees for 20 minutes or until crisp and a meat thermometer inserted in the center of the pork chops registers 160 degrees for medium or 170 degrees for well done. Remove the pork chops to serving plates. Garnish with lemon wedges and orange wedges.

Serve with a Pinot Blanc, such as Hugal from the Alsace region of France.

Serves 4

Marinades

- Oil marinades are great for lean meats. They add moisture and give their outer edge a nice crispness.
- Rubs simply provide flavor to the outside of the meat.
- Vinegar and acidic marinades serve as tenderizers.
- Paste marinades make a savory crust for the meat.

Pork with Dried Plums

1¹/₃ cups pitted dried plums
1¹/₃ cups water
²/₃ cup sherry cooking wine vinegar
¹/₂ cup sugar
¹/₄ cup olive oil
6 garlic cloves
2 tablespoons chopped fresh rosemary
2 teaspoons cracked black pepper
1¹/₂ pounds pork tenderloins
¹/₈ teaspoon crushed red pepper
10 cups sliced escarole (2 large heads)
1 cup chicken broth

Combine the plums, water, vinegar and sugar in a saucepan and mix well. Bring to a boil. Boil until the sugar dissolves, stirring constantly. Reduce the heat to medium. Cook for 20 minutes or until the mixture is of a syrupy consistency, stirring frequently. Remove from the heat. Cover to keep warm.

Combine the olive oil, garlic, rosemary and black pepper in a food processor. Process until blended. Place the pork tenderloins in a roasting pan. Pat 3¹/₂ tablespoons of the garlic mixture over the tenderloins. Roast at 400 degrees for 30 minutes or until a meat thermometer registers 160 degrees for medium or 170 degrees for well done.

Heat the remaining garlic mixture and crushed red pepper in a large saucepan over high heat, stirring occasionally. Add the escarole and broth and mix well. Cook, covered, for 5 minutes or until the escarole wilts.

To serve, slice the pork. Bring the plum mixture to a simmer, stirring occasionally. Divide the escarole mixture evenly among 6 serving plates. Top with the sliced pork and spoon some of the plum mixture over each serving. Serve immediately.

Serves 6

Curried Pork Tenderloin

1 teaspoon cumin seeds
1 teaspoon coriander seeds
¹/₂ cup olive oil
2 tablespoons red curry paste
1 tablespoon minced garlic
1 tablespoon minced shallot
2 teaspoons kosher salt
2 (12-ounce) pork tenderloins, trimmed

Spread the cumin seeds and coriander seeds in a skillet. Toast over high heat until fragrant and brown, stirring frequently. Grind the cumin mixture in a spice grinder until finely ground. Mix the ground cumin mixture, olive oil, red curry paste, garlic, shallot and salt in a bowl.

Place the tenderloins and cumin mixture in a large sealable plastic bag and seal tightly. Turn to coat. Marinate in the refrigerator for 2 hours, turning occasionally. Grill the tenderloins with the lid down over hot coals for 25 minutes or until cooked through, turning once. Let rest for 10 minutes before slicing.

Serves 6

Chipotle Burgers with a Kick

1 tablespoon olive oil
1/2 cup chopped onion
2 pounds ground pork
1 egg, lightly beaten
1 tablespoon adobo sauce (from can of
    chipotle chiles in adobo sauce)
1 canned chipotle chile in adobo sauce, seeded
    and finely chopped
2 tablespoons dry bread crumbs
2 tablespoons chopped fresh parsley
1/2 teaspoon salt
1/8 teaspoon sugar
2 avocados, chopped
Juice of 1 lime
3/4 cup sour cream

Heat the olive oil in a small sauté pan over medium-high heat. Stir in the onion. Reduce the heat to medium-low. Cook for 4 minutes or until the onion is tender, stirring frequently. Remove the onion to a plate to cool.

Combine the cooled onion, ground pork, egg, adobo sauce, chipotle chile, bread crumbs, parsley, salt and sugar in a large bowl and mix well. Shape the ground pork mixture into 6 patties. Grill the patties over hot coals to the desired degree of doneness, turning frequently.

Toss the avocados with the lime juice in a bowl. Top each burger with chopped avocado and 2 tablespoons of the sour cream.

Serves 6

Basic Dry Rub for Ribs
Combine 1 tablespoon coarse salt, 1 tablespoon freshly ground pepper, 1 tablespoon paprika, 1 teaspoon brown sugar, 1 1/2 teaspoons chili powder and 1 teaspoon garlic powder in a bowl and mix well. Sprinkle on ribs. Grill over hot coals.

Buffalo Chili

1 tablespoon olive oil
1 pound ground buffalo meat or lean ground
    beef
1 (15-ounce) can whole kernel corn, drained
1 (15-ounce) can diced tomatoes
1 (15-ounce) can red beans, drained, rinsed
1 (15-ounce) can black beans, drained, rinsed
1 red onion, chopped
1 red bell pepper, chopped
1 yellow bell pepper, chopped
1 green bell pepper, chopped
2 tablespoons chili powder
1 tablespoon salt, or to taste
1 tablespoon cumin
1 tablespoon red pepper flakes
1/4 teaspoon black pepper
2 garlic cloves, minced
1 (11-ounce) can tomato juice
Sour cream
Chopped fresh cilantro

Heat the olive oil in a large Dutch oven over medium-high heat. Brown the ground buffalo meat in the hot olive oil, stirring until crumbly. Drain if using ground beef. Stir in the drained corn, undrained tomatoes, red beans, black beans, onion, bell peppers, chili powder, salt, cumin, red pepper flakes, black pepper and garlic. Add the tomato juice and mix well.

Simmer, covered, for 40 to 45 minutes, stirring frequently. Ladle into chili bowls. Top each serving with a dollop of sour cream and sprinkle with cilantro, or serve with your favorite chili toppings.

You may substitute Bloody Mary mix for the tomato juice and add one 4-ounce can chopped green chiles for a spicier chili.

Serves 4

contents

176 Steamed Mussels
176 Scallops with Ginger Sauce
177 Curried Shrimp with Coconut Milk and Spiced Masala
178 Thai Shrimp Curry
179 Spicy Mango Shrimp on Wilted Greens
180 Sizzling Garlic and Citrus Shrimp
180 Spice-Crusted Tuna
181 Cumin Tuna Steaks with Lime Cream and Salsa
182 Seared Ahi Napoleon
184 Wasabi and Sesame Encrusted Ahi Tuna with Jicama Slaw
185 Grilled Halibut with Ginger Butter
186 Halibut Kabobs with Chile Lime Sauce
188 Halibut with Roasted Red Pepper Sauce
189 Sea Bass in Tomato Fennel Sauce
190 Grilled Salmon in Thai Curry Sauce with Vegetable Slaw
     and Potatoes
191 Salmon Saltimbocca
191 Sweet Barbecue Salmon
192 Salmon with Citrus Soy Glaze
193 Pan-Fried Trout with Bacon
194 Sole with Almonds, Pine Nuts and Currants
194 Grilled Swordfish
195 Grilled Pineapple Salsa
195 Cilantro Tomato Salsa
196 Grilled Swordfish Tostados with Black Beans

SEAFOOD

Steamed Mussels

2 pounds mussels in shells
2 tablespoons olive oil
1/4 cup chopped onion
1/4 cup chopped celery
2 garlic cloves, chopped
1/2 cup dry white wine
1 bay leaf

Rinse the mussels in cold water and debeard. Heat the olive oil in a large stockpot. Sauté the onion, celery and garlic in the hot olive oil for 2 to 3 minutes or just until the vegetables are tender. Add the mussels, wine and bay leaf and mix well.

Cook, covered, over medium-high heat for 4 minutes or until the mussels open. Discard any mussels that do not open. Discard the bay leaf. Ladle the mussels and broth into soup bowls or pasta bowls. Serve with orzo or risotto and crusty bread to soak up the broth.

Serves 2 or 3 as main course, 4 to 6 as appetizer

Scallops with Ginger Sauce

1 pound sea scallops or shrimp
Salt and pepper to taste
3 tablespoons unsalted butter
2 tablespoons minced fresh gingerroot
1 garlic clove, minced
1/2 cup dry white wine
2 tablespoons rice vinegar
1/2 cup whipping cream
2 tablespoons unsalted butter
3 tablespoons chopped fresh cilantro
2 green onions, finely chopped

Cut any large scallops into halves. Sprinkle the scallops with salt and pepper. Heat 3 tablespoons butter in a large skillet over high heat. Sear the scallops in the butter for 1 minute per side or until brown. Remove the scallops to a bowl with a slotted spoon, reserving the pan drippings. Sauté the gingerroot and garlic in the reserved pan drippings for 30 seconds. Stir in the wine and vinegar. Bring to a boil. Boil for 2 minutes, stirring to dislodge any browned bits. Add the whipping cream and 2 tablespoons butter.

Simmer for 3 minutes or just until the sauce thickens enough to coat the back of a spoon, stirring frequently. Return the scallops to the skillet. Simmer for 2 minutes or until the scallops are opaque in the center, stirring frequently. Add the cilantro and green onions and mix well. Serve with hot cooked rice and a green vegetable, such as sugar snap peas.

Serves 4

Curried Shrimp with Coconut Milk and Spiced Masala

In Indian cuisine, a "masala" is a mixture of spices, seasonings, and herbs combined to form a powder or paste. "Garam" means hot, so a "garam masala" is a hot spice mix, which can be found in the spice sections of some supermarkets.

Spiced Masala

2 tablespoons vegetable oil
2 cups chopped onions
4 large garlic cloves, minced
1 1/2 teaspoons garam masala (optional)
1 1/2 teaspoons curry powder
1 1/2 teaspoons coriander
1 teaspoon turmeric
1/2 teaspoon cayenne pepper
1 (28-ounce) can diced tomatoes
1 cup plain whole milk yogurt
Salt and black pepper to taste

Shrimp

2 tablespoons vegetable oil
2 pounds large shrimp, peeled and deveined
1 (13-ounce) can unsweetened coconut milk
1/2 cup chopped fresh cilantro
1/4 cup chopped green onion tops
1 1/2 tablespoons fresh lemon juice
Salt and pepper to taste
Steamed basmati rice
1/2 cup slivered almonds, toasted

For the masala, heat the oil in a large nonstick skillet over medium heat. Sauté the onions in the hot oil for 20 minutes or until golden brown. Stir in the garlic, garam masala, curry powder, coriander, turmeric and cayenne pepper. Process the undrained tomatoes and yogurt in a food processor until almost smooth. Add the onion mixture. Process until almost smooth. Season with salt and black pepper. You may prepare up to 1 day in advance and store, covered, in the refrigerator.

For the shrimp, heat the oil in a large heavy deep skillet over medium-high heat. Add the shrimp. Sauté for 2 minutes or until partially cooked. Stir in the coconut milk, cilantro, green onion tops, lemon juice and masala.

Simmer for 3 minutes or until the shrimp turn pink, stirring frequently. Season with salt and pepper. Serve over rice, sprinkled with the almonds.

Serves 8

Thai Shrimp Curry

Curry Paste

1/2 cup chopped onion
3 large shallots, chopped
3 tablespoons chopped lemon grass (from
    bottom 3 inches of about 5 peeled stalks)
3 tablespoons chopped cilantro stems
3 tablespoons chopped fresh gingerroot
1 tablespoon turmeric
2 teaspoons cumin
1 teaspoon crushed dried red pepper

Shrimp

2 cups canned unsweetened coconut milk
2 (8-ounce) bottles clam juice
1 head (about 1 1/2 pounds) bok choy
2 tablespoons vegetable oil
2 pounds large shrimp, peeled and deveined
1 pound snow peas, strings removed
Salt to taste
Fresh cilantro leaves

For the paste, process the onion, shallots, lemon grass, cilantro stems, gingerroot, turmeric, cumin and red pepper in a food processor until a paste forms, scraping the side of the bowl occasionally. Store, covered, in the refrigerator for up to 4 days.

For the shrimp, bring the coconut milk and clam juice to a boil in a saucepan. Boil for 20 minutes or until reduced to 2 cups, stirring occasionally. You may prepare up to 1 day in advance and store, covered, in the refrigerator.

Cut the white stalks of the bok choy crosswise into 1/4-inch slices. Cut the dark green leaves crosswise into 1-inch slices. Heat the oil in a large heavy skillet over high heat. Stir in 1/2 cup of the paste.

Cook for 1 minute, stirring constantly. Add the shrimp and mix well. Sauté for 2 minutes or just until the shrimp begin to turn pink. Remove the shrimp to a plate with a slotted spoon, reserving the pan drippings. Add the reduced coconut milk mixture to the reserved pan drippings and mix well. Bring to a boil.

Boil for 4 minutes or until slightly thickened, stirring frequently. Stir in the white part of the bok choy. Cook for 2 minutes, stirring frequently. Add the dark green leaves of the bok choy, snow peas and shrimp and mix well.

Simmer, covered, for 5 minutes, stirring occasionally. Season with salt. Spoon into a serving bowl. Sprinkle with cilantro leaves. Serve with hot Jasmine rice.

Serves 6

Spicy Mango Shrimp on Wilted Greens

Sauce

- 1/2 cup sugar
- 1/3 cup chopped mango, puréed or mashed
- 2 tablespoons light soy sauce
- 1 tablespoon dark rum
- 1 tablespoon fresh lime juice

Shrimp

- 2 tablespoons flour
- 1 tablespoon cornstarch
- 1/2 teaspoon baking soda
- 1 egg, lightly beaten
- 1 teaspoon soy sauce
- 1 1/4 pounds large shrimp, peeled, deveined and cut lengthwise into halves
- 2 green onions, thinly sliced
- 1 tablespoon minced fresh gingerroot
- 2 or 3 dried red chiles, crushed
- 1 tablespoon minced garlic
- 1 cup vegetable oil

Wilted Greens and Assembly

- 2 tablespoons vegetable oil
- 1 tablespoon sherry
- 1 tablespoon soy sauce
- 1 teaspoon sugar
- 8 to 10 cups loosely packed mixed spring greens and spinach
- 1/2 cup fresh basil or cilantro, chopped
- 1 mango, sliced
- 1 carambola (star fruit), sliced (optional)

For the sauce, combine the sugar, mango purée, soy sauce, rum and lime juice in a small bowl and mix well.

For the shrimp, combine the flour, cornstarch and baking soda in a bowl and mix well. Stir in the egg and soy sauce. Pat the shrimp dry with paper towels. Add the shrimp to the flour mixture and toss to coat. Chill, covered, for 1 hour or longer.

Combine the green onions, gingerroot, red chiles and garlic in a bowl and mix well. Heat the oil in a wok or deep skillet. Add half the shrimp. Stir-fry for 3 minutes or until the shrimp turn whitish-pink. Remove the shrimp to paper towels to drain using a slotted spoon. Repeat the process with the remaining shrimp.

Drain all but 2 tablespoons of the oil from the wok. Add the green onion mixture. Stir-fry over high heat until the mixture begins to color. Stir in the sauce ingredients. Cook until bubbly, stirring constantly. Return the shrimp to the wok and toss to coat with the sauce. Remove the shrimp mixture to a bowl. Cover to keep warm.

For the greens, heat the oil in a wok. Stir in the sherry, soy sauce and sugar. Cook until heated through, stirring constantly. Add the greens mixture. Stir-fry over high heat just until the greens wilt. Add the basil and toss to mix. Remove from the heat.

To serve, divide the greens equally among 4 serving plates. Arrange the shrimp mixture evenly over the greens. Top with sliced mango and sliced carambola.

Serves 4 as main course, 6 to 8 as first course

Sizzling Garlic and Citrus Shrimp

24 jumbo shrimp (about 1¹/₂ pounds)
¹/₂ cup (1 stick) unsalted butter, melted
¹/₃ cup fresh lime juice
¹/₃ cup fresh lemon juice
¹/₃ cup orange juice
¹/₄ cup fresh cilantro, chopped
10 garlic cloves, finely chopped
¹/₄ teaspoon salt
¹/₄ teaspoon cayenne pepper

Peel the shrimp, leaving the tails intact; devein. Arrange the shrimp in a single layer in a large shallow nonreactive baking dish. Combine the unsalted butter, lime juice, lemon juice, orange juice, cilantro, garlic, salt and cayenne pepper in a bowl and mix well. Pour the butter mixture over the shrimp.

Broil for 8 minutes or until the shrimp turn pink, turning once or twice. Serve over thin slices of French bread or with hot cooked rice, orzo or angel hair pasta. Garnish with citrus slices and additional cilantro.

Serves 4 to 6

Spice-Crusted Tuna

2 tablespoons coriander seeds, crushed
1 tablespoon fennel seeds, crushed
1¹/₂ teaspoons coarsely ground pepper
1 teaspoon salt
4 (6-ounce) fresh tuna steaks,
    ³/4 to 1 inch thick
3 tablespoons olive oil
Lemon wedges

Mix the coriander seeds, fennel seeds, pepper and salt in a small bowl. Spread the spice mixture on a large plate. Coat each tuna steak on both sides with the spice mixture and press lightly to ensure the mixture adheres.

Heat the olive oil in a large heavy skillet over high heat. Add the tuna. Cook for 2 to 3 minutes per side for medium or until the coating is deep brown in color. The tuna will continue to cook after being removed from the heat. Serve with lemon wedges. You may substitute ground coriander for the crushed coriander seeds.

This tuna is delicious served in a Salad Niçoise.

Serves 4

Cumin Tuna Steaks with Lime Cream and Salsa

Mango Salsa

1 cup chopped mango
1/2 cup chopped red bell pepper
1/4 cup chopped red onion
1 Anaheim chile, minced
1/2 cup fresh cilantro, chopped
1 tablespoon honey
1 tablespoon olive oil

Lime Cream Sauce

6 tablespoons sour cream
6 tablespoons mayonnaise
2 1/2 tablespoons fresh lime juice
1 garlic clove, crushed
Salt to taste

Tuna

Salt and pepper to taste
4 (6-ounce) tuna steaks
4 teaspoons cumin

For the salsa, combine the mango, bell pepper, onion, Anaheim chile, cilantro, honey and olive oil in a bowl and mix gently. Chill, covered, for several hours.

For the sauce, whisk the sour cream, mayonnaise, lime juice and garlic in a small bowl. Season with salt. Spoon the sauce into a squeeze bottle and chill. The sauce may also be placed in a sealable plastic bag. Snip one corner of the bag to squeeze just before serving.

For the tuna, sprinkle salt and pepper over both sides of the tuna. Sprinkle with the cumin and press lightly to make sure it adheres. Arrange the tuna on an oiled grill rack. Grill, covered, over medium-high heat for 6 minutes per side for rare or to the desired degree of doneness. Remove the tuna to serving plates. Spoon some of the salsa on each plate. Drizzle the sauce over the tuna and salsa. Serve immediately.

This is a quick and easy recipe for entertaining since the salsa and sauce can be prepared in advance.

Serves 4

Asian Fish Sauce

Asian fish sauce is a popular condiment in Southeast Asia. It is dark brown in color and is made from fermented fish. It has a strong aroma but a subtle, salty taste.

Seared Ahi Napoleon

Sweet Potato Purée

4 medium sweet potatoes
2 tablespoons butter
2 tablespoons minced candied ginger or
    stem ginger in syrup
1/2 cup chicken stock, heated
1 tablespoon minced fresh chives
Salt and pepper to taste

Asian Coleslaw

1/4 cup rice vinegar
1/4 cup sugar
1 tablespoon Thai sweet chili sauce
1 tablespoon finely chopped fresh mint
2 cups finely shredded napa cabbage

Tuna

2 cups canola oil (optional)
8 won ton wrappers (optional)
3/4 teaspoon freshly ground pepper
1/2 teaspoon salt
1/4 cup sesame seeds
1 pound ahi tuna, cut into 2-inch squares
1/2 cup kecap manis (optional)

For the purée, arrange the sweet potatoes on a foil-lined baking sheet. Bake at 400 degrees for 50 to 60 minutes or until tender. Cool slightly. Scoop the sweet potato pulp into a mixing bowl. Add the butter, ginger, 1/4 cup of the stock and chives. Beat until puréed. Add the remaining 1/4 cup stock if needed for the desired consistency and mix well. Season with salt and pepper. Spoon the purée into a baking dish. Keep warm in the oven.

For the coleslaw, combine the vinegar, sugar, chili sauce and mint in a bowl and stir until the sugar dissolves. Add the cabbage and mix well. Chill, covered, in the refrigerator.

For the tuna, heat the canola oil in a heavy skillet. Test oil for correct temperature by dropping a small piece of a won ton wrapper in the hot oil. Bubbles should appear around the outer edges of the wrapper when the oil is the correct temperature. Fry for 30 seconds per wrapper or until golden brown; drain.

Mix the pepper, salt and sesame seeds in a shallow dish. Coat the tuna on all sides with the pepper mixture. Heat a heavy skillet over high heat until water dropped in the skillet beads up and sizzles immediately. Sear the tuna in the hot skillet on all sides for rare or cook longer for the desired degree of doneness. Cut into 1/4-inch slices.

To serve the napoleons, bring the coleslaw to room temperature. Place 1 won ton in the center of each of 4 serving plates. Spoon 1/8 of the purée on top of each. Layer with several slices of the tuna. Repeat the process with the remaining won tons, remaining purée and remaining tuna. Spoon 1/2 cup of the coleslaw on the top. Pour the kecap manis into a squeeze bottle. Squeeze over the napoleons and edges of the plates in a decorative pattern if desired. Serve immediately with Champagne or sparkling wine.

Kecap manis is a dark brown, thick Indonesian condiment that can be found in Asian markets or prepared using this simple recipe. Boil 1/2 cup soy sauce, 1/3 cup sugar, 1 tablespoon water and 2 star anise until the mixture is reduced to 1/3 of the original volume. Discard the star anise and let stand until cool.

Serves 4

Wasabi and Sesame Encrusted Ahi Tuna with Jicama Slaw

Jicama Slaw

1 large jicama, peeled and julienned or grated
2 large carrots, julienned or grated
1 red bell pepper, chopped
1/4 head red cabbage, finely shredded
Juice of 1/2 large lime
1/4 cup rice wine vinegar
2 tablespoons sugar
3/4 teaspoon salt
3/4 teaspoon pepper
1/3 cup canola oil

Ahi Tuna

6 (6-ounce) ahi tuna steaks
6 tablespoons soy sauce
4 to 6 tablespoons wasabi paste
1/2 cup sesame seeds
3 tablespoons canola oil

For the slaw, mix the jicama, carrots, bell pepper, cabbage and lime juice in a bowl. Combine the vinegar, sugar, salt and pepper in a bowl and mix well. Whisk in the canola oil. Add the dressing to the jicama mixture and toss to coat. Chill, covered, for 1 hour or longer.

For the tuna, arrange the tuna in a single layer in a shallow dish. Pour the soy sauce over the tuna and turn to coat. Marinate, covered, in the refrigerator for no more than 1 hour, turning occasionally; drain. Bring to room temperature. Spread 1 to 1 1/2 teaspoons of the wasabi paste on both sides of the tuna. Sprinkle each side with 2 teaspoons of the sesame seeds and press firmly so the coating adheres.

Heat the canola oil in a large sauté pan over medium-high heat. Sear the tuna in the hot canola oil for 2 minutes per side for rare or 3 minutes per side for medium-rare, turning once. You will see the sides of the tuna cooking. When the cooked parts of the sides almost meet, the tuna is rare and warm inside. Remove the tuna to a serving platter. Mix about 2 teaspoons additional wasabi paste and 2/3 cup additional soy sauce and serve in individual bowls as a dipping sauce if desired. Serve the tuna with the slaw.

If wasabi paste is not available, combine 6 tablespoons wasabi powder with 3 tablespoons water to make 1/4 cup wasabi paste.

Serves 6

Wasabi

A Japanese version of horseradish, wasabi is derived from the root of an Asian plant. It is used to make a green-colored condiment that has a sharp, pungent, fiery flavor. It is available in paste and powdered form—or fresh, which can be grated like horseradish.

Grilled Halibut with Ginger Butter

Ginger Butter

6 tablespoons butter
2 green onions, finely chopped
1 tablespoon minced fresh gingerroot
Juice of 1 lemon
Salt and pepper to taste

Halibut

2 tablespoons sesame oil
2 tablespoons soy sauce
2 tablespoons lemon juice or rice vinegar
2 tablespoons chopped fresh parsley
2 green onions, chopped
1/2 teaspoon dried thyme, or 2 teaspoons
   chopped fresh thyme
1/8 teaspoon cayenne pepper
4 (6-ounce) halibut or orange roughy
   fillets or steaks

For the butter, process the butter, green onions, gingerroot and lemon juice in a food processor until blended. Season with salt and pepper. Let stand at room temperature until time to serve.

For the halibut, combine the sesame oil, soy sauce, lemon juice, parsley, green onions, thyme and cayenne pepper in a shallow dish and mix well. Add the halibut and turn to coat. Marinate, covered, in the refrigerator for 1 to 4 hours, turning occasionally.

Grill the halibut over high heat for 10 to 12 minutes or until the fillets flake easily, turning midway through the grilling process. Or broil 6 inches from the heat source for 10 to 12 minutes. Top each fillet with 1 to 2 tablespoons of the butter.

The Ginger Butter is delicious on grilled chicken, swordfish and tuna.

Wine recommendation, serve with a New Zealand Sauvignon Blanc. Try Nobilo or Whitehaven, both from the Marlborough region.

Serves 4

Pile unpeeled, boiled shrimp on a platter. Serve with coleslaw, crusty bread, and cold beer. Line picnic tables with newspaper, place buckets at both ends for shells, and have fun.

Halibut Kabobs with Chile Lime Sauce

Chile Lime Sauce

3/4 cup fresh lime juice

1/3 cup chopped fresh cilantro

3 tablespoons olive oil

3 tablespoons sugar

2 teaspoons (or more) minced serrano chiles

1 teaspoon finely grated lime zest

Salt and pepper to taste

Halibut

1 1/2 pounds halibut fillets, cut into 1- to
1 1/2-inch cubes (about 3 dozen cubes)

2 medium red bell peppers, cut into 1- to
1 1/2-inch pieces (about 3 dozen pieces)

8 green onions, cut into 2-inch pieces
(about 3 dozen pieces)

Salt and pepper to taste

2 tablespoons olive oil

For the sauce, whisk the lime juice, cilantro, olive oil, sugar, serrano chiles and lime zest in a bowl until the sugar dissolves. Reserve 1/2 of the sauce for the marinade. Season the remaining sauce with salt and pepper. Let stand at room temperature until time to serve.

For the halibut, arrange the halibut in a shallow dish. Pour the reserved sauce over the halibut and turn to coat. Marinate, covered, in the refrigerator for 30 minutes, turning occasionally. Thread the halibut, bell peppers and green onions alternately on six 12-inch metal skewers. Sprinkle with salt and pepper and brush with the olive oil.

Grill the kabobs over medium-high heat for 6 minutes or until the halibut turns opaque in the center, turning occasionally. Remove the kabobs to a platter or individual plates. Serve with the remaining seasoned sauce.

For an added twist, thread whole limequats on the skewers if desired.

Serves 6

Fresh or dried basil, oregano, tarragon, or parsley are excellent herbs to combine with olive oil for basting fish or grilled vegetables.

Halibut with Roasted Red Pepper Sauce

The Roasted Red Pepper Sauce is based on a Spanish sauce called romesco and can be used with a variety of grilled or poached fish or as a dip for fresh vegetables.

Roasted Red Pepper Sauce

1 1/2 pounds red bell peppers, stems removed,
    cut into quarters and seeded, or
    1 (12-ounce) jar roasted red peppers
1/2 cup slivered almonds, toasted
1/4 cup olive oil
2 tablespoons red wine vinegar or balsamic
    vinegar
1 1/2 tablespoons tomato paste
1/4 teaspoon cayenne pepper

Halibut

Salt to taste
4 to 6 (6-ounce) halibut fillets

For the sauce, arrange the bell peppers skin side up on a baking sheet. Broil until the skin is blistered and charred. Place the roasted peppers in a sealable plastic bag and seal tightly. Cool for 10 minutes. Discard the blackened skins. Combine the bell peppers, almonds, olive oil, vinegar, tomato paste and cayenne pepper in a food processor. Process for 1 to 2 minutes or until the almonds are finely ground. Heat the sauce in a saucepan just until warm. You may prepare up to 1 day in advance and store, covered, in the refrigerator. Heat before serving.

For the halibut, bring a large skillet of salted water to a simmer. Add the halibut. Simmer, covered, for 5 minutes or until the halibut is opaque in the center, turning once. Remove the halibut to serving plates using a slotted spoon. Drizzle with the warm sauce.

Serves 4 to 6

Orange Herb Sauce

Combine 1/2 cup orange juice, 2 tablespoons lemon juice, 1/4 cup sliced green onions and 1 1/2 tablespoons chopped fresh dill in a small saucepan and cook until heated through. Serve over fish.

Sea Bass in Tomato Fennel Sauce

1¹/₂ cups coarsely chopped fennel
¹/₂ cup coarsely chopped onion
1 teaspoon minced garlic
1 tablespoon olive oil
¹/₂ cup Pernod
3 cups chopped fresh or canned tomatoes
1³/₄ cups tomato juice
¹/₂ cup dry white wine
³/₄ teaspoon salt
³/₄ teaspoon ground pepper
4 to 6 (5-ounce) sea bass fillets or halibut
   fillets

Sauté the fennel, onion and garlic in the olive oil in a large skillet for 5 minutes or until the fennel and onion are tender. Add the Pernod and mix well. Cook for 3 minutes or until most of the liquid evaporates, stirring frequently. Add the tomatoes, tomato juice, wine, salt and pepper and mix well.

Simmer for 15 minutes, stirring occasionally. Process the tomato mixture in a blender or food processor until puréed. Strain, discarding the solids. Return enough of the strained sauce to the skillet to measure 2 to 3 cups, adding some of the solids back to the liquid if needed. You may prepare up to this point 1 day in advance and store, covered, in the refrigerator.

Bring the sauce to a simmer, stirring occasionally. Add the fillets and spoon some of the sauce over the top of each. Simmer, covered, for 10 to 15 minutes or until the fillets are opaque and flake easily. Remove the fillets to serving plates. Spoon some of the sauce over each serving.

Serves 4 to 6

Olive Butter

Put ¹/₂ pound room temperature unsalted butter into a medium bowl and beat with a wooden spoon until smooth. Add ¹/₂ cup chopped pitted kalamata olives, chopped leaves from 2 sprigs of parsley and 1 minced peeled garlic clove and mix well. Season to taste with coarse salt. Serve at room temperature with toasted baguette slices. Makes 1¹/₂ cups.

Grilled Salmon in Thai Curry Sauce with Vegetable Slaw and Potatoes

This is a flavorful and complete meal for entertaining and to the eye appears much too difficult. All of the recipes, except grilling the salmon, may be prepared in advance.

Thai Curry Sauce

1 tablespoon minced fresh gingerroot
1 teaspoon minced garlic
1 tablespoon vegetable oil
1 teaspoon ground coriander seeds
1 teaspoon curry powder
1 teaspoon Thai red curry paste
1 teaspoon paprika
1 teaspoon cumin
1 (13-ounce) can unsweetened coconut milk
2 tablespoons brown sugar
3 tablespoons tomato purée
1 tablespoon soy sauce

Mashed Potatoes

2 pounds russet potatoes, peeled and
cut into quarters
4 garlic cloves
Salt to taste
1/3 cup milk or cream
3 tablespoons butter
Pepper to taste

Vegetable Slaw

3 cups shredded cabbage
1 cup julienned peeled English cucumber
3 tablespoons minced fresh cilantro
3 tablespoons minced fresh mint leaves
3 tablespoons rice vinegar
1 tablespoon soy sauce

Salmon

6 (6-ounce) salmon fillets
1 tablespoon vegetable oil

For the sauce, sauté the gingerroot and garlic in the oil in a medium saucepan until golden brown. Stir in the coriander, curry powder, curry paste, paprika and cumin. Sauté for 1 minute. Add the coconut milk, brown sugar, tomato purée and soy sauce and mix well. Bring to a boil; reduce the heat. Simmer for 15 minutes, stirring occasionally. Cover to keep warm. You may prepare 1 day in advance and store, covered, in the refrigerator. Reheat before serving.

For the potatoes, combine the potatoes, garlic and salt with enough water to cover in a saucepan. Bring to a boil. Boil for 20 to 25 minutes or until the potatoes are tender; drain. Add the milk and butter. Mash until creamy. Season with salt and pepper. Spoon into a baking dish and cover. Keep warm in the oven.

For the slaw, combine the cabbage, cucumber, cilantro and mint in a bowl and mix well. Add a mixture of the vinegar and soy sauce and toss to coat. Chill, covered, for 1 hour.

For the salmon, brush the fillets with the oil. Grill over medium-high heat for 5 to 6 minutes per side or until the fillets flake easily and are opaque in the center.

To serve, mound about 1 cup of the mashed potatoes in the center of each serving plate. Spoon some of the warm sauce around the potatoes. Arrange 1 salmon fillet over each serving of potatoes. Top with the slaw.

Serves 6

Salmon Saltimbocca

6 (6-ounce) center-cut salmon fillets, skinned
    and cut crosswise into halves
Salt and freshly ground pepper to taste
12 fresh sage leaves
4 ounces prosciutto, cut into 12 thin slices
3 tablespoons olive oil

Sprinkle the salmon with salt and pepper. Place 1 sage leaf on each portion of salmon and wrap each with a slice of prosciutto, leaving the ends of the salmon uncovered. Arrange in a buttered large shallow baking dish. Sprinkle with pepper. You may prepare up to this point 1 hour in advance. Store, covered with foil, in the refrigerator.

Brush each portion of salmon with olive oil. Place the baking dish on the middle oven rack. Bake at 425 degrees for 8 to 10 minutes or just until cooked through. Place 2 portions of the salmon on each serving plate and serve immediately.

Serves 6

Sweet Barbecue Salmon

4 (6-ounce) salmon fillets
1/2 cup soy sauce
2 tablespoons honey
1 tablespoon Dijon mustard
1 tablespoon minced fresh parsley
2 or 3 garlic cloves, minced

Pierce the salmon with a fork and place in a sealable plastic bag. Combine the soy sauce, honey, Dijon mustard, parsley and garlic in a bowl and mix well. Pour the soy sauce mixture over the salmon and seal tightly. Turn to coat.

Marinate in the refrigerator for 1 to 4 hours, turning occasionally. Grill over medium-high heat for 5 minutes per side or until the fillets flake easily. Great served in a salad.

Serves 4

Salmon with Citrus Soy Glaze

Here is an alternative method for cooking the salmon that guarantees an easy cleanup and won't smoke up your kitchen. Wrap the salmon in a large piece of foil and crimp the edges so the packet is airtight. Bake at 400 degrees for 20 minutes.

Arrange the fillets in a single layer in a large shallow dish. Combine the orange juice and lime juice in a bowl and mix well. Pour the juice mixture over the fillets, turning to coat. Marinate, covered, in the refrigerator for 1 to 2 hours, turning occasionally.

Combine the cabbage, spinach, bell pepper and carrot in a bowl and mix well. Set aside. Whisk the vinegar, 1/4 cup vegetable oil, 1 tablespoon soy sauce and sesame oil in a bowl until blended. Set the vinaigrette aside.

Drain the salmon, reserving the marinade. Sprinkle with salt and pepper. Arrange the fillets in a broiler pan lined with foil. Broil on the top oven rack for 8 to 10 minutes or until the fillets flake easily.

While the salmon is broiling, sauté the gingerroot and garlic in 1 tablespoon vegetable oil in a small skillet over medium heat for 1 minute. Add the reserved marinade and 1 teaspoon soy sauce. Bring to a boil. Boil for 5 to 6 minutes or until the mixture is reduced to 1/2 cup and is the consistency of a glaze, stirring frequently.

To serve, whisk the vinaigrette. Add the vinaigrette to the cabbage mixture and toss to coat. Divide the cabbage mixture equally among 6 serving plates. Discard the skin from the salmon and arrange 1 fillet on each plate. Drizzle with the glaze. Serve with crusty French bread.

Serves 6

6 (6-ounce) salmon fillets
3/4 cup fresh orange juice
1/3 cup fresh lime juice
4 cups thinly sliced napa cabbage
4 cups packed thinly sliced fresh spinach
1 red bell pepper, julienned
1 carrot, julienned
1/4 cup rice vinegar
1/4 cup vegetable oil
1 tablespoon soy sauce
1 tablespoon oriental sesame oil
Salt and pepper to taste
1 tablespoon minced fresh gingerroot
1 garlic clove, minced
1 tablespoon vegetable oil
1 teaspoon soy sauce

Pan-Fried Trout with Bacon

5 to 6 tablespoons unsalted butter
1 1/2 cups thinly sliced green onions
1/4 cup fresh lemon juice
2 tablespoons rinsed drained capers
1 1/2 tablespoons chopped fresh tarragon, or
    1 1/2 teaspoons dried tarragon
8 slices bacon
4 (8- to 10-ounce) trout fillets, boned
Salt and pepper to taste
Flour

Heat 4 tablespoons of the unsalted butter in a skillet over medium heat. Sauté 1 1/4 cups of the green onions in the butter for 3 minutes. Stir in the lemon juice, capers and tarragon. Remove from the heat. Cover to keep warm.

Fry the bacon in a large skillet for 8 minutes or until crisp. Remove the bacon to a paper towel to drain, reserving the pan drippings. Crumble the bacon and add to the green onion mixture.

Sprinkle the fillets with salt and pepper and coat the fish with flour, shaking off the excess. Drain all but 3 tablespoons of the reserved pan drippings. Add 1 tablespoon of the unsalted butter to the pan drippings. Heat over medium heat until the butter melts. Arrange 2 of the fillets skin side up in the skillet. Cook for 2 minutes; turn. Cook for 2 minutes longer or just until opaque in the center. Remove the fillets to ovenproof serving plates. Keep warm in the oven. Repeat the process with the remaining trout, adding 1 tablespoon unsalted butter to the skillet if needed. Reheat the green onion mixture if needed and spoon over the top of each serving. Sprinkle each with 1 tablespoon of the remaining green onions.

Serves 4

Citrus Ideas

- Float lemon or orange slices in pitchers of water for serving at the table.
- Scoop out oranges, lemons, and limes and insert small votive candles. Trim the bottoms off a bit so they don't topple.
- Use a lemon zester to carve patterns on citrus and pile in a silver bowl as an aromatic centerpiece.

Sole with Almonds, Pine Nuts and Currants

Pine nuts, or pignoli, have a high fat content so it is best to keep them refrigerated or frozen to prevent them from turning rancid.

1 1/2 pounds sole or flounder fillets
Juice and grated zest of 1 lemon
Salt and pepper to taste
2 tablespoons unsalted butter
1/4 cup pine nuts
1/4 cup sliced almonds
1/4 cup dry white wine or sherry
1/4 cup currants or raisins
3 tablespoons apricot jelly or preserves
1/4 cup (1/2 stick) unsalted butter

Arrange the fillets in a single layer in a glass or plastic dish. Drizzle with the lemon juice and sprinkle with the lemon zest, salt and pepper.

Heat 2 tablespoons unsalted butter in a medium skillet. Stir in the pine nuts and almonds. Cook until light brown, stirring frequently. Add the wine, currants and jelly and mix well. Simmer for 3 to 5 minutes or until the sauce is reduced by 1/3, stirring frequently. Remove from the heat. Cover to keep warm. Heat 1/4 cup unsalted butter in a large skillet over medium heat. Add the fillets. Sauté for 3 minutes per side. Remove the fillets to a serving platter. Drizzle with the sauce. Serve immediately.

Serves 4

Grilled Swordfish

6 (6-ounce) swordfish, halibut or mahimahi
   fillets
1/2 cup soy sauce
1/2 cup sherry
1/4 cup vegetable oil
1 1/2 tablespoons lemon juice
1 garlic clove, crushed or minced
Grilled Pineapple Salsa (page 195)
Cilantro Tomato Salsa (page 195)

Arrange the fillets in a single layer in a shallow dish. Mix the soy sauce, sherry, oil, lemon juice and garlic in a bowl. Pour the soy sauce mixture over the fillets, turning to coat. Marinate, covered, in the refrigerator for 1 to 2 hours, turning occasionally.

Brush the grill rack with additional oil. Arrange the fillets on the prepared grill rack. Grill over medium-high heat for 6 to 8 minutes per side or until the fillets flake easily and the center is opaque. Serve alone or with Grilled Pineapple Salsa or Cilantro Tomato Salsa.

Serves 6

Grilled Pineapple Salsa

1 medium pineapple, peeled and cut into
 1/2-inch rounds
3/4 cup finely chopped red onion
3/4 cup chopped fresh cilantro or mint, or a
 combination of the two
1 or 2 jalapeño chiles, seeded and minced
1 teaspoon sugar
1 garlic clove, minced
1/4 teaspoon salt

Arrange the pineapple rounds on an oiled grill rack. Grill over medium heat for 10 minutes or until light brown on both sides. Cool the pineapple and finely chop, discarding the tough center core.

Combine the pineapple, onion, cilantro, jalapeño chiles, sugar, garlic and salt in a bowl and mix well. Marinate at room temperature for 2 hours or longer, stirring occasionally. You may store, covered, in the refrigerator for up to 3 days.

Serves 6

Cilantro Tomato Salsa

1/2 cup finely chopped red onion
1/2 cup fresh cilantro, chopped
1 medium tomato, chopped
1 avocado, chopped
Juice of 1 large lime
2 garlic cloves, minced
1 jalapeño chile, seeded and minced (optional)
1 teaspoon olive oil

Combine the onion, cilantro, tomato, avocado, lime juice, garlic, jalapeño chile and olive oil in a bowl and mix well. Let stand at room temperature for 30 minutes to allow the flavors to blend.

Serves 6

Coring Pineapple Rings

Remove the hard central core and trim the edges of fresh pineapple slices with metal cookie cutters. Use a small, round cookie cutter to stamp out the central core, and a large one to trim the skin and remove the "eyes" from the slice.

Grilled Swordfish Tostados with Black Beans

Avocado Salsa

    1 cup commercially prepared salsa verde
    1 avocado, chopped
    1/3 cup chopped fresh cilantro

Black Beans

    1 tablespoon olive oil
    1 jalapeño chile, seeded and minced
    1 teaspoon cumin
    1/2 teaspoon chili powder
    1 (15- to 16-ounce) can black beans, drained
        and rinsed
    3 tablespoons sour cream

Tostados

    2 (12-ounce) swordfish, halibut or mahimahi
        steaks
    1 medium red onion, cut into 1/3-inch slices
    1 red bell pepper, cut into 1/3-inch rings
    1 yellow bell pepper, cut into 1/3-inch rings
    1 cup fresh lime juice
    1/2 cup olive oil
    Salt and pepper to taste
    4 (7-inch) flour tortillas

For the salsa, combine the salsa verde, avocado and cilantro in a bowl and mix gently. Chill, covered, for up to 3 hours.

For the beans, heat the olive oil in a heavy saucepan over low heat. Stir in the jalapeño chile. Sauté for 3 minutes or until tender. Add the cumin and chili powder and mix well. Sauté for 20 seconds. Stir in the beans and sour cream. Cook for 3 minutes or until heated through, mashing the beans lightly with a spoon and stirring frequently. You may prepare up to 1 day in advance and store, covered, in the refrigerator. Reheat before serving.

For the tostados, arrange the swordfish, onion and bell peppers in a shallow dish or place in a sealable plastic bag. Whisk the lime juice and olive oil in a bowl. Pour the lime juice mixture over the swordfish mixture. Marinate, covered, in the refrigerator for 1 to 4 hours, turning occasionally. Drain, discarding the marinade.

Grill the swordfish over medium-high heat for 5 minutes per side or just until cooked through. Cut the swordfish into 1-inch cubes and place on a serving platter. Cover to keep warm. Grill the onion and bell peppers in a grill basket over medium-high heat for 4 minutes per side or until golden brown and tender. The vegetables may be sautéed in a skillet if desired. Grill the tortillas for 1 minute or until crisp.

To serve, place 1 tortilla on each of 4 serving plates. Layer each tortilla with 1/4 of the bean mixture, 1/4 of the vegetables and 1/4 of the swordfish. Spoon some of the salsa over the top of each. Serve immediately.

Serves 4

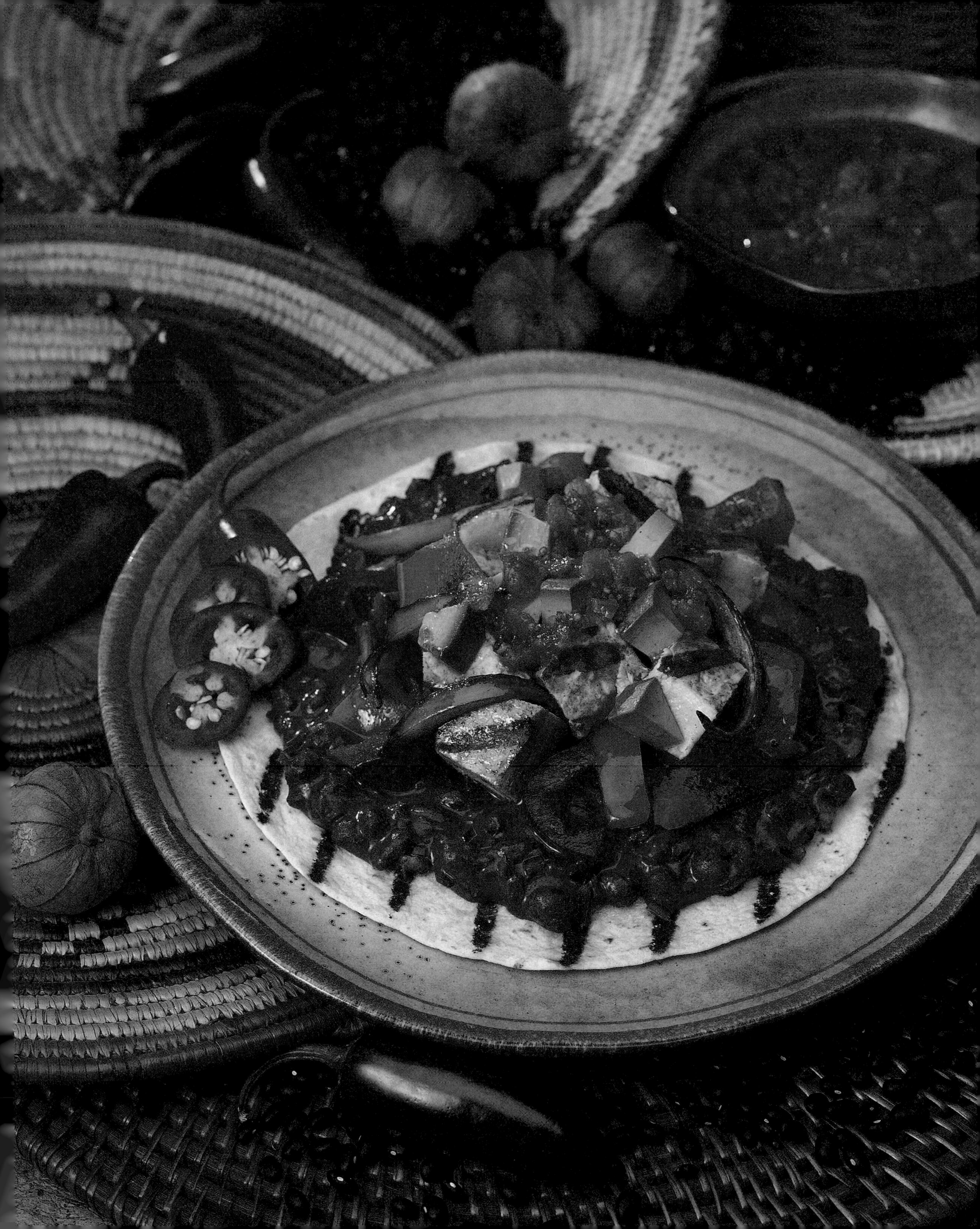

contents

200   Chicken and Shrimp Pad Thai

201   Thai Sweet-and-Sour Sauce

201   Pasta Portofino

202   Malay Curried Noodles

203   Tagliatelle with Mussels, Clams and Pesto

204   Chilled Hunan Noodles

205   Mint and Scallion Soba Noodles

205   Chilled Sesame Noodles with Shrimp and Lime

206   Fusilli Rustica

208   Curried Chicken with Fusilli

209   Fusilli with Prosciutto and Gruyère

210   Spaghetti with Chicken and Lemon Caper Cream

210   Thin Spaghetti with Crab, Asparagus and Sun-Dried Tomatoes

211   Triple-Tomato Pasta

212   Farfalle with Asparagus, Roasted Shallots and Bleu Cheese

214   Farfalle with Pan-Seared Tuna, Lemon and Garlic

215   Greek Penne

215   Sausage Fettuccine Torta

216   Artichoke Heart Ravioli with Three-Pepper Sauce

217   Crab, Cheese and Dill Stuffed Shells

218   Tortellini with Roast Beef and Broccoli

219   Autumn Pumpkin Gnocchi with Butter Thyme Sauce

NOODLES

Chicken and Shrimp Pad Thai

7 ounces stir-fry rice noodles (linguini-style)

1/4 cup peanut oil

1 tablespoon coarsely chopped garlic

1 egg, lightly beaten

8 ounces boneless skinless chicken breasts,
cut into bite-size pieces

6 tablespoons fresh lemon juice

2 tablespoons Thai fish sauce

8 ounces deveined peeled cooked medium
shrimp

8 ounces fresh mung bean sprouts, rinsed
and drained

4 green onions with 3 inches green tops,
thinly sliced crosswise

1/3 cup peanuts, coarsely chopped

1/2 cup coarsely chopped fresh cilantro

1 cup Thai Sweet-and-Sour Sauce
(page 201)

Bring a large saucepan of water to a boil. Remove from the heat. Add the rice noodles and mix gently. Let stand for 5 minutes or until tender; drain.

Heat the peanut oil in a wok or large skillet over medium heat. Sauté the garlic in the hot peanut oil for 2 minutes or until golden brown. Add the egg. Stir-fry until cooked through. Add the chicken. Stir-fry until almost tender. Add the noodles and toss to mix.

Stir the lemon juice and fish sauce into the chicken mixture. Add the shrimp, bean sprouts and green onions and toss gently. Stir-fry for 2 minutes or just until heated. Spoon the chicken mixture into a large shallow serving bowl. Sprinkle with the peanuts and cilantro. Serve immediately with small bowls of the sweet-and-sour sauce. You may substitute crab meat for the chicken and/or the shrimp.

Serves 4

Pad Thai Noodles

Also called Banh Pho (Vietnam), these white rice stick noodles are slightly wider than the thread-like rice stick noodles. They are briefly boiled in salted water before being added to many dishes. These noodles are becoming more popular and may be found in Asian markets and in many larger supermarkets.

Thai Sweet-and-Sour Sauce

1 cup rice wine vinegar
1/2 cup water
1/2 cup sugar
1/4 cup packed light brown sugar
1 to 2 tablespoons finely chopped seeded
    fresh red chiles
1 teaspoon salt
1 teaspoon minced garlic
1 teaspoon finely chopped fresh cilantro
    stems and roots, strings removed
1 cup thinly sliced seeded cucumber
8 fresh cilantro leaves

Combine the vinegar, water, sugar, brown sugar, red chiles, salt, garlic and chopped cilantro in a saucepan and mix well. Cook over low heat for 2 minutes, stirring constantly until the sugar dissolves. Pour the sauce into a bowl. Let stand until room temperature.

Add the cucumber slices to the sauce and mix gently. Garnish with the cilantro leaves. Serve immediately. Store leftovers, covered, in the refrigerator.

Makes 2 cups

Pasta Portofino

12 ounces linguini
1 tablespoon olive oil
1/4 cup (1/2 stick) butter
12 green onions, chopped
4 ripe tomatoes, chopped
4 medium shallots, chopped
1/2 cup black olives, sliced
1/2 cup green olives, sliced
Freshly ground pepper to taste
1/2 cup dry white wine
Fresh parsley (optional)

Cook the pasta using package directions; drain. Cover to keep warm. Heat the olive oil in a large skillet over medium-high heat. Add the butter, green onions and tomatoes and mix gently. Sauté for 2 minutes. Add the shallots, black olives, green olives and pepper and mix well. Sauté for 2 minutes longer. Stir in the wine. Reduce the heat to low. Simmer to the desired consistency, adding additional wine if the mixture becomes too dry. Place the pasta in a large serving bowl. Spoon the tomato sauce over the pasta. Garnish with fresh parsley. Serve immediately.

Serves 4

Malay Curried Noodles

4 ounces angel hair pasta
1 egg, lightly beaten
3 tablespoons vegetable oil
1 medium onion, cut into long strips
1 tablespoon curry powder
1 red bell pepper, julienned
1 pound peeled medium shrimp
2 cups bean sprouts
2 green onions, sliced
Salt and pepper to taste
1/4 cup slivered fresh basil leaves

Cook the pasta using package directions until al dente; drain and rinse. Cover to keep warm. Heat a small skillet sprayed with nonstick cooking spray over medium-high heat. Add the egg, tilting the skillet to ensure even coverage. Turn the omelet gently and cook until firm. Cut the omelet into strips and set aside. Heat the oil in a wok or large deep skillet over medium-high heat. Add the onion. Cook for 10 minutes or until tender, stirring frequently. Stir in the curry powder. Cook for 1 minute, stirring constantly. Add the bell pepper and mix well.

Cook for 2 minutes, stirring frequently. Add the shrimp. Sauté for 6 to 8 minutes or until the shrimp turn pink. Add the pasta, bean sprouts and green onions and mix well. Cook just until heated through, stirring frequently. Season with salt and pepper. Serve immediately, topped with egg strips and basil.

Serves 4

Cellophane Noodles

Cellophane noodles are made from the starch of mung beans. Opaque in their dried form, they become clear and gelatin-like once soaked in hot water. These noodles are enjoyed for their texture, because they have virtually no flavor.

Tagliatelle with Mussels, Clams and Pesto

Basil pesto has a tendency to discolor quickly. Adding a little parsley helps to keep the color green without distracting the basil flavor.

16 to 18 littleneck clams, scrubbed

16 to 18 mussels, scrubbed, debearded
   (green-lipped mussels preferred)

1 cup dry white wine

9 ounces fresh tagliatelle or linguini

Salt to taste

6 tablespoons commercially prepared pesto

1/4 cup sliced drained oil-pack sun-dried
   tomatoes

1/4 teaspoon crushed dried red pepper

Black pepper to taste

Combine the clams, mussels and wine in a stockpot. Bring to a boil over medium-high heat. Cook, covered, for 7 minutes or until the shellfish open; discard any shellfish that do not open. Remove the shellfish to a bowl with tongs, reserving the pan juices. Cover the bowl with foil.

Cook the pasta in boiling salted water in a saucepan until al dente. Drain the pasta and return to the saucepan. Add the reserved shellfish juices, pesto, sun-dried tomatoes and red pepper to the pasta and mix gently. Cook over medium heat just until the pesto coats the pasta, stirring frequently. Season with salt and black pepper. Divide the pasta mixture evenly between 4 bowls. Top with the shellfish. Serve immediately.

Serves 4

How to Clean Mussels

Clean mussels just before cooking; once they've been debearded they will start to spoil. Soak mussels in a large bowl of cool water, turning them over with your hands and scrubbing at the dirt on the shells with a hard-bristled brush. Discard any opened mussels. Rinse, change the water, and repeat, if necessary, until the grit is all gone. Tug on the "beard"—the coarse string sticking out of the shell. It should pull away easily.

Chilled Hunan Noodles

10 ounces Chinese wheat noodles
2¹/₂ tablespoons sesame oil
4¹/₂ tablespoons soy sauce
2 tablespoons rice wine vinegar
2 tablespoons sugar
1 tablespoon chili oil
1 teaspoon grated fresh gingerroot
²/₃ cup frozen peas, thawed
²/₃ cup carrots, grated
2 green onions with tops, sliced

Cook the noodles using package directions; drain. Toss the noodles with the sesame oil in a bowl until evenly coated. Whisk the soy sauce, vinegar, sugar, chili oil and gingerroot in a bowl. Pour the soy sauce mixture over the noodle mixture and toss to coat. Chill, covered, in the refrigerator for up to 24 hours.

Add the peas, carrots and green onions to the noodle mixture 2 hours before serving and toss to mix. Chill, covered, until serving time.

For variation, add cooked chicken, beef or shrimp for a picnic entrée.

Serves 6 to 8 as side dish

Mint and Scallion Soba Noodles

Soba noodles are from Asia and are made mostly from buckwheat flour with wheat flour added to it so its gluten helps with their cooking performance. They look like light-gray spaghetti and have a very distinctive hearty flavor.

12 ounces soba noodles (Japanese buckwheat noodles)
1/3 cup unseasoned rice vinegar
1 tablespoon vegetable oil
1 tablespoon soy sauce
1 1/4 teaspoons sugar
Salt to taste
1/2 cup chopped fresh mint
1 1/2 cups thinly sliced scallions with tops

Cook the noodles in boiling water in a saucepan for 5 minutes or just until tender. Drain the noodles in a colander and rinse with cold water to stop the cooking process; drain. Combine the vinegar, oil, soy sauce, sugar and salt in a bowl, stirring until the sugar dissolves. Toss the noodles, mint and scallions in a bowl. Add the soy sauce mixture and toss gently to coat. Great with lamb.

Serves 6

Chilled Sesame Noodles with Shrimp and Lime

Thai fish sauce is an ingredient that is a "must" in Thai cooking. This condiment is very versatile and just a small spoonful makes a world of difference in Thai dishes.

16 ounces fine egg noodles
2 tablespoons Asian sesame oil
1/2 cup smooth natural peanut butter
2 tablespoons fish sauce
2 tablespoons fresh lime juice
1 tablespoon soy sauce
1 tablespoon sugar
1/2 teaspoon hot sauce, or to taste
1 small garlic clove, chopped
1/2 cup (about) hot water
8 ounces shrimp, cooked, peeled, chopped
1 cup mung bean sprouts, chopped
4 green onions with tops, finely chopped
1/4 cup roasted unsalted peanuts, chopped
1 lime, cut into wedges
Fresh lime juice to taste

Cook the noodles using package directions; drain. Toss the noodles with the sesame oil in a bowl. Chill, covered, for at least 2 hours or for up to 24 hours. Combine the peanut butter, fish sauce, 2 tablespoons lime juice, soy sauce, sugar, hot sauce and garlic in a food processor. Process until smooth. Add the hot water 1 tablespoon at a time until the sauce is the consistency of heavy cream, processing constantly. You may cover the sauce at this point and set aside for several hours.

To serve, toss the peanut sauce, chilled noodles, shrimp, bean sprouts and green onions in a bowl until coated. Sprinkle with the peanuts and top with the lime wedges. Drizzle with lime juice to taste.

Serves 4 to 6

Fusilli Rustica

Pancetta is Italian bacon cured with salt and spices (not smoked) and then rolled up into a sausage shape. Its flavor is different from that of ordinary bacon.

1/2 cup extra-virgin olive oil
3 cups thinly sliced yellow onions
2 tablespoons finely chopped flat-leaf parsley
1 teaspoon finely chopped garlic
1/2 teaspoon red pepper flakes
3 ounces pancetta, cut into thin strips
1 large yellow or red bell pepper, or a
    combination of the two, cut into
    1/2-inch strips
1 pound fresh ripe plum tomatoes, peeled,
    seeded, cut into 1/2-inch pieces
1/2 cup pitted green olives or pimento-stuffed
    green olives, thinly sliced
2 tablespoons drained rinsed capers
Salt to taste
2 tablespoons fresh basil, torn
1 teaspoon coarsely chopped fresh oregano
16 ounces fusilli (longer length preferred)
1/4 cup freshly grated Pecorino Romano
1/4 cup freshly grated Parmigiano-Reggiano

Heat the olive oil in a large skillet over medium-low heat. Add the onions. Cook for 10 minutes or until the onions are tender and golden brown, stirring frequently. Increase the heat to medium-high. Stir in the parsley, garlic and red pepper flakes. Sauté for 30 seconds. Add the pancetta and mix well.

Cook until the pancetta is light brown but not crisp, stirring frequently. Stir in the bell pepper. Cook for 5 to 6 minutes or until tender, stirring occasionally. Add the tomatoes and mix well. Cook for 5 to 6 minutes or until most of the liquid has evaporated, stirring frequently. Stir in the olives and capers. Season with salt. Add the basil and oregano and mix well. Cook for 30 seconds. Remove from the heat.

Cook the pasta in boiling salted water in a saucepan until al dente; drain. Remove the pasta to a heated serving bowl. Add the sauce and cheeses and toss to mix. Serve immediately.

You may substitute crumbled crisp-cooked bacon for the pancetta, adding the bacon in the same sequence as the pancetta.

Serves 6

Extra-virgin olive oil is essential when it is the main flavoring agent in a pasta sauce.

Curried Chicken with Fusilli

8 ounces fusilli
1 1/2 pounds boneless skinless chicken thighs, cut into 2-inch pieces
2 tablespoons flour
6 tablespoons vegetable oil
1 cup coarsely chopped red bell pepper
1 tablespoon minced garlic
1 tablespoon curry powder
2 tablespoons flour
2 cups reduced-sodium chicken broth
1 cup whole cashews, roasted and salted
6 ounces (1/2 cup) fresh snow peas, julienned
1/4 cup sliced green onions
3 tablespoons currants
1 cup plain low-fat yogurt, at room temperature

Cook the pasta using package directions; drain. Cover to keep warm. Combine the chicken and 2 tablespoons flour in a sealable plastic bag and seal tightly. Shake to coat the chicken.

Heat 4 tablespoons of the oil in a large skillet over medium heat. Sauté the chicken in the hot oil for 8 minutes or until cooked through and golden brown and crisp on all sides. Drain the chicken on paper towels.

Drain the pan drippings from the skillet. Add the remaining 2 tablespoons oil to the skillet. Sauté the bell pepper, garlic and curry powder in the hot oil for 2 minutes or until the bell pepper is tender. Sprinkle with 2 tablespoons flour and toss to coat. Stir in the broth. Bring to a boil; reduce the heat. Simmer for 15 minutes, stirring occasionally.

Add the chicken, cashews, snow peas, green onions and currants to the sauce and mix well. Cook just until heated through, stirring occasionally. Remove from the heat. Whisk in the yogurt gradually; if the yogurt is cold the mixture will curdle. Add the pasta and toss to coat. Spoon the pasta mixture onto a large serving platter.

Serves 6

An Added Touch!

Use a vegetable peeler and shave large curls of Parmesan cheese to be placed decoratively atop your pasta dishes or salads.

Fusilli with Prosciutto and Gruyère

Prosciutto is an Italian ham that is seasoned, salt-cured, and air-dried. It is pressed into a dense-textured meat and typically sliced thin and eaten uncooked or lightly cooked. Prosciutto is typically found in Italian delis or large supermarkets.

12 ounces fusilli
1 cup milk
2/3 cup half-and-half
5 ounces Gruyère cheese, shredded
3 eggs
1/8 teaspoon nutmeg, or to taste
4 ounces prosciutto, cut into strips
Salt and pepper to taste
2 tablespoons freshly grated Parmesan cheese

Cook the pasta using package directions; drain. Whisk the milk, half-and-half, 1/2 of the Gruyère cheese, eggs and nutmeg in a bowl until mixed.

Layer the pasta and prosciutto 1/2 at a time in a buttered 8×8-inch baking pan. Pour the egg mixture over the prepared layers and stir just until slightly mixed. Season with salt and pepper. Sprinkle with the remaining Gruyère cheese and the Parmesan cheese.

Bake, covered, at 375 degrees for 20 minutes; remove the cover. Bake for 5 to 10 minutes longer or until golden brown. Serve immediately with a salad for a complete meal.

Serves 4

A Little Music with Dinner

A successful dinner party depends on the right mix of guests and menu. But don't forget that there is another element that can make your evening memorable—the music. For an outdoor summer party, try some bold and fun South American music. For a formal sit-down dinner, experiment with some calming classical piano or instrumentals. The most important thing to remember though is not to compete with the music, but rather just let it complement a wonderful time of conversing with your family and friends.

Spaghetti with Chicken and Lemon Caper Cream

1/4 cup (1/2 stick) unsalted butter
4 medium shallots, finely chopped
1 pound boneless skinless chicken breasts, cut
    crosswise into 1/2-inch strips
1/2 cup lemon juice
2 cups heavy cream
1/4 cup rinsed drained capers, or to taste
12 ounces thin spaghetti, cooked and drained
1/3 cup chopped fresh parsley

Heat the unsalted butter in a large skillet over medium heat. Sauté the shallots in the butter for 1 minute. Increase the heat to high. Add the chicken. Sauté for 3 to 5 minutes or until light brown. Stir in the lemon juice. Cook until most of the liquid has evaporated, stirring with a wooden spoon to dislodge any browned bits. Stir in the cream.

Bring to a gentle boil. Boil for 10 to 12 minutes or until thickened, stirring frequently. Stir in the capers. Spoon the sauce over the hot spaghetti on a serving platter. Sprinkle with the parsley.

Serves 4

Thin Spaghetti with Crab, Asparagus and Sun-Dried Tomatoes

1/4 cup olive oil
3 medium garlic cloves, minced
2 cups chopped fresh tomatoes
3/4 cup drained oil-pack sun-dried tomatoes,
    sliced
3/4 teaspoon crushed dried red pepper
Salt and black pepper to taste
1 pound fresh asparagus, trimmed and cut
    diagonally into 1 1/2-inch pieces
12 ounces thin spaghetti
8 ounces mascarpone cheese
8 ounces fresh crab meat
1/4 cup fresh basil, thinly sliced

Heat the olive oil in a large heavy skillet over medium-high heat. Sauté the garlic in the hot olive oil for 2 minutes. Stir in the fresh tomatoes, sun-dried tomatoes and red pepper. Simmer, covered, for 5 minutes or until the sun-dried tomatoes soften, stirring occasionally. Season with salt and black pepper.

Cook the asparagus in boiling salted water in a saucepan until tender-crisp. Remove the asparagus to the skillet with the tomato sauce, reserving the liquid. Return the reserved liquid to a boil. Add the pasta. Cook just until tender but still firm, stirring occasionally; drain. Bring the tomato sauce to a simmer, stirring occasionally. Stir in the mascarpone cheese. Add the pasta and crab meat and toss just to warm. Divide the pasta equally among serving plates. Sprinkle with the basil.

Serves 4 to 6

Triple-Tomato Pasta

Use only the freshest, most flavorful summer tomatoes.

Balsamic Vinaigrette
1/4 cup olive oil

3 tablespoons white balsamic vinegar or dark balsamic vinegar (white is preferred)

2 tablespoons fresh lemon juice

1/8 teaspoon salt

Freshly ground pepper to taste

Pasta
16 ounces campanelle or other curly pasta

12 ounces ripe red tomatoes, chopped

12 ounces ripe yellow tomatoes or yellow pear tomatoes, chopped

1 (8-ounce) jar oil-pack sun-dried tomatoes, drained

3 or 4 green onions with tops, chopped

1/4 cup chopped fresh flat-leaf parsley

2 tablespoons chopped fresh basil

2 large avocados

Salt to taste

For the vinaigrette, whisk the olive oil, balsamic vinegar, lemon juice, salt and pepper in a bowl.

For the pasta, cook the pasta using package directions until al dente. Drain and rinse with cold water; drain. Place the pasta in a large serving bowl. Add the red tomatoes, yellow tomatoes, sun-dried tomatoes, green onions, parsley and basil and mix gently. Add the vinaigrette and toss to coat. Peel the avocados, chop and sprinkle with salt. Add the avocados to the pasta mixture just before serving and toss to mix. Serve at room temperature.

Wine recommendation, serve with an Italian Sangiovese, "Rubizzo" from Rocca della Macie.

Serves 8 to 10

Beverage Tips

• Carbonated beverages need very little stirring and certainly no shaking. A few turns of a swizzle will distribute the bubbles; more agitation and they'll go flat.
• A cold drink in a frosty glass is heaven on a hot day. Arrange glasses upside down in a bucket of ice next to the beverages.
• For a fun way to dress up the standard Mimosa, try coating the glass rims with sugar. Simply moisten the rims with a cut lemon and dip into a plate of sugar. Garnish with an edible flower.

Farfalle with Asparagus, Roasted Shallots and Bleu Cheese

12 medium shallots, cut lengthwise into halves
3 tablespoons olive oil
Salt and pepper to taste
1 cup fresh bread crumbs (made from French bread)
1 pound fresh thin asparagus spears, trimmed and cut diagonally into 1½-inch pieces
12 ounces farfalle (bow tie)
4 ounces creamy bleu cheese, Saga bleu cheese or Gorgonzola cheese

Toss the shallots with 1 tablespoon of the olive oil on a baking sheet. Spread in a single layer. Sprinkle with salt and pepper. Bake at 375 degrees for 35 minutes or until tender and golden brown, stirring occasionally.

Sauté the bread crumbs in the remaining 2 tablespoons olive oil in a skillet over medium heat for 4 minutes or until brown. The shallots and bread crumbs may be prepared up to 8 hours in advance and stored separately in closed containers at room temperature.

Steam the asparagus until tender-crisp; drain. Cook the pasta using package directions until al dente; drain. Place the hot pasta in a large serving bowl. Add the bleu cheese, shallots and asparagus immediately. Toss until the cheese melts. Season with salt and pepper. Sprinkle with the bread crumbs.

Serves 6

Making Bread Crumbs

Bread that is day old works the best. Cut off the crusts and crumble the bread between your fingers, or put chunks of bread in the food processor and pulse for a moment. Alternatively, you can dry out slices of bread in the oven, then crush them with a rolling pin. It's useful to have both fresh and dried bread crumbs available.

Farfalle with Pan-Seared Tuna, Lemon and Garlic

1 (12-ounce) tuna steak, 1¹/2 inches thick
3 teaspoons olive oil
3 garlic cloves, minced
Salt and black pepper to taste
12 ounces farfalle (bow tie)
¹/4 teaspoon red pepper flakes, or to taste
Finely grated zest of 1 lemon
2 tablespoons fresh lemon juice
20 kalamata olives or other brine-cured olives,
     slivered
¹/2 cup coarsely chopped fresh flat-leaf parsley

Pat the tuna dry with paper towels. Rub ¹/2 teaspoon of the olive oil and ¹/2 teaspoon of the minced garlic over the surface of the tuna. Chill, covered, for 20 minutes. Heat an ovenproof skillet over high heat until hot. Add ¹/2 teaspoon of the olive oil, tilting the skillet to coat the bottom evenly.

Season the tuna with salt and black pepper. Brown the tuna on both sides in the hot oil for 5 minutes. Place the skillet on the middle oven rack. Roast at 400 degrees for 10 minutes or just until the tuna is cooked through; the time will depend on the thickness of the steak. Remove the tuna to a cutting board and flake into bite-size pieces. Place in a bowl and cover to keep warm.

Cook the pasta in boiling salted water in a 6-quart stockpot until al dente. Drain the pasta, reserving 1 cup of the liquid. Sauté the remaining garlic and red pepper flakes in the remaining 2 teaspoons olive oil in a small skillet over medium-high heat for 1 minute or until the garlic is light brown. Remove from the heat. Toss the pasta with the tuna, ²/3 cup of the reserved liquid, lemon zest, lemon juice, sautéed garlic mixture, olives, parsley, salt and black pepper in a serving bowl, adding the remaining ¹/3 cup reserved liquid if needed for the desired consistency. Serve immediately.

Serves 4

Never rinse drained semolina pasta under running water when finished cooking. This only cools it down, makes it taste watery, and removes some of the starch coating that helps the sauce adhere to the noodles.

Greek Penne

8 ounces penne
1/4 cup extra-virgin olive oil
3 tablespoons red wine vinegar
1 (14-ounce) can artichoke hearts, drained
    and sliced
1 (14-ounce) can hearts of palm, drained and
    sliced
4 medium Roma tomatoes, coarsely chopped
1 medium cucumber, peeled and sliced
1/4 cup kalamata olives, sliced
2 tablespoons rinsed drained capers
1 teaspoon dill weed
Salt and pepper to taste
4 ounces fresh feta cheese, crumbled
Chopped fresh parsley
1 avocado, chopped

Cook the pasta in a saucepan using package directions; drain. Rinse the pasta with cold water and drain. Return the pasta to the saucepan. Add the olive oil and vinegar and toss to coat. Add the artichokes, hearts of palm, tomatoes, cucumber, olives, capers and dill weed and mix well. Season with salt and pepper. Toss to mix well.

Spoon the pasta salad into a serving bowl. Sprinkle with the cheese and parsley. Arrange the chopped avocado over the top. Serve chilled or at room temperature.

Serves 4 to 6

Sausage Fettuccine Torta

16 ounces fettuccine
2 tablespoons butter
1 pound Italian sausage
1 medium onion, chopped
1 green bell pepper, chopped
1/4 cup fresh parsley and fresh basil, mixed
3 eggs, beaten
3 or 4 tomatoes, sliced
1/2 cup (2 ounces) shredded Gruyère cheese
1/2 cup (2 ounces) shredded mozzarella cheese
2 tablespoons grated Parmesan cheese

Butter and flour a springform pan. Cook the pasta using package directions until al dente; drain. Toss the hot pasta with 2 tablespoons butter in a large bowl.

Brown the sausage in a skillet, stirring until crumbly; drain. Add the onion and bell pepper and mix well. Cook for 5 minutes, stirring frequently. Stir in the parsley mixture. Remove from the heat.

Add the eggs to the pasta mixture and mix well. Stir in the sausage mixture. Pat 1/2 of the pasta mixture over the bottom of the prepared springform pan. Layer with 1/2 of the tomatoes. Sprinkle with the Gruyère cheese and mozzarella cheese. Layer with the remaining pasta mixture and remaining tomatoes. Sprinkle with the Parmesan cheese. Bake, covered with foil, at 375 degrees for 50 minutes or until set. Slice into wedges to serve.

Serves 6 to 8

Artichoke Heart Ravioli with Three-Pepper Sauce

Cheese Filling

1/2 cup (2 ounces) shredded fontina cheese
2 tablespoons mild soft goat cheese such as Montrachet
1/4 cup finely chopped drained marinated artichoke hearts
Freshly ground pepper to taste

Three-Pepper Sauce

3 medium red, yellow or orange bell peppers, julienned
1 tablespoon olive oil
1 cup chicken broth
1 garlic clove, chopped

Ravioli

24 to 30 won ton wrappers
Salt to taste
Grated Parmesan cheese
Chopped flat-leaf parsley

For the filling, combine the fontina cheese, goat cheese, artichokes and pepper in a bowl and mix well. Chill, covered, for 1 hour or until cold.

For the sauce, cook the bell peppers in the olive oil in a skillet over medium-low heat until tender and slightly darkened. Stir in 1/2 cup of the broth and garlic. Simmer for 15 minutes, stirring occasionally. Remove 2 tablespoons of the bell peppers to a bowl with a slotted spoon and set aside. Spoon the remaining bell pepper mixture into a blender. Add the remaining 1/2 cup broth. Process until puréed. Pour the purée into a small saucepan. Cover and keep warm over low heat.

For the ravioli, place 1 of the won ton wrappers on a lightly floured surface. Spoon 1 teaspoon of the filling in the center of the won ton wrapper. Brush the edges lightly with water. Layer with another won ton wrapper, pressing down around the filling to force out any air. Trim to within 1/4-inch of the filling and seal the edges. Place on a clean tea towel to drain and slightly dry, turning occasionally. Repeat the process with the remaining won ton wrappers and remaining filling.

Bring a large saucepan of salted water to a gentle boil. Carefully add the ravioli to the boiling water. Boil for 2 minutes or until the ravioli rise to the surface and are tender. Do not let the water boil vigorously. Remove the ravioli to a tea towel to drain. Arrange the ravioli on serving plates. Drizzle with the sauce and sprinkle with the reserved bell peppers, Parmesan cheese and chopped parsley. Serve with crusty bread and a green salad for a complete meal.

Makes 12 to 15 ravioli

Crab, Cheese and Dill Stuffed Shells

20 to 22 jumbo pasta shells
6 ounces fresh or thawed frozen crab meat,
    drained and patted dry
15 ounces ricotta cheese
2/3 cup shredded mozzarella cheese
1/4 cup chopped fresh dill weed
2 green onions, sliced
1 egg, beaten
1/4 teaspoon freshly ground pepper
Salt to taste
2 tablespoons olive oil
1 small onion, minced
1 garlic clove, minced
2 (14-ounce) cans tomato purée
1 or 2 tomatoes, peeled, seeded, chopped
Chopped fresh dill weed to taste

Cook the pasta shells in boiling water in a stockpot until tender; drain. Rinse the shells with cold water and drain. Spread the shells on a clean tea towel or waxed paper to drain and dry.

Combine the crab meat, ricotta cheese, mozzarella cheese, 1/4 cup dill weed, green onions, egg, pepper and salt in a bowl and mix gently. Stuff about 2 1/2 tablespoons of the crab meat mixture into each pasta shell.

Heat the olive oil in a skillet. Sauté the onion and garlic in the hot oil until the onion is tender. Stir in the tomato purée and tomatoes. Spread 1/2 of the tomato sauce in the bottom of a 9×13-inch baking dish. Arrange the stuffed shells over the prepared layer. Top with the remaining tomato sauce. Bake, loosely covered with foil, at 350 degrees for 20 minutes or until heated through. Garnish each shell with dill weed to taste.

Serves 6

Tortellini with Roast Beef and Broccoli

Red Wine Vinaigrette
1/3 cup olive oil
3 tablespoons red wine vinegar
1/2 teaspoon salt
1/4 teaspoon coarsely ground pepper
1 garlic clove, crushed

Tortellini
9 ounces fresh or frozen cheese tortellini
2 cups broccoli florets and stems
    (1-inch pieces)
12 ounces (1/2-inch-thick) cooked roast beef,
    cut into 1/4×2-inch strips
1/2 cup thinly slivered red onion
1/2 cup thinly slivered red bell pepper
1/4 cup kalamata olives, pitted
2 tablespoons coarsely chopped fresh
    flat-leaf parsley

For the vinaigrette, whisk the olive oil, vinegar, salt, pepper and garlic in a bowl until mixed.

For the tortellini, cook the tortellini using package directions until al dente; drain. Rinse the tortellini with cool water and drain in a colander until dry. Steam the broccoli and broccoli stems for 3 minutes or until tender-crisp; drain. Let stand until cool.

Combine the tortellini, broccoli, beef, onion, bell pepper, olives and parsley in a large bowl and mix gently. Pour the vinaigrette over the pasta mixture and toss gently to coat. Let stand at room temperature for 30 minutes before serving. You may prepare in advance and store, covered, in the refrigerator. This is a great recipe to use leftover roast beef or deli roast beef.

Serves 4

When stuffing shells or manicotti, coat the filled shells with tomato sauce. The sauce helps to keep them moist. Also, covering the baking dish with foil will keep the pasta moist.

Autumn Pumpkin Gnocchi with Butter Thyme Sauce

Gnocchi, made either from flour, from flour and potatoes, or from semolina, are little cakes or dumpling-like pasta nuggets that are sauced and treated very much like pasta.

Pumpkin Gnocchi

    1 (15-ounce) can pumpkin
    2 tablespoons butter
    1¼ cups flour
    1 egg, lightly beaten
    1 egg yolk, lightly beaten
    1 teaspoon nutmeg
    Salt and freshly ground pepper to taste
    5 cups chicken broth

Butter Thyme Sauce and Assembly

    ⅓ cup butter
    2 tablespoons chopped fresh thyme
    Freshly grated Parmesan cheese
    Sprig of thyme

For the gnocchi, combine the pumpkin and butter in a saucepan. Cook over low heat until thickened, stirring frequently. Remove from the heat. Add the flour, egg, egg yolk, nutmeg, salt and pepper gradually, stirring constantly until a soft dough forms.

Shape 1 to 1½ tablespoons of the dough into a flat disk with floured hands. Place the disk on a baking sheet and press with a fork to indent. Repeat the process with the remaining dough. Bring the broth to a boil in a large stockpot. Drop the gnocchi 12 at a time into the boiling broth. Boil until they rise to the surface. Remove the gnocchi to a bowl using a slotted spoon. Repeat the process with the remaining dough.

For the sauce, combine the butter and chopped thyme in a small saucepan. Simmer over low heat for 2 minutes, stirring frequently.

To serve, spoon the sauce over the gnocchi in a serving bowl. Sprinkle with Parmesan cheese and garnish with a sprig of thyme.

Serves 2 to 4 as main dish, 4 to 6 as side dish

CONTENTS

222 Herb Dumplings with Baby Spinach
224 Country French Onion Gratin
225 Ginger Island Gumbo
226 Rustic Cherry Tomato Melt
227 Soft Polenta with Caramelized Onions, Garlic and Spinach
228 Feta Cheese Polenta with Two-Tomato Salsa
229 Pesto Mozzarella Panini Skewers
229 The Big Veg
230 Herb Shiitake Mushroom Burgers
231 Sautéed Vegetable Wraps with Garlic Bean Purée
232 Spicy Asian Wraps
232 Cherry Tofu Lettuce Wraps
234 Asian Pan-Fried Tofu
234 Silken Tofu Fettuccine
235 Tuscan Cauliflower Rigatoni
236 "Soon To Be Your Favorite" Spaghetti
237 Herb Fontina Orecchiette
238 Mediterranean Risotto and Zucchini Cakes
239 Wild Mushroom Risotto
240 Twice-Baked Harvest Squash
242 Spaghetti Squash Lasagna
243 Coconut Lime Summer Squash Sauté
244 Chanterelle and Portobello Mushrooms in Puff Pastry
245 Savory Stuffed Portobello Mushrooms
246 Thai Peanut Stir-Fry
248 Ultimate Pizza Crust
249 Pizza Dell' Erba di Pesto
249 Pizza Marguerite

VEGETARIAN

Herb Dumplings with Baby Spinach

You can use any of your favorite fresh herbs for the dumplings. This is a light, healthy, and satisfying dish.

1 cup flour
1¹/2 tablespoons minced fresh herbs
1 teaspoon baking powder
¹/2 teaspoon salt
1¹/2 teaspoons shortening
¹/2 cup milk or soy milk
6 cups vegetable broth
4 cups fresh baby spinach

Combine the flour, herbs, baking powder and salt in a bowl and mix well. Cut in the shortening until crumbly. Add the milk and stir with a wooden spoon until mixed. Place the dough on a lightly floured surface. Knead for 1 minute. Pat the dough into a ¹/2-inch-thick rectangle. Cut into 32 pieces.

Bring the broth to a simmer in a stockpot. Add the dough pieces. Cook, covered, for 10 to 13 minutes; do not remove the lid until the dumplings are cooked through. Fold in the spinach with a heatproof rubber spatula. Cook for 1 to 2 minutes. Serve immediately.

Serves 4

Have Too Many Fresh Herbs?

Try making a centerpiece with the extra herbs from your garden. Mix different shapes and textures and add color with edible flowers and herb blossoms. Or, try washing herbs and patting them dry. Remove the leaves and discard the stems. Chop finely in a food processor and slowly drizzle in olive oil until it becomes a paste. Spoon into ice cube trays and freeze for a few hours. Remove from trays and store in freezer bags. Use in sauces, soups, and stews.

Country French Onion Gratin

This French onion soup is unique in that it uses vegetable broth.

Garlic Croutons

 6 (¼-inch-thick) slices French bread
 2 tablespoons butter, melted
 2 tablespoons extra-virgin olive oil
 1 teaspoon garlic salt

Soup

 2 pounds sweet onions, cut into quarters
  and thinly sliced
 ¼ cup (½ stick) butter
 8 cups vegetable broth
 ¼ cup dry sherry
 1 (¾-ounce) package dried shiitake
  mushrooms
 1 large bay leaf
 1 teaspoon kosher salt
 1 teaspoon paprika
 ½ teaspoon steak seasoning
 6 slices smoked provolone cheese

For the croutons, brush both sides of the bread slices with a mixture of the butter and olive oil. Sprinkle each side with garlic salt. Arrange the slices in a single layer on a baking sheet. Toast at 400 degrees for 10 to 12 minutes or until golden brown, turning once.

For the soup, cook the onions in the butter in a skillet over medium heat for 35 to 40 minutes or until tender and caramelized, stirring occasionally. Add the broth, sherry, mushrooms, bay leaf, salt, paprika and steak seasoning. Bring to a simmer. Simmer for 30 to 40 minutes or to the desired consistency, stirring occasionally. Discard the bay leaf.

Ladle the soup into ovenproof soup bowls and place the bowls on a baking sheet. Top each serving with 1 garlic crouton and 1 slice of cheese. Broil until brown and bubbly. Serve immediately.

Serves 6

Onions

There are many varieties of onions available now. Try some of the sweeter types depending on the season and region: Torpedo, Vidalia, Maui, Walla Walla, and Cippolini.

Ginger Island Gumbo

Spicy and sweet, this combination of flavors is quite refreshing. This is a great vegan choice. It is recommended that you wear plastic gloves when handling the jalapeño chile.

1 tablespoon extra-virgin olive oil
1 cup chopped red onion
1/2 cup chopped red bell pepper
1/2 cup chopped yellow bell pepper
1 jalapeño chile, seeded and minced
2 teaspoons minced garlic
1 tablespoon minced fresh gingerroot
1/2 teaspoon thyme
1/2 teaspoon allspice
1 (15-ounce) can black beans, drained and rinsed
1 (15-ounce) can black-eyed peas, drained and rinsed
1 cup fresh or frozen okra, cut into 1/2 inch pieces
1/3 cup fresh orange juice
1/3 cup jalapeño pepper jelly
1 (11-ounce) can mandarin orange sections, drained
3 cups cooked basmati rice or jasmine rice

Heat the olive oil in a large skillet over medium-high heat. Sauté the onion, bell peppers, jalapeño chile and garlic in the hot oil for 6 minutes or until tender. Stir in the gingerroot, thyme and allspice.

Cook for 3 minutes, stirring frequently. Add the beans, peas, okra, orange juice and jelly and mix well. Bring to a boil; reduce the heat. Simmer for 10 minutes or until the okra is tender, stirring occasionally. Stir in the orange sections. Cook for 2 minutes longer, stirring frequently. Spoon over the hot cooked rice on a serving platter.

Serves 4

Seeding a Bell Pepper

To make quick work of seeding a bell pepper, simply set the pepper on a cutting surface stem side up. Slice off the four sides, which will fall away to leave the stem, membranes, and seeds standing. Discard the stem, membranes, and seeds and cut the pepper pieces into strips.

Rustic Cherry Tomato Melt

This makes an especially good main course when the tomato harvest comes in! Use yellow pear cherries for added color. Dice tomatoes and use on small bread rounds for a delicious appetizer.

2 pints cherry tomatoes, cut into halves
2 green onions, coarsely chopped
1/4 cup fresh parsley, minced
1 tablespoon minced fresh rosemary
3 garlic cloves, minced
1/3 cup extra-virgin olive oil
3 tablespoons balsamic vinegar
Salt and freshly ground pepper to taste
4 to 6 tablespoons extra-virgin olive oil
3 garlic cloves, minced
4 (1 1/2-inch-thick) slices crusty bread
4 slices provolone cheese
1/4 cup shredded Parmesan cheese

Toss the tomatoes, green onions, parsley, rosemary and 3 garlic cloves in a bowl. Add 1/3 cup olive oil and the balsamic vinegar and mix well. Season with salt and pepper. Marinate, covered, at room temperature for 1 hour, stirring occasionally.

Combine 4 to 6 tablespoons olive oil and 3 garlic cloves in a bowl and mix well. Let stand for 10 minutes. Brush 1 side of each bread slice with the olive oil mixture. Arrange the slices olive oil side up in a single layer on a baking sheet. Broil until light brown.

Top each slice with 1 slice of the provolone cheese and a generous sprinkling of the Parmesan cheese. Broil until bubbly. Place each bread slice in a shallow bowl. Top each serving with 3/4 cup of the tomato mixture. Sprinkle with the remaining Parmesan cheese. Serve immediately.

Serves 4

Wild Mushrooms

To store fresh, wild mushrooms, arrange them in a single layer on a paper plate and cover with a damp paper towel. Before using, wipe the mushrooms with another damp towel and dry thoroughly. It is best not to soak them in water as this can make the mushrooms mushy.

Soft Polenta with Caramelized Onions, Garlic and Spinach

This is a fresh yet hearty entrée. For a vegan choice, substitute extra-virgin olive oil for the butter.

Soft Polenta

    2 cups vegetable broth
    2 cups water
    1 cup medium-ground cornmeal
    1/4 cup (1/2 stick) butter
    1 teaspoon salt
    1 teaspoon sugar

Spinach and Onion Topping

    1/4 cup extra-virgin olive oil
    2 medium onions, thinly sliced
    6 garlic cloves, slivered
    1 1/2 pounds baby spinach, trimmed
    3/4 teaspoon salt

For the polenta, bring the broth and water to a boil in a large saucepan over high heat. Add the cornmeal in a steady stream to the boiling broth mixture, whisking constantly until smooth. Reduce the heat.

Simmer for 20 to 30 minutes or to the desired consistency, stirring occasionally. Remove from the heat. Stir in the butter, salt and sugar. Cover to keep warm.

For the topping, heat the olive oil in a large saucepan over medium heat. Sauté the onions in the hot oil for 5 to 8 minutes or until tender. Stir in the garlic. Sauté until the garlic is golden brown. Add the spinach and mix well. Sauté for 1 minute. Sprinkle with the salt. Spoon the topping over the polenta on a serving platter.

Serves 4

Leftover Polenta

If you have any leftover polenta, you can enjoy it by frying squares of it in olive oil until golden brown on each side. Serve with sprinkled, freshly grated Parmesan cheese.

Feta Cheese Polenta with Two-Tomato Salsa

While this polenta is wonderful lightly warmed when serving, the salsa is best at room temperature.

Two-Tomato Salsa

1/4 cup sun-dried tomatoes, chopped

1 fresh medium tomato, coarsely chopped

1/4 cup fresh basil, chopped

1/3 cup kalamata olives or other black olives, chopped

3 tablespoons balsamic vinegar

1 garlic clove, minced

1/4 teaspoon sugar

1/4 teaspoon salt

1/4 teaspoon pepper

Polenta

3 cups vegetable broth

1 cup yellow cornmeal

4 ounces feta cheese, crumbled

1/2 teaspoon salt

For the salsa, reconstitute the sun-dried tomatoes in hot water in a bowl; drain. Combine the sun-dried tomatoes, fresh tomato, basil, olives, balsamic vinegar, garlic, sugar, salt and pepper in a bowl and mix well. Let stand at room temperature for 20 minutes to allow the flavors to blend, stirring occasionally.

For the polenta, bring the broth to a boil in a large saucepan over high heat. Add the cornmeal to the boiling broth in a steady stream, whisking constantly until smooth. Reduce the heat.

Simmer for 20 minutes, stirring frequently to prevent the polenta from sticking. Be aware that as the mixture thickens it takes on volcanic qualities. Remove the polenta from the heat. Stir in the cheese. Add the salt and mix well.

Spoon the polenta into a greased 8-inch baking pan, leveling the top with a palette knife. Cool for 10 minutes or until firm. Cut into 6 wedges. Spoon some of the salsa over each serving. You may sauté the wedges in extra-virgin olive oil until golden brown if you prefer a crispy edge.

Serves 6

What is Broccolini?

Broccolini is the trademarked name for a cross between broccoli and Chinese kale. This bright green vegetable has long, tender stalks topped with a bouquet of tiny buds reminiscent of a miniature broccoli head. The flavor is sweet with a subtle, peppery edge; the texture is slightly crunchy.

Pesto Mozzarella Panini Skewers

You need to eat this "sideway sandwich" with a knife and fork. It is a simple dinner that makes quite an impression. Complete the meal with a leafy green salad.

Pesto Sauce

2 cups firmly packed fresh basil leaves

2 1/2 tablespoons pine nuts

2 medium garlic cloves

1/2 cup extra-virgin olive oil

1/3 cup freshly grated Parmesan cheese

Salt to taste

Mozzarella Panini

1 pound fresh water-pack mozzarella cheese

1 French baguette, cut into sixteen
   1/2-inch slices

1/3 cup extra-virgin olive oil

Salt and freshly ground pepper to taste

For the sauce, combine the basil, pine nuts and garlic in a food processor. Process until the mixture is finely ground, scraping the side of the bowl occasionally. Add the olive oil gradually, processing constantly until smooth. Pour the sauce into a bowl. Stir in the cheese and season with salt.

For the panini, remove the mozzarella cheese from the water and pat dry with paper towels. Cut the mozzarella cheese into twelve 1/4-inch slices. Thread 4 slices of the bread and 3 slices of the cheese on each of 4 skewers, beginning and ending with the bread. Brush a medium baking sheet with 1 tablespoon of the olive oil. Arrange the skewers on the prepared baking sheet and brush with the remaining olive oil. Sprinkle with salt and pepper.

Bake at 450 degrees for 4 to 5 minutes or just until the edges of the bread turn golden brown. Do not overbake or the cheese may become runny. Slide the sandwiches from the skewers onto individual serving plates. Drizzle each with some of the pesto sauce. Serve immediately.

Serves 4

The Big Veg

1 (12-inch) focaccia, sliced horizontally into
   halves

1 cup pesto

8 ounces smoked provolone cheese, sliced

1 cup roasted red bell pepper

1/2 cup thinly sliced red onion

4 cups mixed baby salad greens

Arrange the focaccia halves on a baking sheet. Spread 1/2 cup of the pesto on each half. Bake at 425 degrees for 8 to 10 minutes or until heated through. Remove from the oven. Arrange the cheese on the bottom half. Bake the bottom half for 3 to 5 minutes or until the cheese melts. Layer the bell pepper, onion and salad greens over the cheese. Top with the remaining half. Cut into 6 to 8 wedges.

Serves 6 to 8

Herb Shiitake Mushroom Burgers

This is an amazing alternative to meat. Serve with a basket of French fries and enjoy with a cold beer.

3/4 cup dried shiitake mushrooms
2 cups boiling water
3 (1-ounce) slices firm sandwich bread
1 pound fresh shiitake mushrooms, stems
    removed and caps cut into quarters
2 teaspoons extra-virgin olive oil
1 medium onion, finely chopped
1 carrot, finely chopped
3 garlic cloves, minced
2/3 cup bulgur
1/4 cup whole grain mustard
1 tablespoon minced fresh basil
1 1/4 teaspoons salt
1/4 teaspoon rosemary, crumbled
3 ounces mozzarella cheese, shredded
3 ounces sharp Cheddar cheese, shredded
1 teaspoon extra-virgin olive oil
Buns
Lettuce
Sliced red onion
Sliced fresh tomatoes
Sliced provolone cheese

Combine the dried mushrooms and boiling water in a heatproof bowl. Let stand for 20 minutes to reconstitute. Remove the mushrooms from the liquid to a cutting board and finely chop, reserving the liquid. Strain the reserved liquid through a fine mesh sieve into a bowl and set aside.

Process the bread in a food processor until finely crumbled. Remove to a bowl. Process the fresh mushrooms in the food processor until finely chopped. Heat 2 teaspoons olive oil in a large saucepan over low heat. Add the onion, carrot and garlic. Cook for 7 minutes or until the onion is tender, stirring frequently. Stir in the fresh mushrooms and reconstituted mushrooms. Add the reserved liquid, bulgur, mustard, basil, salt and rosemary and mix well. Increase the heat to medium.

Cook, covered, for 10 minutes, stirring occasionally; remove the cover. Cook for 5 to 7 minutes or until the bulgur is tender and the liquid has been absorbed, stirring occasionally. Spoon the mushroom mixture into a large bowl. Cool to room temperature.

Add the bread crumbs, mozzarella cheese and Cheddar cheese to the mushroom mixture and mix well. Shape the mushroom mixture into 1/2-inch-thick patties. Heat 1 teaspoon olive oil in a large nonstick skillet over medium heat. Brown the patties on both sides in the hot oil, turning once; drain.

To serve, arrange the patties on buns topped with lettuce, sliced red onion, sliced fresh tomatoes and sliced provolone cheese.

Serves 6 to 8

Sautéed Vegetable Wraps with Garlic Bean Purée

Garlic Bean Purée

1 head garlic
2 teaspoons plus 1 tablespoon extra-virgin olive oil
3 cups cooked white beans, drained and rinsed
1/3 cup sour cream
3 tablespoons minced fresh chives
1/2 teaspoon freshly ground pepper
Salt to taste

Guacamole

2 ripe avocados, cut into halves
2 shallots, coarsely chopped
2 fresh green chiles, seeded and coarsely chopped
Juice of 2 limes

Wraps

1 tablespoon extra-virgin olive oil
1 garlic clove, minced
2 red bell peppers, cut into 3/4-inch pieces
2 yellow bell peppers, cut into 3/4-inch pieces
1 small red onion, thinly sliced
3 tomatoes, seeded and chopped
4 green onions with tops, thinly sliced
1 tablespoon balsamic vinegar
1/2 cup fresh cilantro, minced
12 (10-inch) tortillas
Sour cream
Minced fresh chives to taste
1 lime, cut into wedges

For the purée, slice off the top 1/2 inch of the garlic head. Discard the papery skin, leaving the cloves intact. Rub 2 teaspoons of the olive oil over the garlic head. Place the garlic in a small roasting pan and cover with foil. Roast at 325 degrees for 40 to 45 minutes or until the garlic feels soft when gently squeezed. Let stand until cool. Squeeze the pulp from the cloves into a food processor. Add the remaining 1 tablespoon olive oil, beans, sour cream, chives and pepper to the food processor. Process until blended. Season with salt and set aside.

For the guacamole, combine the avocados, shallots, green chiles and lime juice in a food processor. Process for 1 minute or until smooth. Scrape the guacamole into a bowl. Chill, covered, in the refrigerator.

For the wraps, heat 1 tablespoon olive oil in a large nonstick skillet over medium heat. Sauté the minced garlic in the hot oil for 30 to 60 seconds or until fragrant. Stir in the bell peppers, red onion, tomatoes, green onions and balsamic vinegar. Sauté for 1 minute. Remove from the heat. Stir in the cilantro. Heat a large skillet over medium heat; do not use nonstick. Heat the tortillas 1 at a time in the hot skillet for 20 seconds per side or until softened.

To serve, place 2 tortillas on each of 6 serving plates. Spread 2 tablespoons of the garlic bean purée down the center of each tortilla. Divide the vegetable mixture among the tortillas. Fold in both sides and the bottom of each tortilla up over the filling and then roll to enclose the filling. Top each with a dollop of sour cream and a dollop of the guacamole. Sprinkle with chives to taste and top with a lime wedge.

Serves 6

Spicy Asian Wraps

Serve with an Asian beer such as Asahi or Kirin.

1 pound coleslaw mix with red cabbage and
  carrots
2 teaspoons sesame oil
1/3 cup bottled stir-fry sauce
1/8 teaspoon red pepper flakes
4 (12-inch) flour tortillas
1/2 cup fresh bean sprouts
1/4 cup chopped green onions
8 ounces Pepper Jack cheese, shredded
1/4 cup bottled stir-fry sauce
2 tablespoons chopped green onions

Sauté the coleslaw mix in the sesame oil in a skillet until tender. Stir in 1/3 cup stir-fry sauce and red pepper flakes and mix well. Remove from the heat. Heat the tortillas 1 at a time in a hot nonstick skillet for 20 seconds per side.

To serve, layer the coleslaw mixture, bean sprouts, 1/4 cup green onions and cheese evenly on each of the 4 tortillas. Wrap, folding the ends in first, before rolling to enclose the filling. Drizzle with 1/4 cup stir-fry sauce and sprinkle with 2 tablespoons green onions. Serve immediately.

Serves 4

Cherry Tofu Lettuce Wraps

Crisp lettuce leaves make a crunchy and refreshing wrapper for the cherry tofu mixture.

1 tablespoon peanut oil
1 1/4 pounds firm tofu, cut into bite-size pieces
1 tablespoon minced fresh gingerroot
1/3 cup sliced almonds
2 tablespoons rice vinegar
2 tablespoons teriyaki sauce
1 tablespoon peanut oil
1 tablespoon honey
1 pound dried cherries
1 1/2 cups shredded carrots
1/2 cup chopped green onions
12 lettuce leaves

Heat 1 tablespoon peanut oil in a large nonstick skillet over medium-high heat. Sauté the tofu and gingerroot in the hot oil for 4 to 5 minutes. Remove from the heat. Toast the almonds in a small skillet over medium heat until light brown, stirring frequently. Remove to a bowl to cool immediately.

Whisk the vinegar, teriyaki sauce, 1 tablespoon peanut oil and honey in a bowl. Stir in the tofu mixture, almonds, cherries, carrots and green onions. Spoon some of the tofu mixture in the center of each lettuce leaf and roll to enclose the filling. Serve immediately.

Serves 6

Asian Pan-Fried Tofu

1 pound extra-firm tofu, drained and
　　cut into 1/2-inch cubes
2 tablespoons canola oil
1 1/2 tablespoons sesame seeds
3 bunches watercress, stems removed
1/2 cup fresh orange juice
3 tablespoons soy sauce
1 1/2 tablespoons Asian sesame oil
1 tablespoon grated fresh gingerroot
2 garlic cloves, minced
1/8 teaspoon freshly ground pepper

Pat the tofu dry with paper towels. Sauté the tofu
in 1 tablespoon of the canola oil in a nonstick
skillet over medium-high heat for 8 to 10 minutes
or until golden brown on all sides, turning
frequently. Remove the tofu to a plate with a
slotted spoon, reserving the pan drippings. Toast
the sesame seeds in a small skillet over medium
heat until golden brown, stirring frequently.
Remove to a bowl to cool immediately.

Heat the remaining 1 tablespoon canola oil with
the reserved pan drippings over medium-high
heat. Add the watercress. Cook just until wilted,
turning frequently. Stir in the sesame seeds.
Remove the watercress mixture to a serving platter,
reserving the pan drippings. Arrange the tofu over
the watercress.

Stir the orange juice, soy sauce, sesame oil,
gingerroot, garlic and pepper into the reserved
pan drippings. Simmer for 5 minutes, stirring
frequently. Drizzle over the tofu and watercress.

Serves 4

Silken Tofu Fettuccine

12 ounces fettuccine
3 garlic cloves
2 tablespoons butter
1 pound silken tofu
2/3 cup freshly grated Parmesan cheese
1/2 cup milk or soy milk
1 1/4 teaspoons salt
2 tablespoons minced fresh flat-leaf parsley
1/4 cup freshly grated Parmesan cheese

Cook the pasta in boiling water in a saucepan for
10 to 12 minutes or until al dente; drain. Cover to
keep warm.

Crush the garlic with the side of a knife. Sauté the
garlic in the butter in a sauté pan over medium-low
heat for 2 to 3 minutes or until golden brown.
Remove from the heat and discard the garlic to
make a garlic-infused butter.

Combine the garlic-infused butter, silken tofu,
2/3 cup cheese, milk and salt in a food processor.
Process until smooth and creamy. Combine the
hot pasta and tofu sauce in a large serving bowl
and toss to mix. Sprinkle with the parsley and
1/4 cup cheese.

Serves 4 to 6

Tuscan Cauliflower Rigatoni

Look for cauliflower with plenty of outside leaves since these keep the flowers fresher.

6 quarts water
2 tablespoons salt
1¹/2 pounds fresh cauliflower
¹/4 cup extra-virgin olive oil
3 cups thinly sliced red onion
6 mint leaves, minced
¹/2 teaspoon red pepper flakes
16 ounces rigatoni
1 cup grated pecorino cheese
¹/3 cup fresh flat-leaf parsley, minced
1¹/2 teaspoons salt
¹/2 teaspoon freshly ground black pepper

Bring the water and 2 tablespoons salt to a boil in a stockpot. Core the cauliflower and chop the base into ¹/4-inch pieces. Break the florets into bite-size pieces.

Heat the olive oil in a large sauté pan just until smoking. Add the onion, mint leaves and red pepper flakes. Cook for 5 to 6 minutes or until the onion is tender, stirring frequently. Stir in the cauliflower. Cook over medium heat for 12 to 15 minutes or until the cauliflower is tender and light brown but not mushy, stirring frequently.

Add the pasta to the boiling water. Cook for 8 to 12 minutes or until al dente; drain. Toss the hot pasta with the cauliflower mixture, cheese, parsley, 1¹/2 teaspoons salt and black pepper in a large pasta bowl. Serve immediately.

Serves 6

Introducing Tofu

With its growing popularity, tofu has become easy to find in supermarkets everywhere. Tofu, also known as bean curd, is one of the most versatile protein foods in the world. It is made by curding the mild "milk" of the soybean. Tofu is available in many forms. Fresh tofu, which is packed in water and sealed in one-pound plastic containers in the refrigerated section, comes in several consistencies: soft, regular, firm, and extra-firm. Silken tofu is sold in aseptically sealed cartons and can be stored unopened on pantry shelves for several months. Silken tofu has a silkier, smooth surface, and it also comes in soft, regular, firm, and extra-firm. Tofu can be adapted to many of your own recipes. It fits easily as a salad dressing or dip; as an alternative to meat, fish, poultry, or cheese; or in desserts and baked goods.

"Soon To Be Your Favorite" Spaghetti

Whole wheat spaghetti has a nice heartiness to pair with the balsamic vinegar and cherry tomatoes. You may prepare the sauce and bread crumbs in advance; just make sure you don't add the bread crumbs until right before serving. The crunchy bread crumbs make this dish!

6 quarts water
1 tablespoon salt
2 pints cherry tomatoes, cut into halves
1/2 cup extra-virgin olive oil
1/4 cup balsamic vinegar
1/4 teaspoon kosher salt
1/8 teaspoon freshly ground pepper
7 (1/2-inch-thick) slices French bread
1/4 cup extra-virgin olive oil
1 teaspoon kosher salt
16 ounces whole wheat spaghetti
3 tablespoons minced fresh basil
1 tablespoon minced fresh sage
1/2 cup freshly grated Parmesan cheese

Bring the water and 1 tablespoon salt to a boil in a stockpot. Toss the tomatoes with 1/2 cup olive oil, balsamic vinegar, 1/4 teaspoon kosher salt and pepper in a bowl until coated. Marinate at room temperature while preparing the remainder of the recipe.

Toast the bread slices in a toaster until light brown. Place the toast in a food processor. Pulse until finely ground. Spread the bread crumbs on a baking sheet. Drizzle with 1/4 cup olive oil, sprinkle with 1 teaspoon kosher salt and stir until evenly coated. Place the baking sheet on the middle oven rack. Toast at 400 degrees for 8 minutes or until golden brown; stir.

Add the pasta to the boiling water. Cook using package directions; drain. Toss the hot pasta with the cherry tomato mixture in a large pasta bowl. Add the basil, sage and 1/2 of the bread crumbs and mix gently. Top each serving with 1 heaping teaspoon of the remaining bread crumbs and 4 teaspoons of the cheese. Serve immediately.

Serves 6

Outdoor Lighting

If you have a pool, float white candles and gardenias in the water. The candles' soft light blends with the sweet aroma of the flowers to create a tropical feeling.

Use your Christmas lights in the summer, too. Wrap them around branches or porch columns to add warmth and festivity.

Herb Fontina Orecchiette

6 quarts water

1 tablespoon salt

5 (1/2-inch-thick) slices French bread

1/4 cup extra-virgin olive oil

1 teaspoon kosher salt

2 garlic cloves, minced

1 tablespoon finely chopped shallots

2 tablespoons butter

1 1/2 tablespoons minced fresh basil

1 1/2 tablespoons minced fresh chives

1 1/2 tablespoons minced fresh oregano

1 1/2 tablespoons minced fresh flat-leaf parsley

1 1/2 cups half-and-half

16 ounces orecchiette or medium pasta shells

2 cups (8 ounces) shredded fontina cheese

1/3 cup freshly grated Parmigiano-Reggiano cheese

1/4 teaspoon freshly grated nutmeg

Salt and pepper to taste

3 tablespoons freshly grated Parmigiano-Reggiano cheese

Bring the water and 1 tablespoon salt to a boil in a stockpot. Toast the bread in a toaster until light brown. Place the toast in a food processor. Pulse until finely ground. Spread the bread crumbs on a baking sheet. Drizzle with the olive oil, sprinkle with 1 teaspoon kosher salt and stir until evenly coated. Place the baking sheet on the middle oven rack. Toast at 400 degrees for 8 minutes or until golden brown; stir. Set aside. Maintain the oven temperature.

Sauté the garlic and shallots in the butter in a skillet over medium heat for 3 minutes. Add the basil, chives, oregano and parsley and mix well. Sauté for 2 minutes longer. Remove from the heat. Heat the half-and-half in a small saucepan. Remove from the heat. Cover to keep warm.

Add the pasta to the boiling water. Cook for 1 to 2 minutes short of al dente; drain. Toss the pasta and sautéed herb mixture in a large pasta bowl. Add the warm half-and-half, fontina cheese and 1/3 cup Parmigiano-Reggiano cheese and stir until the cheese melts. Season with the nutmeg and salt and pepper to taste.

Spoon the pasta mixture into a 9×13-inch baking dish sprayed with nonstick cooking spray. Sprinkle with the bread crumbs and 3 tablespoons Parmigiano-Reggiano cheese. Bake for 20 minutes or until brown and bubbly. Add 2 cups of your favorite cooked vegetables for variety.

Serves 6

Mediterranean Risotto and Zucchini Cakes

Warm bread with a leafy green salad will round out this light but satisfying meal.

Risotto and Zucchini Cakes

 2 tablespoons extra-virgin olive oil
 1 cup chopped onion
 3/4 cup arborio rice
 3 garlic cloves, minced
 1/2 cup white wine
 1/2 teaspoon salt
 2 1/2 cups simmering water
 1 medium zucchini, grated
 2/3 cup freshly grated Parmesan cheese
 1/4 teaspoon freshly ground pepper
 2 tablespoons extra-virgin olive oil

Mediterranean Compote and Assembly

 3 ripe medium tomatoes, chopped
 1/2 cup minced onion
 1 cup pitted kalamata olives,
  coarsely chopped
 1/3 cup fresh basil, thinly sliced
 1/2 teaspoon kosher salt
 1/4 teaspoon freshly ground pepper
 Freshly grated Parmesan cheese
 1/4 cup fresh basil, thinly sliced

For the cakes, heat 2 tablespoons olive oil in a large skillet over medium-high heat. Sauté the onion in the hot oil for 5 minutes. Stir in the rice and garlic. Sauté for 2 minutes. Add the wine and salt and mix well.

Cook until the wine has almost evaporated, stirring frequently. Add 1/2 cup of the simmering water. Cook until the water has been absorbed, stirring frequently. Add the remaining simmering water in 1/2-cup increments, stirring frequently and cooking until the water is absorbed after each addition. This will take approximately 20 minutes. Note the time you first begin adding the water and add the zucchini after 10 minutes. When the risotto tests done, the rice will be tender but a little chewy and the risotto will be creamy but not too wet.

Remove the risotto from the heat. Stir in the cheese and pepper. Chill, covered, for 30 minutes or longer. Shape the chilled mixture into six 1-inch-thick cakes. Heat 2 tablespoons olive oil in a nonstick skillet over high heat. Add the cakes. Reduce the heat to medium-high. Sear the cakes on 1 side for 5 to 7 minutes or until golden brown; turn. Sear for 5 to 7 minutes longer. Remove to a platter. Cover to keep warm.

For the compote, heat the tomatoes in a skillet over medium heat, stirring occasionally. Stir in the onion. Cook for 1 minute, stirring frequently. Remove from the heat. Stir in the olives, 1/3 cup basil, salt and pepper.

To serve, spoon some of the compote over each cake on a serving plate. Sprinkle with cheese and 1/4 cup fresh basil.

Serves 6

Wild Mushroom Risotto

This is a hearty meal that tastes wonderful. Use half the butter to reduce the fat if desired.

1 (3/4-ounce) package dried porcini
    mushrooms
1 cup hot water
2 tablespoons unsalted butter
1 tablespoon olive oil
1 medium red onion, chopped
1 garlic clove, minced
10 to 12 button mushrooms, sliced
2 cups arborio rice
1/2 cup red wine
6 cups vegetable stock, heated
1/4 cup (1/2 stick) unsalted butter
2 ounces Parmigiano-Reggiano cheese, grated
Salt and pepper to taste

Soak the porcini mushrooms in the hot water in a bowl for 30 minutes. Drain, reserving the liquid. Rinse the mushrooms and slice.

Heat 2 tablespoons unsalted butter and olive oil in a large skillet. Sauté the onion and garlic in the butter mixture for 2 minutes. Stir in the button mushrooms. Sauté for 3 minutes. Add the rice and mix well.

Sauté for 1 minute. Stir in the wine. Cook until the wine evaporates, stirring constantly. Add 1 cup of the hot stock. Cook until the stock is absorbed, stirring constantly. Add the porcini mushrooms and 1 cup of the remaining stock. Cook until the stock is absorbed, stirring constantly. Pour the reserved mushroom liquid through a fine strainer into the rice mixture and mix well.

Add the remaining stock 1 cup at a time, stirring constantly and cooking until the stock is absorbed after each addition. This will take approximately 20 minutes. Remove from the heat. Stir in 1/4 cup unsalted butter and cheese. Season with salt and pepper. Serve immediately.

Serves 4

Eggplant: To Salt or Not to Salt

To reduce bitterness and to prevent eggplant from absorbing excess oil when sautéed, it is important to salt the eggplant. Place sliced or chopped eggplant in a colander and sprinkle all over with salt. Let drain for about 1 hour. Rinse well and pat dry before cooking.

If you are using large eggplant, select the hardest ones you can find, as they will have the fewest seeds.

Twice-Baked Harvest Squash

3½ cups water

1 cup wild rice blend

3 (10- to 12-ounce) orange acorn squash, cut into halves and seeded

¼ cup (½ stick) butter

2 cups finely chopped onions

2 teaspoons crumbled dried sage leaves

2 tablespoons fresh lemon juice

½ cup dried cranberries

½ cup hazelnuts, roasted and coarsely chopped

¼ cup fresh parsley, minced

1 tablespoon brown sugar

Salt and pepper to taste

3 tablespoons cranberries

3 tablespoons hazelnuts, roasted and coarsely chopped

Bring the water and wild rice to a boil in a large heavy saucepan; reduce the heat. Simmer, covered, for 1 hour or until the rice is tender; drain. Remove the rice to a large bowl.

Arrange the squash halves cut side down on an oiled baking sheet. Bake at 375 degrees for 40 minutes or until tender; reduce the oven temperature to 350 degrees. Let stand until cool. Scoop out the squash pulp carefully, leaving a ¼-inch shell. Place the pulp in a small bowl.

Heat the butter in a large nonstick skillet over medium heat. Sauté the onions in the butter for 15 minutes or until very tender. Stir in the sage. Sauté for 2 minutes. Add the wild rice, squash pulp and lemon juice, mixing well and breaking up the squash pulp into smaller pieces. Stir in ½ cup dried cranberries, ½ cup hazelnuts, parsley and brown sugar. Season with salt and pepper.

Mound the rice mixture evenly in the reserved shells. You may prepare up to this point 6 hours in advance and store, covered, in the refrigerator. Arrange the shells in a roasting pan. Bake for 25 minutes or until heated through. Remove the stuffed shells to a serving platter. Sprinkle with 3 tablespoons cranberries and 3 tablespoons hazelnuts. If time is of the essence, pierce the squash with a fork and microwave for about 10 minutes or until tender.

Serves 6

Roast Hazelnuts/Filberts

Place the nuts in a single layer on a baking sheet and bake at 350 degrees for 20 minutes or until the skins rub off easily and the nuts underneath are golden brown. Hazelnuts/filberts may be roasted a few days before using. Store in an airtight container.

Spaghetti Squash Lasagna

If you like spaghetti squash you will love this lasagna. This improvisation of lasagna is fun to eat and a favorite with children.

1 (2- to 3-pound) spaghetti squash
1 tablespoon extra-virgin olive oil
4 ounces shiitake mushrooms, stems removed
    and caps sliced
2 garlic cloves, minced
1 (16-ounce) can whole tomatoes, drained
15 ounces ricotta cheese
8 ounces mozzarella cheese, shredded
1 (6-ounce) can black olives, drained and
    sliced
1 teaspoon minced fresh basil
1 teaspoon dried oregano
Salt and pepper to taste
3/4 cup grated Parmesan cheese

Pierce the squash several times with a fork and arrange the squash on a baking sheet. Bake at 350 degrees for 45 to 60 minutes or until making an indentation in the shell with a spoon is easy. To save time, pierce the skin in several places with a fork and microwave on High for 10 to 15 minutes or until tender. Let stand until cool. Cut the squash into halves and remove the seeds and stringy pulp. Using a fork, gently scrape the remaining pulp to remove the spaghetti-like strands of squash and place in a bowl.

Heat the olive oil in a nonstick skillet over medium-high heat. Sauté the mushrooms and garlic in the hot oil until the mushrooms are tender. Remove from the heat. Add the mushroom mixture, tomatoes, ricotta cheese, mozzarella cheese, olives, basil, oregano, salt and pepper to the squash and mix well. Spoon the squash mixture into a 9×13-inch baking pan or lasagna pan sprayed with nonstick cooking spray. Sprinkle with the Parmesan cheese. Bake at 350 degrees for 45 minutes or until bubbly.

For variety, cook the spaghetti squash as directed and scrape the strands into a bowl. Toss with softened butter or olive oil and freshly grated Parmesan cheese. Season with salt and pepper.

Try Terrale Primitivo or Candido Salice Salentino, both great wine choices from Southern Italy.

Serves 6

Coconut Lime Summer Squash Sauté

This dish is rich and soupy. An excellent vegan choice. To save time, use frozen corn.

1 teaspoon canola oil
1 pound extra-firm tofu, drained and cut into
    1/2-inch cubes
1 cup chopped yellow squash
1 cup chopped zucchini
1 teaspoon salt
2 cups fresh corn kernels (about 4 ears of
    corn)
1 cup canned light coconut milk
3/4 cup chopped green onions
1/3 cup water
2 tablespoons minced fresh basil
2 tablespoons minced fresh cilantro
2 jalapeño chiles, seeded and chopped
1 teaspoon soy sauce
1/4 teaspoon freshly ground pepper
2 tablespoons fresh lime juice
2 cups hot cooked basmati rice or jasmine rice
1/2 cup chopped unsalted cashews, toasted

Heat the canola oil in a large nonstick skillet over medium-high heat. Add the tofu, yellow squash and zucchini. Sprinkle with 1/2 teaspoon of the salt. Sauté for 8 minutes or until light brown. Add the remaining 1/2 teaspoon salt, corn, coconut milk, green onions, water, basil, cilantro, jalapeño chiles, soy sauce and pepper and mix well; reduce the heat.

Simmer for 8 minutes or until the corn is tender, stirring occasionally. Add the lime juice and mix well. Spoon over the rice on a serving platter. Sprinkle with the cashews.

Serves 4

Outdoor Entertaining

Like that old standby citronella, lavender oil and basil repel pests. Fill torches with lavender oil and place bouquets or pots of basil around the party. Keep them, as well as citronella candles, away from food; their scent interferes with the flavors of the food.

Chanterelle and Portobello Mushrooms in Puff Pastry

1 (6-count) package frozen puff pastry shells
1 (³/4-ounce) package dried chanterelle
    mushrooms
4 tablespoons (¹/2 stick) butter
¹/2 cup minced leeks (white and pale green
    parts only)
1 large shallot, chopped
6 ounces portobello mushrooms, stems and
    gills removed and caps chopped
²/3 cup dry white wine
6 tablespoons fresh soft goat cheese, such as
    Montrachet
2 tablespoons minced fresh flat-leaf parsley
Salt and pepper to taste ·
Fresh flat-leaf parsley leaves

Bake the pastry shells using package directions. Place the chanterelle mushrooms in a small heatproof bowl. Add enough hot water to cover. Let stand for 30 minutes or until softened. Drain the mushrooms and chop.

Heat 2 tablespoons of the butter in a large nonstick skillet over medium-high heat. Sauté the leeks and shallot in the butter for 2 minutes. Add the remaining 2 tablespoons butter. Stir in the chanterelle mushrooms and portobello mushrooms. Sauté for 5 minutes or until the mushrooms are tender. Add the wine and mix well.

Simmer for 2 minutes or until the liquid is reduced by ¹/2, stirring frequently. Add the goat cheese. Cook for 1 minute or until slightly thickened, stirring frequently. Stir in the minced parsley and season with salt and pepper. Fill each pastry shell with ¹/6 of the mushroom mixture. Replace the pastry tops and garnish with parsley leaves.

Spoon the mushroom mixture into miniature pastry shells and serve as an appetizer if desired.

Serves 6

Chanterelle Mushrooms

Chanterelle mushrooms have a delicate flavor, which has been described as peppery, rich, and fruity. Season these delicate mushrooms lightly as they can be easily overshadowed. Wash thoroughly in cold water before using. Hydrate in warm water or white wine until saturated, then enjoy them in your favorite recipe.

Savory Stuffed Portobello Mushrooms

Brown rice and mushrooms share the same deep, earthy flavor. Serve with mixed baby greens for a complete meal.

4 large portobello mushrooms, stems and
    gills removed
1/4 teaspoon salt
1/8 teaspoon pepper
3 cups instant brown rice
1 teaspoon vegetable bouillon granules
1/2 cup (1 stick) butter
1/3 cup chopped red bell pepper
1/2 cup chopped green onions
1/3 cup pecan pieces, toasted
1/4 cup dry sherry
1/4 cup minced fresh parsley
1/4 cup grated Parmesan cheese
2 eggs, lightly beaten
1/2 teaspoon crushed garlic
1/4 teaspoon freshly ground pepper
4 slices baby Swiss cheese
1/4 cup pecan pieces, toasted
1 tablespoon minced fresh parsley

Arrange the mushrooms skin side down on a lightly greased baking sheet. Sprinkle with the salt and 1/8 teaspoon pepper. Cook the brown rice using package directions and substituting vegetable bouillon granules for the salt and butter.

Heat the butter in a large sauté pan. Sauté the bell pepper in the butter. Add the brown rice, green onions, 1/3 cup pecans, sherry, 1/4 cup parsley, cheese, eggs, garlic and 1/4 teaspoon pepper. Stuff the mushrooms with the rice mixture.

Bake at 350 degrees, covered with foil, for 25 to 30 minutes; remove the foil. Top each mushroom with 1 slice of the cheese. Bake for 10 to 15 minutes longer or until the cheese melts. Sprinkle with 1/4 cup pecans and 1 tablespoon parsley.

Serves 4

How to Clean a Leek

- Fill the sink with water and add a few drops of lemon juice or wine vinegar.
- Cut off the root end and the top few inches of greens. Slit it lengthwise so it unscrolls.
- Loosen the layers and soak the leek for about 10 minutes. Rinse it well with fresh water and pat dry with absorbent towels.

Thai Peanut Stir-Fry

Authentic and delicious. Try it chilled for a warm-weather treat.

Peanut Sauce

1/2 cup water
1/3 cup sesame oil
1/4 cup peanut butter
3 tablespoons soy sauce
4 teaspoons minced garlic
4 teaspoons minced fresh gingerroot
4 teaspoons rice vinegar
2 teaspoons sugar
1 teaspoon Asian chili paste

Stir-Fry

12 ounces cellophane noodles
12 ounces oyster mushrooms, sliced
8 ounces snow peas, ends trimmed
1 pound firm tofu, cut into 1/2-inch cubes
1 (8-ounce) can sliced water chestnuts, drained
1/2 cup fresh cilantro, minced
1/4 cup peanuts, chopped

For the sauce, combine the water, sesame oil, peanut butter, soy sauce, garlic, gingerroot, vinegar, sugar and chili paste in a food processor. Process until puréed.

For the stir-fry, prepare the noodles using package directions. Heat a wok or large skillet coated with nonstick cooking spray over high heat. Add the mushrooms to the hot wok. Stir-fry for 4 minutes or until light brown. Add the snow peas. Stir-fry for 2 to 3 minutes or until the snow peas are tender-crisp. Add the tofu and water chestnuts and mix well.

Stir-fry until heated through. Add the noodles and sauce and mix well. Cook until heated through, stirring frequently. Spoon the stir-fry mixture onto a serving platter. Sprinkle with the cilantro and peanuts.

Serves 4

To speed stir-frying time, avoid using a nonstick pan, which slows down stir-frying. Also, be sure to use very high heat, which is essential for searing the food so that it cooks quickly.

Ultimate Pizza Crust

1 1/4 teaspoons dry yeast
1 cup warm (100 degrees) water
2 cups bread flour
1/4 cup grated Parmesan cheese
2 teaspoons oregano
2 tablespoons extra-virgin olive oil
1 teaspoon salt
Cornmeal
2 tablespoons extra-virgin olive oil

Dissolve the yeast in the warm water in a medium bowl. Add the bread flour 1/2 cup at a time, stirring well after each addition until the mixture is of a doughy consistency. Add the cheese, oregano, 2 tablespoons olive oil and salt and mix with your hands until the ingredients are incorporated. Knead for 1 to 3 minutes or until the dough is smooth and elastic; shape into a ball. Coat the dough with a small amount of additional olive oil and place in a bowl.

Let rise, covered, for 1 1/2 hours or until doubled in bulk. When the dough has risen, preheat a 12-inch pizza stone at 450 degrees in the upper 1/3 of the oven. Skip this step if you are using a pizza pan. Roll the dough into a 1/4-inch-thick 12-inch circle on a lightly floured surface.

Sprinkle the preheated pizza stone lightly with cornmeal. Reverse roll the dough onto a rolling pin (as for a pie pastry) and roll it out onto the stone or a pizza pan. Drizzle with 2 tablespoons olive oil. Bake at 450 degrees for 5 minutes. Complete the pizza with one of the two recipes on page 249.

For a sandwich variation, shape the dough into 4 small loaves and drizzle with olive oil. Arrange the loaves on a pizza stone or baking sheet. Bake for 15 to 20 minutes. Fill the loaves with whole basil leaves, fresh buffalo mozzarella cheese and sliced red onion. Drizzle with olive oil and sprinkle with salt and pepper.

Serves 8

Pizza Topping Ideas

- Pesto, sun-dried tomatoes, basil, feta
- Roasted garlic, caramelized onions, fontina
- Sliced fresh figs, mint, Gorgonzola
- Grilled eggplant, fresh basil, pine nuts, mozzarella
- Cilantro, fresh salsa, fresh-roasted chiles, Monterey Jack

Pizza Dell' Erba di Pesto

2 tablespoons extra-virgin olive oil
1/2 yellow bell pepper, julienned
1/2 red bell pepper, julienned
1 portobello mushroom cap, gills removed,
    cut into 1/4-inch slices
1 teaspoon salt
3 garlic cloves, minced
1/4 teaspoon freshly ground pepper
1/2 cup lightly packed fresh basil leaves,
    minced
8 to 10 ounces fresh salted mozzarella cheese,
    cut into 1/4-inch cubes
2 tablespoons commercially prepared pesto
1/2 cup freshly grated Parmigiano-Reggiano
    cheese

Heat the olive oil in a large skillet over medium-high heat. Cook the bell peppers in the hot olive oil for 10 minutes, stirring occasionally. Add the mushroom and salt and mix well. Cook for 10 minutes or until the mushroom is golden brown, stirring frequently.

Spread the bell pepper mixture on the Ultimate Pizza Crust. Bake at 450 degrees for 12 minutes. Sprinkle with the garlic, pepper and basil. Mix the mozzarella cheese and pesto in a bowl. Spoon the mozzarella mixture over the pizza. Sprinkle with the Parmigiano-Reggiano cheese. Bake for 10 to 15 minutes longer or just until the cheese is beginning to brown and is bubbly.

Serves 8

Pizza Marguerite

4 garlic cloves, chopped
1/2 cup fresh basil, minced
4 ounces goat cheese, cut into 10 to 12 slices
2 Roma tomatoes, thinly sliced
Salt and pepper to taste
Olive oil to taste

Sprinkle the garlic and basil over the Ultimate Pizza Crust. Arrange the cheese slices and tomato slices evenly over the top. Sprinkle generously with salt and pepper and drizzle with olive oil, especially over the tomato slices. Bake at 450 degrees for 12 minutes. Remove from the oven. Let rest for 3 minutes before serving.

Serves 8

CONTENTS

252   Tahitian Bananas Foster

253   Banana Crème Brûlée

254   Tuxedo Cheesecake

255   Western Chocolate Stack-Ups

256   Port Flan with Citrus Essence

257   Chai Chocolate Custard

258   Espresso Frizzante

259   Mango Tango Gelato

259   Chocolate Valencia Pie

260   Lemonade Pie with Blueberry Sauce

260   Modern Mincemeat Pear Tart

261   Cranberry Tart

262   Lemon Hazelnut Tart

263   Rustic Berry Galette

264   Rhubarb Blueberry Cobbler with Pistachio Topping

266   Black Cherry Almond Cake

267   Toffee Cake with Caramel Sauce

268   Warm Chocolate Decadence Cakes

269   Celestial Sugar Cookies

269   Chocolate Snowflake Cookies

270   Colorado Ranch Cookies

270   Sweetheart Straws

271   Caramel Apple Bars

271   Colorado Cherry Bars

DESSERTS

Tahitian Bananas Foster

1/4 cup (1/2 stick) butter
1/2 cup packed dark brown sugar
1/4 cup mango nectar
1 tablespoon dark rum
1 tablespoon minced candied ginger
1/8 teaspoon nutmeg
1 cup chopped fresh pineapple
1 large banana, diagonally sliced
1 cup chopped peeled fresh mango
Vanilla ice cream (optional)
Toasted shredded coconut (optional)

Heat the butter in a large heavy skillet over medium heat. Add the brown sugar, nectar and rum and mix well. Cook until the brown sugar dissolves, stirring frequently. Increase the heat and bring to a boil.

Boil for 4 minutes or until it is a syrupy consistency, stirring frequently. Stir in the ginger and nutmeg. Add the pineapple, banana and mango and mix gently. Sauté for 1 minute or until heated through. Cool for 2 minutes. Serve warm over vanilla ice cream in dessert bowls. Sprinkle with toasted coconut.

Serves 6

Banana Crème Brûlée

1 tablespoon unsalted butter
3 bananas, coarsely chopped
1 tablespoon sugar
1 tablespoon lemon juice
3 tablespoons rum (optional)
3 cups heavy cream
1 vanilla bean
8 egg yolks
5 tablespoons sugar
1 tablespoon cinnamon
3 tablespoons sugar

Heat the unsalted butter in a large sauté pan over medium heat. Add the bananas and 1 tablespoon sugar and mix well. Cook for 5 minutes or until the bananas begin to caramelize. Mash the bananas with the back of a wooden spoon. Stir in the lemon juice. Increase the heat to high. Stir in the rum. Bring the banana mixture to a boil. Boil for 1 minute, stirring frequently. Remove from the heat. Spoon the banana mixture evenly into 6 shallow crème brûlée dishes or ramekins. Spread the mixture to the edges of the dishes using the back of a spoon. Let stand until cool.

Pour the heavy cream into a saucepan. Slice open 1 side of the vanilla bean with the tip of a paring knife. Open the vanilla bean and run the edge of the knife down the length to scrape out the seeds. Add the bean and seeds to the cream. Bring the cream just to a boil over low to medium heat. Remove from the heat.

Whisk the egg yolks and 5 tablespoons sugar in the top of a double boiler. Cook over simmering water for 15 minutes or until fairly thick, stirring frequently. Strain the cream mixture into the egg yolk mixture and mix well, discarding the solids. Cook over simmering water for 10 minutes longer, stirring frequently. Remove from the heat. Ladle the cream mixture over the banana mixture.

Place the crème brûlée dishes in a roasting pan. Add enough hot water to the roasting pan to reach halfway up the sides of the dishes. Bake at 300 degrees for 40 minutes. Remove the dishes from the roasting pan. Chill, covered, for 3 hours or longer.

Mix the cinnamon and 3 tablespoons sugar in a bowl. Sprinkle 2 teaspoons of the cinnamon-sugar mixture over the top of each serving. Arrange the dishes on a bed of cracked ice in a roasting pan. Broil until the sugar caramelizes. Watch carefully and rotate the dishes so the sugar browns evenly. You may use a propane torch to caramelize the sugar if desired. Serve immediately.

Serves 6

Tuxedo Cheesecake

Crust

    6 ounces chocolate wafer cookies
    1 cup lightly packed flaked sweetened
        coconut
    1/4 cup sugar
    1/4 cup (1/2 stick) unsalted butter, chopped,
        chilled

Chocolate Filling

    5 ounces unsweetened chocolate, finely
        chopped
    1 pound reduced-fat cream cheese, softened
    1 3/4 cups sugar
    3 tablespoons light corn syrup
    1 teaspoon vanilla extract
    1 egg, at room temperature
    2 egg yolks, at room temperature

Topping

    3 cups lightly packed flaked sweetened
        coconut
    6 tablespoons reduced-fat sour cream
    2 ounces reduced-fat cream cheese, softened
    1/4 cup confectioners' sugar
    1/4 cup canned cream of coconut
    1/4 teaspoon coconut extract
    1/3 cup flaked sweetened coconut, toasted

For the crust, combine the cookies, coconut and sugar in a food processor. Process until coarsely ground. Add the unsalted butter. Process until moist crumbs form. Press the crumb mixture over the bottom and 2 inches up the side of a 10-inch springform pan. Bake on the center oven rack at 350 degrees for 10 minutes. Cool on a wire rack. Maintain the oven temperature.

For the filling, heat the chocolate in the top of a double boiler over simmering water until melted, stirring occasionally. Let stand until cool. Combine the cream cheese and sugar in a food processor. Process until blended. Add the chocolate, corn syrup and vanilla. Process until blended, scraping the side of the bowl occasionally. Add the egg and egg yolks. Process for 5 seconds; scrape the side of the bowl. Process for 5 seconds longer. Spread the filling over the baked layer. Bake for 40 minutes or until the outer 2 inches of the cheesecake is puffed and set and the center is soft set. Cool in the pan on a wire rack for 5 minutes.

For the topping, combine 3 cups coconut, sour cream, cream cheese, confectioners' sugar, cream of coconut and flavoring in a food processor. Process for 1 minute or until the coconut is finely chopped, scraping the side of the bowl occasionally. Spread the topping over the baked layer. Bake for 20 minutes longer or until the topping is set and the coconut just begins to brown. Remove the pan to a wire rack. Run a sharp knife around the edge to loosen the crust. Let stand until cool. Chill, covered, for 4 hours or longer. Sprinkle with 1/3 cup toasted coconut just before serving. You may prepare up to 2 days in advance and store, covered, in the refrigerator.

Serves 12

Western Chocolate Stack-Ups

This dessert must be assembled just before serving.

1/2 cup (3 ounces) semisweet chocolate chips
1/2 cup reduced-fat cream cheese
1/4 cup sugar
1/2 teaspoon vanilla extract
8 ounces whipped topping
1/4 cup sugar
1 tablespoon baking cocoa
1/4 teaspoon cinnamon
6 (6-inch) flour tortillas, each cut into
    4 wedges
2 cups sliced fresh strawberries
1/2 cup semisweet miniature chocolate chips
1/2 cup chocolate syrup

Place 1/2 cup chocolate chips in a microwave-safe bowl. Microwave on High for 1 minute; stir. Microwave for 1 minute longer or until almost melted. Combine the cream cheese, 1/4 cup sugar and vanilla in a mixing bowl. Beat at medium speed until blended. Stir in the melted chocolate and whipped topping. Chill, covered, in the refrigerator.

Combine 1/4 cup sugar, baking cocoa and cinnamon in a bowl and mix well. Arrange the tortilla wedges in a single layer on a baking sheet sprayed with nonstick cooking spray. Spray 1 side of each wedge with nonstick cooking spray and sprinkle with the baking cocoa mixture. Bake at 350 degrees for 10 minutes. Remove to a wire rack to cool.

Spread 1 1/2 tablespoons of the cream cheese mixture on the baking cocoa side of 1 tortilla wedge. Layer with 1 tortilla wedge baking cocoa side up, 1/4 cup of the strawberries, 1 tortilla wedge baking cocoa side up and 1 1/2 tablespoons of the cream cheese mixture. Sprinkle with 1 tablespoon of the miniature chocolate chips and drizzle with 1 tablespoon of the chocolate syrup. Repeat the process with the remaining tortilla wedges, cream cheese mixture, strawberries, miniature chocolate chips and chocolate syrup.

Serves 8

After Dinner Cheese

When paired with a ripe fruit, a few nuts, and a glass of wine or port, cheese can be a satisfying and delicious finale to any meal. Choose three ripe cheeses: a bleu, a triple cream, and a goat cheese. Place them on a platter with one type of fruit, such as pears, figs, or grapes; some walnuts; and thinly sliced crusty bread.

Some suggested pairings:

Roquefort and green apples • Feta and watermelon • Mascarpone and strawberries
Chèvre and peaches • Havarti and cantaloupe • Lemon Stilton and blueberries
Gorgonzola and fresh purple figs • Creamy Bleu cheese with ginger cookies

Port Flan with Citrus Essence

1³/₄ cups sugar
Julienned zest of 1 orange
Julienned zest of 1 lemon
2 cups half-and-half
2 cups whipping cream
12 egg yolks
¹/₄ cup Tawny Port

Pour ³/₄ cup of the sugar into a 10- to 12-inch skillet. Heat over high heat for 3 to 5 minutes or until the sugar liquefies and turns amber in color, tilting and shaking the skillet constantly. Pour the syrup into 8 ramekins. The syrup does not need to cover the bottom of each ramekin completely.

Combine the remaining 1 cup sugar, orange zest and lemon zest in the same skillet; do not rinse the skillet. Press the zest with a wooden spoon to release the oils. Add the half-and-half and whipping cream and mix well. Heat over medium-high heat until steaming but not boiling, stirring occasionally. Remove from the heat and cover. Let stand for 10 to 15 minutes.

Whisk the egg yolks and port in a bowl until blended. Pour the hot cream mixture through a fine strainer into a 1-quart measuring cup, discarding the zest. Whisk the cream mixture into the egg yolk mixture until blended.

Arrange the ramekins in a shallow baking pan. Pour the custard mixture into the prepared ramekins. Pour enough boiling water into the baking pan to measure 1 inch. Bake at 350 degrees for 40 to 45 minutes or until the custard barely moves when the ramekins are gently shaken. Remove the custards from the boiling water. Chill until cold. Cover and chill for an additional 12 hours or for up to 2 days. Run a sharp knife around the edge of the flans. Invert a glass plate over each flan. Hold the ramekin and plate together tightly, inverting and allowing the flan and syrup to slide onto the plate. Remove the ramekins. Serve immediately.

Utilize the remaining Tawny Port as a pairing for this dish. Taylor Fladgate is a nice choice.

Serves 8

Forcing Bulbs

Place pebbles or marbles in a waterproof container. Place bulbs in the container an inch apart, leaving the top third exposed to light. Pour in water to reach the bottom of the bulbs. Keep this amount of water in the container and in four to six weeks, the blooms will appear.

Chai Chocolate Custard

2 cups heavy whipping cream
1¹/4 cups chai tea concentrate
¹/2 cup sugar
6 ounces semisweet chocolate, chopped
7 egg yolks
²/3 cup heavy whipping cream
1 tablespoon plus 2 teaspoons confectioners'
    sugar
Cinnamon to taste
Chocolate shavings

Combine 2 cups heavy whipping cream, chai tea concentrate and sugar in a medium saucepan and mix well. Heat just until bubbles form around the edge of the pan. Remove from the heat. Add the chopped chocolate and stir until smooth.

Whisk the egg yolks in a mixing bowl until blended. Whisk a small amount of the warm chocolate mixture into the egg yolks. Add the egg yolk mixture to the warm chocolate mixture and mix well. Pour the chocolate mixture evenly into 8 ramekins or ovenproof dishes. Arrange the ramekins in a shallow baking pan. Pour enough hot water into the baking pan to reach ¹/2 to ¹/3 up the sides of the dishes. Bake at 300 degrees for 25 to 30 minutes or just until set. Chill, covered, for 3 hours or longer. You may prepare up to this point 2 days in advance and store, covered with plastic wrap, in the refrigerator.

Beat ²/3 cup heavy whipping cream in a mixing bowl until soft peaks form. Add the confectioners' sugar and beat until blended. Spoon some of the whipped cream over each custard and sprinkle with cinnamon. Top with chocolate shavings. Serve immediately.

Serves 8

Espresso Frizzante

For serious coffee lovers!

Phyllo Pillows

$^1/_4$ cup sugar

$^1/_4$ teaspoon ginger

4 sheets phyllo pastry

$^1/_4$ cup ($^1/_2$ stick) unsalted butter, melted

Icy Espresso Granita

$^1/_4$ cup simple syrup

$1^1/_4$ cups brewed espresso, at room temperature

$^1/_4$ cup nonfat milk

Sabayon and Assembly

3 egg yolks

$^1/_4$ cup sugar

$^1/_4$ cup milk

$^1/_8$ teaspoon cinnamon

$^1/_3$ cup whipping cream

$^2/_3$ cup mascarpone cheese

Confectioners' sugar to taste

Chocolate curls

For the pillows, butter a baking sheet and dust with sugar, tapping off the excess. Combine $^1/_4$ cup sugar and ginger in a small bowl and mix well.

Lay the pastry on a cool smooth cutting board or marble surface. Cut each sheet crosswise into halves. Work with half a sheet at a time, covering the remaining pastry halves with a clean tea towel to prevent drying out. Brush each pastry half with some of the unsalted butter and sprinkle with some of the sugar mixture. Peel each pastry half off the work surface and fold the corners under to mold into the shape of a disc about 3 inches in diameter. The pastry may tear during the process but it will still make a great disc. Arrange on the prepared baking sheet.

Bake at 350 degrees for 8 to 10 minutes or until the sugar caramelizes and the pastry is golden brown. Remove to a wire rack to cool. You may prepare in advance and store in an airtight container.

For the granita, make a simple syrup by bringing equal portions of sugar and water to a boil in a saucepan. Boil for 1 minute. Cool. Pour the syrup, espresso and nonfat milk into a 9×9-inch metal pan and mix well. Freeze, uncovered, until solid. Cover the frozen granita with plastic wrap if you are not going to serve within 1 to 2 hours of preparing.

For the sabayon, combine the egg yolks, sugar, milk and cinnamon in the top of a double boiler and mix well. Cook over simmering water for 8 to 10 minutes or until thick and foamy, whisking constantly. The tracks of the whisk should remain for an instant before disappearing. Set the top of the double boiler in a bowl of ice cubes. Whisk constantly for 3 minutes or until the mixture is cool. You may prepare up to this point 1 day in advance and store, covered, in the refrigerator.

Beat the whipping cream in a mixing bowl until soft peaks form. Soften the mascarpone cheese in a bowl by stirring with a rubber spatula. Fold the mascarpone cheese and whipped cream into the sabayon. Use the sauce immediately or store, covered, in the refrigerator for up to 4 hours.

To serve, arrange 1 phyllo pillow in a dessert bowl and top with some of the granita and a heaping spoonful of the sabayon. Top with another phyllo pillow. Sprinkle with confectioners' sugar and chocolate curls. Serve immediately.

Serves 4

Mango Tango Gelato

1 cup sugar
1 cup water
3 cups finely chopped peeled mangoes
2 cups passion fruit nectar
1 1/3 cups half-and-half
1 cup finely chopped peeled mango

Combine the sugar and water in a medium saucepan and mix well. Bring to a boil. Boil until the sugar dissolves, stirring occasionally. Cool slightly. Combine the syrup and 3 cups mangoes in a blender or food processor. Process until smooth. Pour the mango mixture into a large bowl. Let stand until cool.

Add the nectar and half-and-half to the mango mixture and mix well. Pour the mango mixture into an ice cream freezer container. Freeze using manufacturer's directions, adding 1 cup chopped mango 5 minutes before the end of the process. Freeze until firm.

Makes 7 (1/2-cup) servings

Chocolate Valencia Pie

1 cup (6 ounces) semisweet chocolate chips
1/3 cup milk
4 ounces cream cheese
1 tablespoon grated orange zest
1 cup heavy whipping cream
1 (8-inch) chocolate cookie crumb pie shell

Combine the chocolate chips and milk in a microwave-safe 1-quart bowl. Microwave on High for 1 to 2 minutes or until blended; stir. Add the cream cheese and orange zest. Beat with an electric mixer until smooth. Let stand until cool.

Beat the whipping cream in a mixing bowl until stiff peaks form. Fold the whipped cream into the chocolate mixture. Spoon the chocolate filling into the pie shell. Freeze, covered, for 4 hours or until firm. Let stand at room temperature for 30 minutes before serving. Garnish with dollops of additional whipped cream, chocolate curls and/or orange slices.

Serves 6 to 8

Lemonade Pie with Blueberry Sauce

Crust

2 cups graham cracker crumbs
(about 40 graham crackers)
6 tablespoons butter, melted
1 tablespoon sugar

Lemonade Pie

4 cups frozen vanilla yogurt, slightly thawed
1/2 cup lemonade concentrate, thawed
1 tablespoon fresh lemon juice

Blueberry Sauce

1 1/2 cups fresh blueberries
2 tablespoons sugar
1 tablespoon fresh lemon juice

For the crust, combine the graham cracker crumbs, butter and sugar in a food processor. Pulse to combine. Pat the crumb mixture over the bottom of a 9-inch springform pan. Freeze for 20 minutes.

For the pie, combine the yogurt, lemonade concentrate and lemon juice in a bowl and mix well. Spread the yogurt mixture evenly in the prepared springform pan. Freeze, covered with foil or plastic wrap, for 6 hours or until firm.

For the sauce, combine the blueberries, sugar and lemon juice in a food processor. Process until puréed. Press the purée through a fine mesh sieve into a bowl. Taste and add additional sugar and/or lemon juice if desired.

To serve, allow the pie to soften slightly at room temperature. Spoon 1 tablespoon of the sauce over each serving. Serve immediately.

To save time and energy use a commercially prepared graham cracker pie shell.

Serves 6 to 8

Modern Mincemeat Pear Tart

1 (1-crust) pie pastry
1 (15-ounce) jar mincemeat pie filling
4 ripe pears, peeled and cut into 1/4- to
1/2-inch slices
1 tablespoon brandy
Cinnamon and sugar

Fit the pastry into a tart pan, reserving the excess pastry for decoration. Combine the mincemeat, pears and brandy in a bowl and mix gently. Spoon the mincemeat mixture into the prepared tart pan. Cut the reserved pastry into stars or leaves or your favorite shapes and sprinkle with cinnamon and sugar. Arrange the decorations over the top of the mincemeat filling. Bake at 375 degrees for 45 minutes. Cool slightly and serve with whipped cream or ice cream.

Serves 8

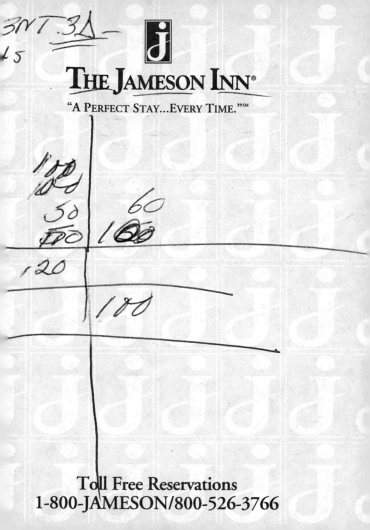

3NT. 3Δ
+5

THE JAMESON INN®

"A PERFECT STAY...EVERY TIME."℠

```
100
100
    50      60
   100    100

120

        100
```

3643.58

(1)

5088.22 —
12708.29 =

17796.51

109266.

Cranberry Tart

Do you know how to tell if a cranberry is ripe? Try dropping a few on your counter.
If they bounce, then they are ripe.

2 cups fresh cranberries, chopped
1/2 cup walnuts, chopped
1 1/2 cups sugar
1 cup flour
1/4 teaspoon salt
3/4 cup (1 1/2 sticks) butter, melted
2 eggs, lightly beaten
1 teaspoon grated orange zest
1/4 teaspoon orange extract
Confectioners' sugar

Combine the cranberries, walnuts and 1/2 cup of the sugar in a bowl and mix well. Pat the cranberry mixture into a buttered 10-inch springform pan.

Combine the remaining 1 cup sugar, flour and salt in a bowl and mix well. Stir in the butter, eggs, orange zest and flavoring. Pour the batter over the cranberry mixture. Place the springform pan on a baking sheet with sides.

Bake at 350 degrees for 40 to 45 minutes. Cool in the pan on a wire rack. Remove the pan cuff when the tart cools. Dust with confectioners' sugar. Serve on a cake pedestal.

Serves 8

Lemon Hazelnut Tart

When in season, use Meyer lemons for a different twist.

Pastry

    10 tablespoons butter, at room temperature
    1/4 cup confectioners' sugar
    1 egg yolk
    1 cup plus 3 tablespoons flour
    1 teaspoon heavy cream

Lemon Hazelnut Filling

    1 cup (2 sticks) unsalted butter
    1 cup sugar
    1/3 cup fresh lemon juice
    3 eggs, lightly beaten
    3 egg yolks
    1 tablespoon grated lemon zest
    1 teaspoon vanilla extract
    3 tablespoons sugar
    4 teaspoons water
    1/2 cup hazelnuts

For the pastry, cut the butter into 10 to 20 pieces. Toss the butter with the confectioners' sugar in a mixing bowl. Beat at medium speed until creamy, scraping the bowl occasionally. Add the egg yolk. Beat until blended. Add 1/2 cup of the flour. Beat until the mixture is crumbly. Add the remaining 1/2 cup plus 3 tablespoons flour and heavy cream. Beat until the dough forms a sticky ball. Shape the dough into a disc. Chill, wrapped in plastic wrap, for 2 hours or until firm.

Knead the dough lightly on a floured surface until malleable, keeping the surface well dusted with flour. Roll the dough into a 12-inch round. Press the dough over the bottom and up the side of a 10-inch tart pan with removable bottom. Trim the excess dough from the edge of the pan using a knife or rolling pin. The dough should be flush with the top of the pan. Prick the pastry several times with a fork. Freeze for 10 minutes. Bake at 375 degrees for 25 to 30 minutes or until golden brown. Cool in the pan on a wire rack.

For the filling, heat the unsalted butter in a heavy saucepan over medium heat. Whisk in 1 cup sugar, lemon juice, eggs, egg yolks, lemon zest and vanilla. Cook for 7 to 10 minutes or until thickened, whisking constantly. The eggs and butter will separate if overcooked. Reduce the heat to low. Whisk for 2 minutes longer. Pour the hot filling into the pastry-lined tart pan. Chill, uncovered, for 2 hours or until set.

Line a small baking sheet with foil. Combine 3 tablespoons sugar and water in a small saucepan and mix well. Cook over low heat until the sugar dissolves, stirring frequently. Increase the heat and bring to a boil. Boil for 6 minutes or until pale and golden brown; do not stir. Stir in the hazelnuts. Spread the hazelnut mixture on the prepared baking sheet. Let stand until cool. Chop the hazelnuts. Remove the tart from the pan and sprinkle with the hazelnuts. Slice and serve.

Serves 8

Rustic Berry Galette

Pâte Brisée
    1/2 cup (1 stick) unsalted butter, frozen
    1 cup flour
    1 tablespoon sugar
    1 teaspoon salt
    1/2 cup cold water

Berry Galette
    1 cup flour
    1/2 cup packed brown sugar
    1/2 cup sugar
    1/2 cup (1 stick) unsalted butter, softened
    1 pound fresh mixed berries (any combination
       of raspberries, blueberries, blackberries or
       strawberries)

For the pastry, cut the unsalted butter into 8 equal slices. Combine the flour, sugar and salt in a food processor fitted with a steel blade. Add the butter slices 1 at a time, processing constantly until fine crumbs form. Place the crumb mixture in a bowl. Add the cold water gradually, stirring constantly until the dough adheres. Chill, covered with plastic wrap, until ready to use. You may freeze for future use.

For the galette, roll the pastry into an 11- or 12-inch round on a lightly floured surface. Arrange the pastry round on a baking sheet. Combine the flour, brown sugar and sugar in a bowl and mix well. Cut in the butter until crumbly.

Arrange the berries over the pastry round. Sprinkle with the crumb mixture. Pull the side of the round up slightly to form a rim. Place the baking sheet on the bottom oven rack. Bake at 400 degrees for 40 minutes. Serve warm with vanilla ice cream.

Serves 10

When you're on vacation, pack up a few of your favorite table-setting props, such as sand and shells, to take home. Pull them out next winter when that summery spot seems very far away; they will make a perfect setting for a midwinter meal.

Rhubarb Blueberry Cobbler with Pistachio Topping

Pistachio Topping

3/4 cup flour

1/3 cup sugar

1/3 cup packed brown sugar

6 tablespoons unsalted butter, chilled and cubed

1/3 cup pistachios, finely chopped

Rhubarb Blueberry Cobbler

1/2 cup sugar

3 tablespoons flour

2 cups fresh or frozen chopped rhubarb

2 cups fresh blueberries

2 tablespoons lemon juice

For the topping, combine the flour, sugar and brown sugar in a bowl and mix well. Cut in the unsalted butter until crumbly. Stir in the pistachios.

For the cobbler, combine the sugar and flour in a bowl and mix well. Add the rhubarb and blueberries and mix gently. Stir in the lemon juice. Spoon the rhubarb mixture into a 2-quart baking dish sprayed with nonstick cooking spray.

Squeeze the topping together a handful at a time and coarsely crumble over the rhubarb mixture. Bake at 375 degrees for 40 minutes or until brown and bubbly.

Serves 6 to 8

Simple Wine and Cheese Pairings

- Hard Cheeses—Savor hard cheeses such as Parmigiano, Romano, and Reggiano with dry Italian red wines such as Chianti Classico, Barolo, and Amarone.
- Semisoft Cheeses—Pair creamy semisoft cheeses such as rich, earthy Brie and Camembert with a Pinot Noir–style red wine.
- Bleu Cheeses—Contrast the tangy taste of bleu cheeses by serving a sweet dessert wine or dry red wine such as a Cabernet Sauvignon.
- Cheddars—Complement the rich taste of Cheddar cheeses with a dry red wine.

Black Cherry Almond Cake

Cherry Filling
8 ounces cream cheese, softened
1/3 cup sugar
1 egg
1 cup fresh or frozen black cherries,
    cut into halves
1/4 cup sliced almonds

Cake
1 1/2 cups flour
2/3 cup sugar
1 teaspoon baking powder
1 teaspoon baking soda
1/2 teaspoon salt
1 cup sour cream
1/2 cup (1 stick) butter or margarine,
    softened
2 eggs
1 teaspoon almond extract
1/2 teaspoon vanilla extract

Confectioners' Sugar Icing
2 cups confectioners' sugar
1/4 to 1/2 cup cream
2 tablespoons butter or margarine, melted
1 teaspoon vanilla extract
1/2 teaspoon almond extract

For the filling, beat the cream cheese, sugar and egg in a mixing bowl until smooth. Fold in the cherries and almonds.

For the cake, sift the flour, sugar, baking powder, baking soda and salt into a bowl and mix well. Beat the sour cream, butter, eggs and flavorings in a mixing bowl until smooth. Add the sour cream mixture to the flour mixture and mix well.

Spoon 1/2 of the batter into a greased and lightly floured bundt pan or tube pan. Spread with the filling and top with the remaining cake batter.

Bake at 350 degrees for 40 to 50 minutes or until the cake tests done. Cool in the pan for 10 minutes. Invert onto a wire rack to cool completely.

For the icing, combine the confectioners' sugar, 1/4 cup cream, butter and flavorings in a mixing bowl. Beat until smooth, adding additional cream if needed for the desired consistency. Spread the icing over the top and side of the cake.

Serves 12

Cherry wine from the Carlson Vineyards in Colorado is recommended. It tastes like "cherry pie in a glass." Serve this wine with dessert, over ice cream, or let it stand alone.

Toffee Cake with Caramel Sauce

Cake

 8 ounces chopped dates
 1 cup boiling water
 1 cup packed brown sugar
 1/2 cup (1 stick) unsalted butter, softened
 4 eggs
 1³/4 cups self-rising flour
 2¹/2 tablespoons instant coffee granules
 1 teaspoon baking soda
 Confectioners' sugar

Caramel Sauce and Assembly

 2 cups whipping cream
 1 cup packed brown sugar
 1/4 cup (1/2 stick) unsalted butter
 Whipped cream
 Chocolate shavings

For the cake, combine the dates and boiling water in a heatproof bowl. Let stand for 1 hour. Process the undrained date mixture in a food processor or blender until finely chopped. Coat the bottom and side of a 9-inch springform pan with butter. Line the bottom with baking parchment and coat the parchment with butter. Beat the brown sugar and unsalted butter in a mixing bowl until blended. Add 2 of the eggs 1 at a time, beating well after each addition. Add 1/2 of the self-rising flour and beat until blended. Add the remaining 2 eggs 1 at a time and beat well after each addition. Beat in the remaining self-rising flour until blended. Combine the coffee granules and baking soda in a bowl and mix well. Add the coffee granule mixture to the date mixture and stir until the coffee granules dissolve. Add the date mixture to the batter. Beat until mixed.

Spoon the batter into the prepared pan and place the pan on a baking sheet with sides. Bake at 350 degrees for 45 minutes or until a wooden pick inserted in the center comes out clean. Cool in the pan for 10 minutes. Remove to a wire rack and sprinkle with confectioners' sugar. Let stand until cool.

For the sauce, combine the whipping cream, brown sugar and unsalted butter in a heavy 2-quart saucepan. Bring to a boil over medium-high heat, stirring frequently. Reduce the heat to medium-low. Simmer for 15 minutes or until the sauce is reduced to 1³/4 cups, stirring occasionally. You may prepare the sauce up to 1 day in advance and store, covered, in the refrigerator. Reheat over medium-low heat before serving.

Cut the cake into 12 slices. Serve with the sauce, whipped cream and chocolate shavings.

Serves 12

Warm Chocolate Decadence Cakes

4 ounces semisweet chocolate, chopped
1 1/2 ounces unsweetened chocolate, chopped
10 tablespoons unsalted butter, softened
1/2 cup plus 2 tablespoons sugar
3 eggs, lightly beaten
1/2 cup plus 2 teaspoons flour
1 1/2 tablespoons baking cocoa
3/4 teaspoon baking powder

Coat six 3/4- to 1-cup ramekins lightly with butter. Combine the semisweet chocolate and unsweetened chocolate in the top of a double boiler. Heat over barely simmering water until smooth, stirring constantly. Add the unsalted butter and sugar. Heat until the butter melts and the sugar dissolves, stirring frequently. Pour the chocolate mixture into a large mixing bowl.

Add the eggs, flour, baking cocoa and baking powder to the chocolate mixture and mix well. Beat for 8 minutes or until thickened and of a mousse consistency. Spoon the chocolate mixture evenly into the prepared ramekins. Freeze, covered with plastic wrap, for 3 hours or longer. You may prepare up to this point 3 days in advance; remove the plastic wrap.

Arrange the ramekins on a baking sheet. Place the baking sheet on the center oven rack. Bake at 375 degrees for 14 minutes or until the edges are set and the tops are moist and shiny. Do not overbake. Let stand for 10 minutes. Invert onto individual dessert plates. Serve warm with ice cream or whipped cream.

Quady Elysium, a dessert wine, pairs perfectly with this decadent dessert.

Serves 6

Star Anise

A long time favorite spice and tea flavoring in China, star anise is now becoming more popular in America. Best known as a component of Chinese five-spice powder, or the liqueur called anisette, star anise is now adding a new flavor to various main dishes and desserts. Look for these licorice-flavored star-shape pods, which are added to foods whole, broken, or ground, in Asian markets and some grocery stores.

Celestial Sugar Cookies

4 1/4 cups flour
1 teaspoon baking soda
1 teaspoon cream of tartar
1 teaspoon salt
1 cup (2 sticks) butter, softened
1 cup vegetable oil
1 cup sugar
1 cup confectioners' sugar
2 eggs
1 teaspoon vanilla extract

Sift the flour, baking soda, cream of tartar and salt together. Beat the butter, oil, sugar and confectioners' sugar in a mixing bowl until creamy, scraping the bowl occasionally. Add the eggs and vanilla and beat until smooth. Add the dry ingredients gradually and beat until blended. Chill, covered, for 1 hour.

Shape the dough into 1-inch balls. Coat the balls with additional sugar. Arrange the balls on an ungreased cookie sheet. Flatten with the bottom of a glass dipped in sugar. Bake at 350 degrees for 8 to 10 minutes or until light brown. Cool on the cookie sheet for 2 minutes. Remove to a wire rack to cool completely. Store in an airtight container.

Try one of these variations for a different twist. Add 1 teaspoon almond extract or lemon extract, add 1/2 cup crushed almonds or hazelnuts, add 1 tablespoon finely chopped lemon zest, add 1 tablespoon crushed peppermint candies, roll in colored sugars for holidays, or use a decorative glass to create a pattern on each cookie.

Makes 4 to 5 dozen cookies

Chocolate Snowflake Cookies

5 ounces unsweetened chocolate
1/2 cup (1 stick) butter
1 1/2 cups sugar
2 cups flour
3 eggs
2 teaspoons baking powder
2 teaspoons vanilla extract
1/8 teaspoon salt
Confectioners' sugar
36 (about) walnut halves (optional)

Heat the chocolate and butter in the top of a double boiler over simmering water until blended, stirring frequently. Pour the chocolate mixture over the sugar in a mixing bowl. Beat until creamy. Add the flour, eggs, baking powder, vanilla and salt and beat until blended. Drop the dough by large teaspoonfuls 1 or 2 at a time into confectioners' sugar to coat each cookie. Press a walnut half in the center of each cookie. Arrange on a cookie sheet. Bake at 350 degrees for 9 to 10 minutes or until crisp around the edges. Cool on the cookie sheet for 2 minutes. Remove to a wire rack to cool completely.

Makes (about) 3 dozen cookies

Colorado Ranch Cookies

2$\frac{1}{2}$ cups flour
2 teaspoons baking soda
1 teaspoon salt
1 cup (2 sticks) butter, softened
1 cup packed brown sugar
1 cup sugar
2 cups rolled oats
1 cup dried cranberries
$\frac{3}{4}$ cup shredded coconut
$\frac{1}{2}$ cup sliced almonds
3 eggs, beaten
$\frac{1}{2}$ teaspoon almond extract

Mix the flour, baking soda and salt together. Beat the butter, brown sugar and sugar in a mixing bowl until creamy. Add the flour mixture and beat until blended. Stir in the oats, cranberries, coconut, almonds, eggs and flavoring. The dough will be very stiff.

Drop the dough by heaping teaspoonfuls onto an ungreased cookie sheet. Bake at 350 degrees for 10 minutes or until light brown. Cool on the cookie sheet for 2 minutes. Remove to a wire rack to cool completely. Store in an airtight container. To enhance the flavor of the cookies, mix the eggs, almond extract and cranberries in a bowl and let stand for 1 hour before adding to the recipe.

Makes 6 dozen cookies

Sweetheart Straws

$\frac{3}{4}$ teaspoon anise seeds
$\frac{1}{2}$ cup chocolate chips
2$\frac{1}{2}$ tablespoons sugar
5 or 6 sheets phyllo pastry
6 tablespoons unsalted butter, melted

Grind the anise seeds in a spice grinder or with a pestle in a mortar. Combine the ground anise seeds, chocolate chips and sugar in a food processor. Process until finely ground.

Cut the pastry sheets crosswise into halves. Cover with plastic wrap and place a damp tea towel over the top. Arrange 1 sheet of the pastry at a time on a work surface with the longest side facing you.

Brush the bottom half with some of the unsalted butter. Spoon a heaping tablespoon of the chocolate mixture lengthwise across the center of the pastry and fold in half toward you to enclose the chocolate. Brush the top with some of the melted butter.

Starting with the chocolate side, roll the pastry tightly to form a straw. Arrange seam side down on a cookie sheet. Repeat the process with the remaining pastry, remaining butter and remaining chocolate mixture. Bake at 375 degrees for 14 minutes or until light golden brown. Remove to a wire rack to cool. Break each straw into halves before serving. Serve with vanilla or coconut ice cream for a real treat.

Makes 20 to 24 straws

Caramel Apple Bars

Crust and Topping

1 cup packed brown sugar
1/2 cup (1 stick) butter, softened
1/4 cup shortening
1 3/4 cups flour
1 cup quick-cooking oats
1 teaspoon salt
1/2 teaspoon baking soda

Apple Filling

5 cups chopped peeled Granny Smith apples
3 tablespoons flour
1 (12-ounce) package caramels

For the crust and topping, beat the brown sugar, butter and shortening in a mixing bowl until creamy. Add the flour, oats, salt and baking soda. Beat until mixed. Reserve 2 cups of the oat mixture. Pat the remaining oat mixture over the bottom of an ungreased 9×13-inch baking pan.

For the filling, toss the apples with the flour in a bowl. Sprinkle the apples over the prepared layer. Heat the caramels in a small saucepan over low heat until melted, stirring frequently. Drizzle the caramel over the apples and sprinkle with the reserved oat mixture. Bake at 350 degrees for 25 to 30 minutes or until brown and bubbly. Cool in the pan on a wire rack. Cut into bars.

Makes 3 to 4 dozen bars

Colorado Cherry Bars

1 1/2 cups flour
1 teaspoon baking powder
1/4 teaspoon salt
1 1/2 cups rolled oats
1 cup packed brown sugar
3/4 cup (1 1/2 sticks) butter, melted
1 (14-ounce) jar cherry preserves

Combine the flour, baking powder and salt in a bowl and mix well. Stir in the oats and brown sugar. Add the butter and mix until crumbly. Reserve 1/3 of the crumb mixture.

Pat the remaining crumb mixture into a greased 8×8-inch baking pan. Spread with the preserves and sprinkle with the reserved crumb mixture. Bake at 375 degrees for 30 to 35 minutes or until light brown and bubby. Cool in the pan on a wire rack. Cut into bars.

Makes 16 bars

menus

MENUS

Let's Do Lunch

Pecan Chicken and Wild Rice Salad, 55
Fresh Seasonal Fruit
High Country Herb Rolls, 92
Lemon Hazelnut Tart, 262

Big Night Dinner

Spicy Sashimi Triangles, 23
Bacon-Wrapped Grissini, 18
Mixed Greens with Baked Goat Cheese and
    Roasted Red Pepper Vinaigrette, 47
Beef en Croûte with Cilantro Walnut Filling, 152
Roasted Asparagus and Portobello
    Mushrooms, 113
Port Flan with Citrus Essence, 256

Seafood on the Grill

Montrachet Spread, 35
Multicolor Southwest Tomato Salad, 46
Rice Pilaf with Almonds and
    Dried Mangoes, 127
Halibut Kabobs with Chili Lime Sauce, 186
Rustic Berry Galette, 263

Southwest Patio Dinner

Avocado Lime Cream Dip with
    Blue Corn Chips, 28
Spicy Rib Eyes with Dueling Salsas, 158
Corn Cheese Boats, 116
Green Salad with Balsamic Vinaigrette, 59
Crusty Bread with Butter
Western Chocolate Stack-Ups, 255

A Feast without the Beast

Chèvre, Marmalade and Ripe
    Pear Crostini, 16
Mediterranean Risotto and
    Zucchini Cakes, 238
Mixed Greens
Baguette with Herbed Olive Oil
Warm Chocolate Decadence Cakes, 268

Thai One On

Asian Salsa with Won Ton Chips, 32
Spicy Carrot Soup with Red Curry, 62
Lemon Grass Beef with Rice Paper, 161
Mango Tango Gelato, 259, or
    purchased Coconut Ice Cream

Sponsors

We would like to thank the special people and companies that came forward and generously supported The Junior League of Denver in our cookbook endeavor to help the community.

Maroon Peak Sponsor
(elevation 14,156 feet)

Murray Motors

Red Cloud Peak Sponsor
(elevation 14,034 feet)

Peppercorn Gourmet Goods

Gold Dust Peak Sponsor
(elevation 13,365 feet)

First Data Corporation
The Seasoned Chef Cooking School
Susan Stevens

Ruby Peak Sponsor
(elevation 12,644 feet)

Cherry Creek Shopping Center
Franklin Mortgage Company—
Kelly Eischen
Urology Research Options—
Dr. and Mrs. Joel Kaufman
U.S. Mix Products

Gray Rock Peak Sponsor
(elevation 12,504 feet)

Horizon Organic Dairy

Individual Sponsors

Marsha Lynn Alpert

Roxanne Fie Anderson

In Loving Memory of Norma Jean Ansted —
 Margaret Ansted

For my Mother and Daughters — Elaine Asarch

Christie L. Austin

Josie Baker

Sharon B. Barnard

Marsha P. Berger

Trish Bloemker

In Loving Memory of Paula F. Boehme —
 Kellye Boehme

Kristen and Martin Boublik

Carey Brandt

Margie and George Browning

Joann Morgan Burstein

Carole Cheley

Cameron Claussen

Kristina Davidson

In Appreciation of Katie Stapleton — Judy DeBord

Diane Eckloff

Chris, Pat, Taryn, Corey, and Shay Elliott

Sara Farren

Tom, Sarah, and Lillian Feist

Karen B. Fisher

In Honor of Mrs. Hilliard Fletcher —
 Janie Fletcher

Cynthia Frandsen

Beverlee Henry Fullerton

Lynn Glassman

In Memory of Dorothy Axel — Marilyn Gottesfeld

Judith Lamme Green

Michelle K. Hanley & Family

In Loving Memory of Grandma Raskie —
 Michelle Hanley

Mrs. James R. Hartley

Arlene Hirschfeld

In Memory of Ruth Rice Rogers — Katy Jacaruso

JLD 2001–2002 Management Team

JLD 2003–2004 VP Elects

JLD 2001–2002 Finance Council

JLD 2001–2002 Ways and Means Council

2002 Holiday Mart Steering Committee

Margaret Kinney for Son, Paul Embleton

In Loving Memory of Marguarite C. Fraser —
 Midge Kral

Cindy Laurnen

Jill Dana Lee

In Loving Memory of Jackie Lind —
 From "Jackie's Angels"

In Loving Memory of Bryn Linkow —
 Susan Linkow

Patty Mack

Judith A. Massie

Honoring my Mother Betty Litten —
 Kathy McConahey

Elizabeth and Sean McDermott

Patrice A. McMonigle

Meghan B. Mortimer

Marion Milton

Mary Peterson

To Sherri Koelbel, "My Pretty Friend" — CR

Melissa Redmond

Michael, Werth, Jackson, and Caroline Roddy

Frances Walthall Roberts & Carol R. Roddy

Catherine W. Rundle

Aline Sandomire

Joan W. Smith

Ronda Barlow Smith

In Loving Memory of Ruth Hollister Smith —
 Ronda Barlow Smith

Cheryl F. Stephens

Sue Sumners

To my Mother and Grandma Katie who
 taught me to cook — Nancy Tankersley

Kathryn Sullivan Terry

Leona (Lee) J. Thrailkill

Barbara J. Webb

For Jamie, Hannah, and Alena Payne.
 Thanks for the extra testing. Love, Mom

submitters

Dolly Adler
Thelma Albrecht
Cindy Alexander
Ann Allison
Lorie Amass
Barb Anderson
Miki Anderson
Lisa Aubrey
Judy Bailey
Natalie Baker
Sally Barker
Patty Barnard
Mary Beckwith
Betty Beeler
Jeffrey Anne Bellows
Sherry Benight
Jeannie Bennington
Sheila Bernardi
Joella Blackburn
Chris A. Blakeslee
Suzanne Nielson Blakeslee
Marci Block
Ann Bohn
Kim Boli
Sarah Booras
Pamela Boosalis
Vicki Bourret
Kathleen Bowen
Anne Bower
Alyson Bradley
Karen Ellis Bradley
Lisle Loosli Bradley
Fred Bramhall
Nancy Breutt
Pat Bringenberg
Lora Louise Broady

Verna J. Broussard
Karol Brown
Sharon Brown
KieAnn Brownell
Marlene Buck
Melissa Burkett
Melissa Burkhart
Carol Ann Burnett
Mrs. James L. Byler
Sally Cadol
Judith Calhoun
John Cardie
Kathy Carlson
Mike Carrington
Marsha Chambers
Antoinette Cheney
Kim Christenson
Joan Christopherson
Mary Clark
Taylor Clark
Bonnie Cleaver
Kathleen Clifford
Katharine Connolly
Cami Cooper
Elizabeth Corbin
Janice Cortez
Ellyn Coughlin
Heather Cracraft
Alissa Gutin Crowley
Holly Curtis
Marilyn Curtis
Connie Cusack
Lee Dabberdt
Claire M. Dallarosa
Sally Davidson-Marovich
Annette Davis

Stephani C. Davis
Susanne deGeus
Tracy DeHoop
Wendy DeBell
Susan Demander
Kelly Laing Director
Amy Dixon
Judi Doherty
Bridget Donnelly
Bonnie Downing
Tina Downs
Pat Duensing
Amy Eckhout
Debra Fagan
Sarah Feist
Nikki Feltz
Terri Fennell
Frieda Fischer
Debby Fisher
Karen Fisher
Janie Fletcher
Karie Fletcher
Jeannie Foss-Turner
Cindy Fowler
Brian I. Fun
Rae Ann Gallegos
Linda Ganter
Margaret Garbe
Nancy Gargan
Susan M. H. Gills
Karen Glassman
Lynn Glassman
Tatyana Golyansky
Dana Good
Marilyn A. Gottesfeld
Mary Ann Gray

Stacy Gray
Susan Gray
Kelley Griffith
Barbara Grob
Stephanie Grogan
Jeanie Grow
Nancy Grubin
Paulette Guenette
Shirley Guiraud
Linda Gutin
Anne Hackstock
Julia Romeo Haen
Carol Hall
Connie Hambrook
Anne Hammer
Katie Harrell
Gail Hartley
Kathy Haruf
Deanna J. Hawes
Haley Hayes
Duane Helfer
Sally Henrich
Mary Ann Henry
Carey Nivens Hicks
Anne Hill
Michele Hobbs
Debbie Hoellen
Miriam Holley
Catherine Hollis
Jeanne Holm
Carolyn House
Janice Hrbaty
Michelle Hunsinger
Kaye Hurtt
Laura Hylbert
Loretta Isaak

Cheri Issel
Anne Jeffries
Becky Johnson
Judy Johnson
Suzanne Jones
Kathy Kahn
Marie Revelle Kalisker
Kathleen Kastles
Marcy Ann Kaufman
Margaret Keefe
Maureen Keefner
Debbie Keesling
Audrey Keller
Mae Jane Keller
Christi Kelsey
Lindy Kennedy
Cara Kimsey
Margaret Kinney
Lisen Kintzele
Bruce Kippur
Merrie Margolin Kippur
Audrey Albrecht Kiszla
Denise Kolb
Sue Krenger
Peter Kroth
Francie Lavin
Sarah Leffen
Mary Lempke
Becke Leo
Marilyn Leonard
Emily Levorsen
Diane Lewis
Randy Lewis
Judith S. Liebman
Meg Littlepage
Barbara Lockhart
Suzy Love
Karen Lozow
Carol Macbride
Janet MacBride
Laura Maddock
Nichola Madigan
Lori Magazine
Lisa Maher
Janet Manning
Meg Mara
Sharon Marks

Christi Stager Martin
Susie Martin
Anne Mayer
Susan Warner McCann
Meredith McClements
Denny McLain
Susie McLain
Sophia McMillon
Bev McMurria
Mary Melick
Diane Metz
Lori Midson
Melanie Milasinovich
Kathryn Blind Miller
Julie Mondschein
Rita Moore
Kelly Moran
Bev Morrato
Kathleen Morton
Carol Moth
Shellie R. Munn
Judy Murray
Kathy Myers
Amy Nemechek
Karen Neville
Pam Newell
Bev Newton
Marcia Norton
Edrie O'Brien
Kelley O'Connor
Kathy Oman
Nancy Orcutt
Lauri Osborne
Lori Ostmeyer
Donna Packard
Susan Pasek
Olga Payne
Jackie Perett
Cecily Peters
Jill Pedicord Peterson
John Peterson
Nell Pickering
Ann Pierson
Sally Pistilli
Karen Ragsdale
Betsy Randall
Pam Read

Karen Reardon
Lorrie Reed
LeaAnn Reitzig
Charlotte Ressegier
Kathryn M. Rhodes
Judy Rieker
Kathye Ripley
Dennis Ritchie
Diane Robinson
Cristelyn Roebuck
Mary Frances Roebuck
Rebecca Roebuck
Kara Rogers
Beth Rohr
Patricia Romeo
Tana Rosenberg
Sabine Rouse
Linda Ryan
Brian Sack, 4th Story
Sarah R. Sandusky
Kim Santangelo
Mike Santangelo
Carol Sarchet
Mildred Mae Sarchet
Sarah Sargent
Persis Schlosser
Melissa Schwab
Carol Selner
Goldie Shapiro
Karen Shuman
Cristina Sigdestad
Jane Siekmeier
Kathryn Simich
Connie Smith
Lorraine Smith
Doug Sottoway
Melissa Sottoway
Susan Spaulding
Judy Spinney
Priscilla Stedman
Jayme Stelbof
Gretchen Stemple
Amy Stern
Susan Stevens
Cristin Stice
Stacy Stokes
Jena Stuckey

Beatrice Szadokierski
Sonnie Talley
Nancy Tankersley
Doug Tannenbaum
Marilyn Shields Taylor
Francine Terrell
Margaret Tezak
Sharon Thomas
Debbie Tilton
Linda Treibitz
Christine McLaughlin-Trigg
Jennifer Turner
Misti Turra
Kate Urich
Jean Liu Urquhart
Karen Valdez
Maria Frances Valdez
Glenda Varnell
Lauri Varsubsky
Norma Varsubsky
Susan Vick
David Vreeman
Yvette Vreeman
Nancy Rae Wait
Sandra Walley
Michelle Weinraub
Phyllis Weinraub
Paula Wheatley
Missy Wiggs
Jeanne W. Wilde
Katie Wilkins
Stacia Wilkins
Bonnie Williams
Erin Williams
Rosemary Wills
Elaine Woodworth
Jane Yale
Meg Yarka
Fran Yeddis
Rebecca Young
Wendy Zerr

testers

TESTERS

Cindy Alexander

Barb Anderson*

Miki Anderson

Gail Berliner*

Karen Blackman

Marci Block

Ann Bohn

Kimberley Bolt

Aleita Cass

Sugar Chalus

Camilla Chaplick

Antoinette Cheney

Toni Cohig

Cami Cooper*

Janice Cortez*

Ellyn Coughlin

Hannah Crowley

John Crowley

Walker Crowley

Holly Curtis

Lee Dabberdt

Lynda Dalton

Caroline Davis

Kim Davis

Madeleine Davis

Glenna Day

Susan Deagle

Linda Dean

Wendy DeBell

Susanne deGeus

Barbara Deline

Mimi deOlloqui

Kelley O'Connor Digby

Kelly Laing Director

Bridget Donnelly

Christina Downs

Stephanie Duncan

Debra Fagan

Judy Fallin

Sarah Feist

Nikki Feltz*

Karen Fisher

Nanette Fishman

Rae Ann Gallegos

Nancy Gargan*

Kimberly Garneau

Laura Gillespie

Debbie Gray

Mary Ann Gray

Susan Gray

Kelley Griffith

Anne Hackstock

Julia Romeo Haen

Connie Hambrook

Anne Hammer

Katie Harrell

Gail Hartley

Haley Hayes*

Debbie Hoellen

Catherine Hollis*

Carolyn Hunter

Susan James*

Suzanne Jenkins

Katie Johnson

Suzanne Jones

Lee Keatinge

Cara Kimsey*

Maria Kinsella

Merrie Margolin Kippur

Annette Kleber

Sally Kneser

Barbara Knight

Rebecca Lawrence

Nancy Leatherman

Mary Lempke

Hanne Lichtenfels

Karen Lozow

Sarah MacMillan

Lori Magazine

Janet Manning

Meg Mara

Susie McLain*

Claire Mindock

Kathleen Morton*

Amy Nemechek

Kellie Newland

Edrie O'Brien

Olga Payne

Martha Persons

Jeanne Phillips

Annette Pluss

Karen Ragsdale

Alexandra Ramsay

Pam Read

Karen Reardon

Melissa Redmond

LeaAnn Reitzig

Sharon Ripps

Suzanne Robinson

Cristelyn Roebuck

Tana Rosenberg*

Sabine Rouse

Kathryn Ryan

Alison Sandler

Sally Sandusky

Karen Schmidt

Kathy Schmidt

Nancy Schotters

Goldie Shapiro

Debbie Shpall

Beth Shure

Jane Siekmeier*

Kathryn Simich

Stacy Stokes*

Nancy Tankersley

Francine Terrell

Page Tredennick

Christine McLaughlin-Trigg*

Jennifer Turner*

Misti Turra

Katherine Van Schaack

Glenda Varnell

Lauri Varsubsky

Michelle Weinraub*

Paula Wheatley

Leslie Williams

Fran Yeddis

Phil Yeddis

Linda Young

Rebecca Young

Mary Youngblood

Sherrie Zeppelin

Bailey Zerr

Brady Zerr

B.Z. Zerr

Nicki Zwick

* Section Head

279

INDEX

Accompaniments. *See also* Salsas
Brie Butter, 24
Butter Thyme Sauce, 219
Cherry Tomato Relish, 157
Chimichurri, 160
Cranberry Orange Preserves, 94
Cranberry Salsa Sorbet, 147
Fresh Mint Vinaigrette for
    Lamb, 164
Garlic Bean Purée, 231
Ginger Butter, 185
Guacamole, 231
Lime-Pickled Red Onions, 163
Olive Butter, 189
Sweet and Spicy Pecans, 41

Appetizers. *See also* Dips; Salsas
Asian Chicken Lettuce Wraps, 22
Bacon-Wrapped Grissini, 18
Bleu Cheese Quesadillas with Pear
    Salsa, 15
Ceviche, 25
Chèvre, Marmalade and Ripe Pear
    Crostini, 16
Cojita Cheese Rounds, 16
Endive with Brandied
    Gorgonzola, 17
Figs with Prosciutto, 30
Grilled Beef and Pepper
    Bundles, 20
King Crab Cups with Avocado, 24
Lemon Shrimp, 26
Mango, Shrimp and Prosciutto
    Kabobs, 26
Marinated Mushrooms, 18
Pesto Hots, 16
Pistachio Shrimp with Dipping
    Sauces, 27
Spicy Black Bean Cakes, 19
Spicy Sashimi Triangles, 23
Zucchini Tomato Bites, 14

Apples
Acorn Squash Apple Rings, 123
Apple Sausage Quiche, 104
Caramel Apple Bars, 271
Farmer's Market Soup, 66
Indian Waldorf Salad, 45

Artichokes
Artichoke Heart Ravioli with
    Three-Pepper Sauce, 216
Artichoke Tart, 104
Chicken with Figs and Artichoke
    Hearts, 138
Greek Penne, 215
Greek Potato Salad, 44
Mediterranean Salsa, 34
Open-Face Tuna Melt, 81
Roasted Red Potatoes with
    Artichokes, 121

Asparagus
Farfalle with Asparagus, Roasted
    Shallots and Bleu Cheese, 212
Mango Chili Chicken, 138
Raspberry Asparagus, 112
Roasted Asparagus and Portobello
    Mushrooms, 113
Savory Baked Eggs and
    Asparagus, 102
Thin Spaghetti with Crab, Asparagus
    and Sun-Dried Tomatoes, 210
Zesty Spring Vegetable Medley, 124

Avocados
Avocado Lime Cream Dip, 28
Avocado Salsa, 196
Cantaloupe and Avocado Salad with
    Chili Dressing, 40
Dueling Salsas, 158
Grilled Swordfish Tostados with
    Black Beans, 196

Guacamole, 231
Island Paradise Salad, 46
King Crab Cups with Avocado, 24
Pecan Chicken and Wild Rice, 55
Sautéed Vegetable Wraps with Garlic
    Bean Purée, 231
Spicy Rib Eyes with Dueling
    Salsas, 158
Spinach Salad with Crisp
    Red Chiles, 53
Triple Tomato Pasta, 211

Bacon
Bacon-Wrapped Grissini, 18
Braised Chicken with Shallots and
    Pancetta, 137
Hearty Baked Beans, 113
Pan-Fried Trout with Bacon, 193
Savory Baked Eggs and
    Asparagus, 102

Beans
Black Beans, 196
Buffalo Chili, 173
Edamame and Cherry Medley, 116
Edamame Salad, 43
Front Range Steak Salad, 54
Garlic Bean Purée, 231
Ginger Island Gumbo, 225
Green and White Bean Salad, 45
Grilled Swordfish Tostados with
    Black Beans, 196
Hearty Baked Beans, 113
Sautéed Vegetable Wraps with Garlic
    Bean Purée, 231
Spicy Black Bean Cakes, 19
Tuna, White Bean and Roasted
    Pepper Salad with Creamy Dijon
    Dressing, 57
Tuscan Green Beans, 119
Zesty Spring Vegetable Medley, 124

Beef. *See also* Ground Beef
  Après Ski Stew, 72
  Beef and Pepper Bundles, 20
  Beef en Croûte with Cilantro Walnut
    Filling, 152
  Beef Tenderloin with Thai Green
    Curry Sauce, 154
  Cold Sliced Beef Sirloin with Herb
    Sauce, 160
  Front Range Steak Salad, 54
  Grilled Tri-Tip Roast with Cherry
    Tomato Relish, 157
  Lemon Grass Beef with Rice
    Paper, 161
  Mediterranean Pot Roast, 155
  Spicy Rib Eyes with Dueling
    Salsas, 158
  Spicy Thai Beef Strips, 162
  Steak Chimichurri, 160
  Tortellini with Roast Beef and
    Broccoli, 218
  Wine-Braised Brisket, 156

Beets
  Balsamic-Glazed Beets, 114
  Roasted Beet, Caraway and Red
    Cabbage Slaw, 50
  Roasted Root Vegetables, 125

Beverages
  Coconut Margarita, 36
  Pear and Ginger Martini, 36
  Pisco Sour, 37
  Ramos Gin Fizz, 37
  Tamarind Water, 132
  The Ruby, 37
  White Wine Sangria, 36

Blueberries
  Bakery Shoppe Blueberry
    Bread, 88
  Blueberry Sauce, 260
  Lemonade Pie with Blueberry
    Sauce, 260
  Rhubarb Blueberry Cobbler with
    Pistachio Topping, 264
  Rustic Berry Galette, 263
  Spinach and Berries Salad
    with Dill, 51

Breads
  Baked French Toast with Cardamom
    and Marmalade, 100
  Bakery Shoppe Blueberry
    Bread, 88
  Bubbly Cinnamon Toast, 100
  Cinnamon Streusel Buns, 90
  English Crumpets, 91
  Garlic Croutons, 224

Hazelnut Chocolate Breakfast
    Bread, 87
  High Country Herb Rolls, 92
  Lemon Poppy Seed Waffles with
    Raspberry Sauce, 98
  Parmesan Sesame Biscuits, 93
  Puffy Pear Pancake, 96
  Rhubarb Sweet Bread, 88
  Sweet Fruit Scones, 94
  The Best Focaccia Ever, 86
  Ultimate Pizza Crust, 248
  Wheat Germ Pancakes, 97

Brunch. *See also* Breads; Egg Dishes
  Artichoke Tart, 104
  Cherry Bruschetta, 93
  Christmas Oranges, 109
  Cranberry Orange Preserves, 94
  Fresh Pineapple in Cinnamon
    Syrup, 109
  Goldilock's Goodness, 108
  Pesto and Prosciutto Breakfast
    Strata, 105
  Strawberry Patch Soup, 101
  Sweet Potato Hash Browns, 108

Cabbage
  Asian Coleslaw, 182
  Grilled Salmon in Thai Curry Sauce
    with Vegetable Slaw and
    Potatoes, 190
  Ham, Gruyère and Cabbage
    Salad, 55
  Herb and Garlic Cheese Stuffed
    Potatoes, 120
  Irish Lamb and Barley Stew, 72
  Jicama Slaw, 184
  Roasted Beet, Caraway and Red
    Cabbage Slaw, 50
  Salmon with Citrus Soy Glaze, 192
  Scallop Dumplings in Asian
    Broth, 70
  Seared Ahi Napoleon, 182
  Tofu Coleslaw, 50
  Vegetable Slaw, 190
  Wasabi and Sesame Encrusted
    Ahi Tuna with Jicama Slaw, 184

Cakes
  Black Cherry Almond Cake, 266
  Toffee Cake with Caramel Sauce, 267
  Warm Chocolate Decadence
    Cakes, 268

Carrots
  Après Ski Stew, 72
  Asian Pear and Watercress Salad
    with Sesame Dressing, 40
  Cherry Tofu Lettuce Wraps, 232

Chicken Tortilla Soup, 68
Chilled Hunan Noodles, 204
Creamy Autumn Vegetable
    Soup, 65
Curried Couscous Salad, 42
Edamame Salad, 43
Greek Potato Salad, 44
Herb Shiitake Mushroom
    Burgers, 230
Irish Lamb and Barley Stew, 72
Jicama Slaw, 184
Layered Ginger Chicken Dip, 31
Roasted Beet, Caraway and Red
    Cabbage Slaw, 50
Roasted Carrots, 115
Roasted Chicken with
    Vegetables, 134
Roasted Root Vegetables, 125
Scallop Dumplings in Asian
    Broth, 70
Spicy Carrot Soup with Red
    Curry, 62
Tofu Coleslaw, 50

Chicken
  Asian Chicken Lettuce Wraps, 22
  Braised Chicken with Shallots and
    Pancetta, 137
  Chicken and Shrimp Pad Thai, 200
  Chicken Tortilla Soup, 68
  Chicken with Figs and Artichoke
    Hearts, 138
  Cinnamon-Cured Smoked Chicken
    with Cherry Barbecue
    Sauce, 140
  Crispy Pan-Fried Chicken with
    Summer Sauce, 141
  Curried Chicken with Fusilli, 208
  Elegant Chicken and Brie
    Croissants, 78
  Feta-Stuffed Chicken, 135
  Front Range Buffalo Chicken
    Burger, 137
  Ginger Chicken and Vegetable
    Stir-Fry, 144
  Green Olive Enchiladas, 142
  Grilled Rosemary Chicken in Herb
    Vinaigrette, 134
  Layered Ginger Chicken Dip, 31
  Lemon Chicken with Rosemary
    Orzo, 139
  Lemon Tarragon Chicken Salad
    Sandwiches, 77
  Mango Chili Chicken, 138
  Pecan Chicken and Wild Rice, 55
  Polynesian Chicken Burgers, 136
  Roasted Chicken with
    Vegetables, 134
  Sautéed Chicken Paprika, 146

Spaghetti with Chicken and Lemon
  Caper Cream, 210
Spinach Salad with Grilled Chicken
  and Mango Chutney, 52
Sticky Glazed Coconut Chicken and
  Coconut Basil Rice, 145
Tarragon Chicken (Poulet a
  l'Estragon), 136
Thai One On Soup, 67

Chocolate
Chai Chocolate Custard, 257
Chocolate Snowflake Cookies, 269
Chocolate Valencia Pie, 259
Hazelnut Chocolate Breakfast
  Bread, 87
Hazelnut Topping, 87
Sweetheart Straws, 270
Tuxedo Cheesecake, 254
Warm Chocolate Decadence
  Cakes, 268
Western Chocolate Stack-Ups, 255

Cookies
Caramel Apple Bars, 271
Celestial Sugar Cookies, 269
Chocolate Snowflake Cookies, 269
Colorado Cherry Bars, 271
Colorado Ranch Cookies, 270
Sweetheart Straws, 270

Corn
Buffalo Chili, 173
Coconut Lime Summer Squash
  Sauté, 243
Corn Cheese Boats, 116
Edamame and Cherry Medley, 116
Mile-High Chili over Rice, 69
Southwestern Shrimp
  Sandwiches, 81

Crab
Crab, Cheese and Dill-Stuffed
  Shells, 217
King Crab Cups with Avocado, 24
Seafood Stew with Basil and
  Tomatoes, 73
Thin Spaghetti with Crab, Asparagus
  and Sun-Dried Tomatoes, 210

Desserts. *See also* Cakes; Cookies; Tarts
Banana Crème Brûlée, 253
Chai Chocolate Custard, 257
Chocolate Valencia Pie, 259
Espresso Frizzante, 258
Lemonade Pie with Blueberry
  Sauce, 260
Mango Tango Gelato, 259
Port Flan with Citrus Essence, 256

Rhubarb Blueberry Cobbler with
  Pistachio Topping, 264
Rustic Berry Galette, 263
Tahitian Bananas Foster, 252
Tuxedo Cheesecake, 254
Western Chocolate Stack-Ups, 255

Dips. *See also* Salsas
Avocado Lime Cream Dip, 28
Danube Dip, 29
Hot Soufflé Dip, 29
Layered Ginger Chicken Dip, 31
Montrachet Spread, 35
Roasted Red Pepper, Feta and
  Mint Dip, 28
Roma Dip, 29
Santa Fe Dip, 29
Stacked Caviar Dip, 35
Sun-Dried Tomato Dip, 29
Sweet Onion Dip, 29

Egg Dishes
Apple Sausage Quiche, 104
Chile Rellenos Soufflé with Sage
  Cheese, 103
Savory Baked Eggs and
  Asparagus, 102
Scrambled Eggs with Smoked
  Salmon and Chives, 101
Spanish Frittata with Fruit
  Salsa, 106

Entertaining Ideas, 15, 17, 19, 20, 23,
  28, 31, 32, 41, 47, 49, 51, 58, 68,
  73, 74, 97, 103, 153, 158, 163, 193,
  209, 211, 236, 243, 255, 256, 263

Fish. *See also* Halibut; Salmon; Tuna
Ceviche, 25
Grilled Swordfish, 194
Grilled Swordfish Tostados with
  Black Beans, 196
Pan-Fried Trout with Bacon, 193
Sea Bass in Tomato Fennel
  Sauce, 189
Sole with Almonds, Pine Nuts and
  Currants, 194

Fruit. *See also* Apples; Avocados;
  Blueberries; Mangoes; Pears;
  Strawberries
Banana Crème Brûlée, 253
Basil-Scented Kumquat Sauce, 148
Black Cherry Almond Cake, 266
Cantaloupe and Avocado Salad with
  Chili Dressing, 40
Cherry Tofu Lettuce Wraps, 232
Christmas Oranges, 109
Colorado Cherry Bars, 271

Cornish Game Hens with Tamarind
  Glaze, 132
Cranberry Orange Preserves, 94
Cranberry Salsa Sorbet, 147
Cranberry Tart, 261
Edamame and Cherry Medley, 116
Fresh Pineapple in Cinnamon
  Syrup, 109
Grilled Pineapple Salsa, 195
Lemon Poppy Seed Waffles with
  Raspberry Sauce, 98
Mustard Greens with
  Grapefruit, 48
Pacific Flavors Salad, 49
Papaya Salsa, 32
Pork with Dried Plums, 171
Raspberry Asparagus, 112
Raspberry Port Sauce, 148
Raspberry Sauce, 98
Rhubarb Blueberry Cobbler with
  Pistachio Topping, 264
Rhubarb Salsa, 54
Rustic Berry Galette, 263
Spinach and Berries Salad
  with Dill, 51
Summer Orange Salad with
  Rhubarb Salsa, 54
Sweet Fruit Scones, 94
Tahitian Bananas Foster, 252
Tamarind Balls, 132
Tamarind Glaze, 133
Tamarind Water, 132
Watermelon Salsa, 34

Game
Buffalo Chili, 173
Cornish Game Hens with Tamarind
  Glaze, 132
Seared Duck Breasts with Two
  Sauces, 148
Venison Steak Sandwiches, 76

Grains
Coconut Basil Rice, 145
Coconut Lime Summer Squash
  Sauté, 243
Curried Couscous Salad, 42
Feta Cheese Polenta with
  Two-Tomato Salsa, 228
Goldilock's Goodness, 108
Irish Lamb and Barley Stew, 72
Mango Chili Chicken, 138
Mediterranean Risotto and Zucchini
  Cakes, 238
Mile-High Chili over Rice, 69
Orange Curry Couscous, 128
Pecan Chicken and Wild Rice, 55
Rice Pilaf with Almonds and Dried
  Mangoes, 127

Savory Stuffed Portobello
    Mushrooms, 245
Soft Polenta with Caramelized
    Onions, Garlic and Spinach, 227
Sticky Glazed Coconut Chicken and
    Coconut Basil Rice, 145
Twice-Baked Harvest Squash, 240
Wild Mushroom Risotto, 239

Ground Beef
Hearty Baked Beans, 113
Southwest-Style Salisbury Steaks
    with Lime-Pickled Onions, 163

Halibut
Grilled Halibut with Ginger
    Butter, 185
Halibut Kabobs with Chili Lime
    Sauce, 186
Halibut with Roasted Red Pepper
    Sauce, 188

Ham. *See also* Prosciutto
Ham, Gruyère and Cabbage
    Salad, 55

Lamb
Grilled Lamb with Roasted Olives
    and Onions, 164
Irish Lamb and Barley Stew, 72
Piquant Spicy Leg of Lamb, 166

Mangoes
Cumin Tuna Steaks with Lime
    Cream and Salsa, 181
Fruit Salsa, 106
Island Paradise Salad, 46
Mango Chili Chicken, 138
Mango Chutney Dressing, 52
Mango Salsa, 181
Mango, Shrimp and Prosciutto
    Kabobs, 26
Mango Tango Gelato, 259
Rice Pilaf with Almonds and Dried
    Mangoes, 127
Slow-Baked Spareribs with Mango
    Chutney Marinade, 167
Spicy Mango Shrimp on Wilted
    Greens, 179
Spinach Salad with Grilled Chicken
    and Mango Chutney, 52
Tahitian Bananas Foster, 252

Marinades
Colorful Marinade for
    Chicken, 141
Herb Marinade for Lamb or
    Beef, 162
Herb Vinaigrette, 134

Marinade, 132
Souvlaki Marinade, 166
Soy Marinade, 22

Meatless Main Dishes
Asian Pan-Fried Tofu, 234
Autumn Pumpkin Gnocchi with
    Butter Thyme Sauce, 219
Chanterelle and Portobello
    Mushrooms in Puff Pastry, 244
Cherry Tofu Lettuce Wraps, 232
Chile Rellenos Soufflé with Sage
    Cheese, 103
Coconut Lime Summer Squash
    Sauté, 243
Farfalle with Asparagus, Roasted
    Shallots and Bleu Cheese, 212
Feta Cheese Polenta with
    Two-Tomato Salsa, 228
Ginger Island Gumbo, 225
Greek Penne, 215
Herb Dumplings with Baby
    Spinach, 222
Herb Fontina Orecchiette, 237
Herb Shiitake Mushroom
    Burgers, 230
Mediterranean Risotto and Zucchini
    Cakes, 238
Pasta Portofino, 201
Pizza Dell' Erba di Pesto, 249
Pizza Marguerite, 249
Rustic Cherry Tomato Melt, 226
Sautéed Vegetable Wraps with Garlic
    Bean Purée, 231
Savory Stuffed Portobello
    Mushrooms, 245
Silken Tofu Fettuccine, 234
Soft Polenta with Caramelized
    Onions, Garlic and
    Spinach, 227
"Soon To Be Your Favorite"
    Spaghetti, 236
Spaghetti Squash Lasagna, 242
Spicy Asian Wraps, 232
Thai Peanut Stir-Fry, 246
Triple Tomato Pasta, 211
Tuscan Cauliflower Rigatoni, 235
Twice-Baked Harvest
    Squash, 240
Wild Mushroom Risotto, 239

Mushrooms
Asian Chicken Lettuce Wraps, 22
Braised Chicken with Shallots and
    Pancetta, 137
Chanterelle and Portobello
    Mushrooms in Puff Pastry, 244
Country French Onion
    Gratin, 224

Edamame and Cherry Medley, 116
Ginger Chicken and Vegetable
    Stir-Fry, 144
Herb Shiitake Mushroom
    Burgers, 230
Marinated Mushrooms, 18
Pizza Dell' Erba di Pesto, 249
Roasted Asparagus and Portobello
    Mushrooms, 113
Savory Baked Eggs and
    Asparagus, 102
Savory Stuffed Portobello
    Mushrooms, 245
Spaghetti Squash Lasagna, 242
Thai One On Soup, 67
Thai Peanut Stir-Fry, 246
Wild Mushroom and Bleu Cheese
    Bread Pudding, 126
Wild Mushroom Risotto, 239

Noodles
Artichoke Heart Ravioli with
    Three-Pepper Sauce, 216
Chicken and Shrimp Pad
    Thai, 200
Chilled Hunan Noodles, 204
Chilled Sesame Noodles with Shrimp
    and Lime, 205
Crab, Cheese and Dill-Stuffed
    Shells, 217
Curried Chicken with Fusilli, 208
Farfalle with Asparagus, Roasted
    Shallots and Bleu Cheese, 212
Farfalle with Pan-Seared Tuna,
    Lemon and Garlic, 214
Fusilli Rustica, 206
Fusilli with Prosciutto and
    Gruyère, 209
Greek Penne, 215
Herb Fontina Orecchiette, 237
Lemon Chicken with Rosemary
    Orzo, 139
Malay Curried Noodles, 202
Mint and Scallion Soba
    Noodles, 205
Orzo with Spinach and
    Taleggio, 126
Pasta Portofino, 201
Sausage Fettuccine Torta, 215
Silken Tofu Fettuccine, 234
"Soon To Be Your Favorite"
    Spaghetti, 236
Spaghetti with Chicken and Lemon
    Caper Cream, 210
Tagliatelle with Mussels, Clams and
    Pesto, 203
Thai Peanut Stir-Fry, 246
Thin Spaghetti with Crab, Asparagus
    and Sun-Dried Tomatoes, 210

Tortellini with Roast Beef and
  Broccoli, 218
Triple Tomato Pasta, 211
Tuscan Cauliflower Rigatoni, 235

Pasta. *See* Noodles

Pears
Asian Pear and Watercress Salad
  with Sesame Dressing, 40
Bleu Cheese Quesadillas with Pear
  Salsa, 15
Chèvre, Marmalade and Ripe Pear
  Crostini, 16
Grilled Salmon and Pear Salad, 56
Modern Mincemeat Pear
  Tart, 260
Pear and Ginger Martini, 36
Pear Salsa, 15
Puffy Pear Pancake, 96

Peas
Chilled Hunan Noodles, 204
Curried Chicken with Fusilli, 208
Curried Couscous Salad, 42
Ginger Chicken and Vegetable
  Stir-Fry, 144
Ginger Island Gumbo, 225
Island Paradise Salad, 46
Orange Curry Couscous, 128
Pecan Chicken and Wild Rice, 55
Scallop Dumplings in Asian
  Broth, 70
Sugar Snap Peas with Toasted
  Sesame Seeds, 127
Thai Peanut Stir-Fry, 246
Thai Shrimp Curry, 178
Zesty Spring Vegetable
  Medley, 124

Pork. *See also* Bacon; Ham; Sausage
Celebrity Ribs, 167
Chipotle Burgers with a Kick, 172
Curried Pork Tenderloin, 171
Pork with Dried Plums, 171
Romano Sage Pork Chops, 170
Slow-Baked Spareribs with Mango
  Chutney Marinade, 167
Sugar-Spiced Pork Chops with
  Chipotle Sauce, 168

Potatoes. *See also* Sweet Potatoes
Après Ski Stew, 72
Baked Potato Soup, 63
Boursin Potatoes, 119
Greek Potato Salad, 44
Grilled Salmon in Thai Curry Sauce
  with Vegetable Slaw and
  Potatoes, 190

Herb and Garlic Cheese Stuffed
  Potatoes, 120
Leek and Sautéed Shrimp Soup, 71
Mashed Potatoes, 190
Roasted Potatoes, 120
Roasted Red Potatoes with
  Artichokes, 121

Poultry. *See* Chicken; Turkey

Prosciutto
Country Picnic Loaf, 82
Figs with Prosciutto, 30
Fusilli Rustica, 206
Fusilli with Prosciutto and
  Gruyère, 209
Mango, Shrimp and Prosciutto
  Kabobs, 26
Pesto and Prosciutto Breakfast
  Strata, 105
Salmon Saltimbocca, 191

Salad Dressings
Asian Sesame Dressing, 59
Balsamic Vinaigrette, 56, 211
Chili Dressing, 40
Cider Dressing, 53
Creamy Dijon Dressing, 57
Dijon Vinaigrette, 41
Easy Balsamic Salad Dressing, 59
Ginger Dressing, 54
Herb Vinaigrette, 45, 134
Honey Lime Dressing, 46
Irish Mist Salad Dressing, 59
Lime Dressing, 48
Mango Chutney Dressing, 52
Mustard Vinaigrette, 44
Orange Curry Dressing, 128
Orange Curry Vinaigrette, 42
Pacific Flavors Dressing, 49
Red Wine Vinaigrette, 51, 218
Roasted Red Pepper
  Vinaigrette, 47
Roquefort Dressing, 55
Sesame Dressing, 40
Walnut Vinaigrette, 78

Salads
Asian Coleslaw, 182
Asian Pear and Watercress Salad
  with Sesame Dressing, 40
Baby Bleu Salad with Sweet and
  Spicy Pecans, 41
Cantaloupe and Avocado Salad with
  Chili Dressing, 40
Cranberry Lemon Tuna Salad, 57
Curried Couscous Salad, 42
Edamame Salad, 43
Front Range Steak Salad, 54

Greek Potato Salad, 44
Green and White Bean Salad, 45
Grilled Salmon and Pear Salad, 56
Ham, Gruyère and Cabbage
  Salad, 55
Indian Waldorf Salad, 45
Island Paradise Salad, 46
Japanese Shrimp Salad, 58
Jicama Slaw, 184
Mixed Greens with Baked Goat
  Cheese and Roasted Red Pepper
  Vinaigrette, 47
Multicolor Southwest Tomato
  Salad, 46
Mustard Greens with
  Grapefruit, 48
Pacific Flavors Salad, 49
Pecan Chicken and Wild Rice, 55
Roasted Beet, Caraway and Red
  Cabbage Slaw, 50
Spinach and Berries Salad
  with Dill, 51
Spinach Salad with Crisp Red
  Chiles, 53
Spinach Salad with Grilled Chicken
  and Mango Chutney, 52
Stuffed Fresh Figs on Greens, 44
Summer Orange Salad with
  Rhubarb Salsa, 54
Tofu Coleslaw, 50
Tuna, White Bean and Roasted
  Pepper Salad with Creamy Dijon
  Dressing, 57
Vegetable Slaw, 190

Salmon
Grilled Salmon and Pear
  Salad, 56
Grilled Salmon in Thai Curry Sauce
  with Vegetable Slaw and
  Potatoes, 190
Open-Face Smoked Salmon
  Sandwiches with Goat
  Cheese, 80
Salmon Saltimbocca, 191
Salmon with Citrus Soy
  Glaze, 192
Scrambled Eggs with Smoked
  Salmon and Chives, 101
Sweet Barbecue Salmon, 191

Salsas
Asian Salsa with Won Ton
  Chips, 32
Avocado Salsa, 196
Cilantro Tomato Salsa, 195
Dueling Salsas, 158
Fruit Salsa, 106
Grilled Pineapple Salsa, 195

Mango Salsa, 181
Mediterranean Salsa, 34
Papaya Salsa, 32
Pear Salsa, 15
Rhubarb Salsa, 54
Two-Tomato Salsa, 228
Watermelon Salsa, 34

Sandwiches. *See also* Wraps
Chipotle Burgers with a Kick, 172
Country Picnic Loaf, 82
Elegant Chicken and Brie
Croissants, 78
Greek Pitas, 83
Herb Shiitake Mushroom
Burgers, 230
Lemon Tarragon Chicken Salad
Sandwiches, 77
Open-Face Smoked Salmon
Sandwiches with Goat Cheese, 80
Open-Face Tuna Melt, 81
Pesto Mozzarella Panini
Skewers, 229
Rustic Cherry Tomato Melt, 226
Southwestern Shrimp Sandwiches, 81
The Big Veg, 229
Venison Steak Sandwiches, 76
Viejo Turkey and Chutney
Sandwiches, 76

Sauces
Basil-Scented Kumquat
Sauce, 148
Blueberry Sauce, 260
Caramel Sauce, 267
Cheese Sauce, 102
Cherry Barbecue Sauce, 140
Chili Lime Sauce, 186
Chipotle Sauce, 168
Ginger Dipping Sauce, 27
Heavenly Horseradish Cream
Sauce, 156
Herb Sauce, 160
Hot Sauce, 22
Lime Cream Sauce, 181
Mint Dipping Sauce, 27
Orange Herb Sauce, 188
Peanut Sauce, 246
Pesto Sauce, 229
Raspberry Port Sauce, 148
Raspberry Sauce, 98
Roasted Red Pepper Sauce, 188
Summer Sauce, 141
Sweet-and-Sour Sauce, 31
Thai Curry Sauce, 190
Thai Green Curry Sauce, 154
Thai Sweet-and-Sour Sauce, 201
Three-Pepper Sauce, 216
Vietnamese Dipping Sauce, 161

Sausage
Apple Sausage Quiche, 104
Mile-High Chili over Rice, 69
Sausage Fettuccine Torta, 215
Wild Mushroom and Bleu Cheese
Bread Pudding, 126

Seafood. *See also* Crab; Fish; Shrimp
Scallop Dumplings in Asian
Broth, 70
Scallops with Ginger Sauce, 176
Seafood Stew with Basil and
Tomatoes, 73
Steamed Mussels, 176
Tagliatelle with Mussels, Clams and
Pesto, 203

Shrimp
Ceviche, 25
Chicken and Shrimp Pad Thai, 200
Chilled Sesame Noodles with
Shrimpand Lime, 205
Cuban Shrimp Stew, 74
Curried Shrimp with Coconut Milk
and Spiced Masala, 177
Japanese Shrimp Salad, 58
Leek and Sautéed Shrimp Soup, 71
Lemon Shrimp, 26
Malay Curried Noodles, 202
Mango, Shrimp and Prosciutto
Kabobs, 26
Pistachio Shrimp with Dipping
Sauces, 27
Seafood Stew with Basil and
Tomatoes, 73
Sizzling Garlic and Citrus
Shrimp, 180
Southwestern Shrimp
Sandwiches, 81
Spicy Mango Shrimp on Wilted
Greens, 179
Thai Shrimp Curry, 178

Side Dishes
Fried Parsley, 128
Orzo with Spinach and
Taleggio, 126
Wild Mushroom and Bleu Cheese
Bread Pudding, 126

Soups. *See also* Stews
Baked Potato Soup, 63
Chicken Tortilla Soup, 68
Chilled Sorrel Soup, 65
Country French Onion Gratin, 224
Creamy Autumn Vegetable
Soup, 65
Curry Pumpkin Soup, 64
Farmer's Market Soup, 66

Ginger Island Gumbo, 225
Herb Dumplings with Baby
Spinach, 222
Leek and Sautéed Shrimp
Soup, 71
Mile-High Chili over Rice, 69
Scallop Dumplings in Asian
Broth, 70
Spicy Carrot Soup with Red
Curry, 62
Strawberry Patch Soup, 101
Thai One On Soup, 67

Spinach
Beef en Croûte with Cilantro
Walnut Filling, 152
Elegant Chicken and Brie
Croissants, 78
Greek Pitas, 83
Greens with Orange and Ginger, 117
Herb Dumplings with Baby
Spinach, 222
Orzo with Spinach and
Taleggio, 126
Salmon with Citrus Soy Glaze, 192
Santa Fe Dip, 29
Soft Polenta with Caramelized
Onions, Garlic and Spinach, 227
Spicy Mango Shrimp on Wilted
Greens, 179
Spinach and Berries Salad
with Dill, 51
Spinach and Leek Sauté, 122
Spinach and Onion Topping, 227
Spinach Salad with Crisp Red
Chiles, 53
Spinach Salad with Grilled Chicken
and Mango Chutney, 52

Squash
Acorn Squash Apple Rings, 123
Coconut Lime Summer Squash
Sauté, 243
Grilled Yellow Squash, 122
Spaghetti Squash Lasagna, 242
Twice-Baked Harvest
Squash, 240

Stews. *See also* Soups
Après Ski Stew, 72
Cuban Shrimp Stew, 74
Irish Lamb and Barley Stew, 72
Seafood Stew with Basil and
Tomatoes, 73

Strawberries
Baby Bleu Salad with Sweet and
Spicy Pecans, 41
Rustic Berry Galette, 263

Spinach and Berries Salad
  with Dill, 51
Strawberry Patch Soup, 101
Western Chocolate Stack-Ups, 255

Sweet Potatoes
  Mashed Sweet Potatoes Brûlée, 124
  Roasted Sweet Potatoes with
    Garlic, 123
  Seared Ahi Napoleon, 182
  Sweet Potato Hash Browns, 108
  Sweet Potato Purée, 182

Tarts
  Artichoke Tart, 104
  Cranberry Tart, 261
  Lemon Hazelnut Tart, 262
  Modern Mincemeat Pear Tart, 260

Tofu
  Asian Pan-Fried Tofu, 234
  Cherry Tofu Lettuce Wraps, 232
  Coconut Lime Summer Squash
    Sauté, 243
  Silken Tofu Fettuccine, 234
  Thai Peanut Stir-Fry, 246
  Tofu Coleslaw, 50

Tomatoes
  Après Ski Stew, 72
  Ceviche, 25
  Cherry Tomato Relish, 157
  Chimichurri, 160
  Cilantro Tomato Salsa, 195
  Country Picnic Loaf, 82
  Crab, Cheese and Dill-Stuffed
    Shells, 217
  Dueling Salsas, 158
  Elegant Chicken and Brie
    Croissants, 78
  Farmer's Market Soup, 66
  Feta Cheese Polenta with
    Two-Tomato Salsa, 228
  Front Range Steak Salad, 54
  Fusilli Rustica, 206
  Greek Penne, 215
  Greek Pitas, 83
  Grilled Tri-Tip Roast with Cherry
    Tomato Relish, 157
  Grilled Yellow Squash, 122
  Lemon Chicken with Rosemary
    Orzo, 139

Mediterranean Risotto and Zucchini
  Cakes, 238
Mediterranean Salsa, 34
Multicolor Southwest Tomato
  Salad, 46
Pasta Portofino, 201
Pesto and Prosciutto Breakfast
  Strata, 105
Pizza Marguerite, 249
Rustic Cherry Tomato Melt, 226
Sausage Fettuccine Torta, 215
Sautéed Vegetable Wraps with Garlic
  Bean Purée, 231
Sea Bass in Tomato Fennel
  Sauce, 189
"Soon To Be Your Favorite"
  Spaghetti, 236
Steak Chimichurri, 160
Sugar-Spiced Pork Chops with
  Chipotle Sauce, 168
Thin Spaghetti with Crab, Asparagus
  and Sun-Dried Tomatoes, 210
Triple Tomato Pasta, 211
Tuscan Green Beans, 119
Two-Tomato Salsa, 228
Zucchini Tomato Bites, 14

Toppings
  Hazelnut Topping, 87
  Pistachio Topping, 264
  Spinach and Onion Topping, 227

Tuna
  Cranberry Lemon Tuna Salad, 57
  Cumin Tuna Steaks with Lime Cream
    and Salsa, 181
  Farfalle with Pan-Seared Tuna,
    Lemon and Garlic, 214
  Open-Face Tuna Melt, 81
  Seared Ahi Napoleon, 182
  Spice-Crusted Tuna, 180
  Spicy Sashimi Triangles, 23
  Tuna, White Bean and Roasted
    Pepper Salad with Creamy Dijon
    Dressing, 57
  Wasabi and Sesame Encrusted
    Ahi Tuna with Jicama
    Slaw, 184

Turkey
  Brown Sugar-Rubbed Turkey
    Breast, 146

Roasted Turkey Breast with Sage
  Corn Bread Crust, 147
Viejo Turkey and Chutney
  Sandwiches, 76

Vegetables. *See also* Artichokes;
    Asparagus; Beans; Beets;
    Cabbage; Carrots; Corn;
    Mushrooms; Peas; Potatoes;
    Spinach; Squash; Tomatoes;
    Zucchini
  Asperation Inspiration, 115
  Baked Bok Choy with Gruyère
    Cheese, 114
  Eggplant Stacks, 117
  Ginger Island Gumbo, 225
  Greens with Orange and Ginger, 117
  Grilled Peppers Stuffed with Goat
    Cheese, 118
  Irish Lamb and Barley Stew, 72
  Roasted Root Vegetables, 125
  Sautéed Brussels Sprouts, 115
  Spicy Mango Shrimp on Wilted
    Greens, 179
  Thai Shrimp Curry, 178
  Tortellini with Roast Beef and
    Broccoli, 218
  Tuscan Cauliflower Rigatoni, 235
  Wasabi and Sesame Encrusted
    Ahi Tuna with Jicama
    Slaw, 184

Vegetarian. *See* Meatless Main Dishes

Wraps
  Asian Chicken Lettuce Wraps, 22
  Cherry Tofu Lettuce Wraps, 232
  Sautéed Vegetable Wraps with Garlic
    Bean Purée, 231
  Spicy Asian Wraps, 232

Zucchini
  Coconut Lime Summer Squash
    Sauté, 243
  Creamy Autumn Vegetable Soup, 65
  Ginger Chicken and Vegetable
    Stir-Fry, 144
  Lemon Chicken with Rosemary
    Orzo, 139
  Mediterranean Risotto and Zucchini
    Cakes, 238
  Zucchini Tomato Bites, 14

 Junior League of Denver

6300 East Yale Avenue • Denver, CO 80222-7184
(800) 552-9244 / (303) 782-9244 • FAX: (303) 753-6846
WWW.JLD.ORG

ORDER DATE: _____

SHIP TO: [   ] *Please check here if billing address is different than shipping address.*

Name: _____

Address: _____

_____

City: _____ State: _____ Zip Code: _____

SOLD TO: *(If different than shipping address)*   Phone: (   ) _____

Name: _____

Street Address: _____

City: _____ State: _____ Zip Code: _____

NUMBER OF BOOKS ORDERED:

Colorado Cache _____ @ $17.95 per book $ _____

Crème de Colorado _____ @ $24.95 per book $ _____

Colorado Collage _____ @ $27.95 per book $ _____

Colorado Colore _____ @ $29.95 per book $ _____

Take 10% off with order of 3 or more books $ _____

TOTAL PRICE FOR COOKBOOKS: $ _____

($4.95 for first book and an additional $2.00 for each additional book) **Shipping / Handling:** $ _____

(2.9% tax if Colorado shipping address or 7.2% tax if city of Denver shipping address) **Tax:** $ _____

TOTAL CHARGE AMOUNT: $ _____

Prices subject to change without notice.

METHOD OF PAYMENT:

Credit Card # _____ Exp. Date: _____

(MasterCard or Visa ONLY)

Signature _____ OR Check # _____